"Project Censored has shined the light for more than forty years on those critical stories and investigative reports that government officials, major media companies, and assorted gatekeepers of 'respectable' journalism too often ignore."

—JUAN GONZÁLEZ, co-host of *Democracy Now!* and professor of journalism and media studies at Rutgers University

"Now, more than ever, press freedom is at stake. In opposition to the undemocratic censorship of information, I proudly stand with Project Censored."

—SHARYL ATTKISSON, Emmy Award–winning investigative journalist and host of *Full Measure with Sharyl Attkisson*

"Project Censored sets the standard for the Fourth Estate, shedding light on important stories that would otherwise remain obscure and allowing citizens to demand justice and solutions."

—TED RALL, syndicated cartoonist and columnist

"In an era when truth and transparency are under assault, Project Censored offers a vitally important guide on how to think critically and provides the proper media literacy tools for everyone to survive this 'post-truth' era."

—MNAR MUHAWESH, editor-in-chief, MintPress News

"If you want a break from 'fake news' and wish instead to witness real journalism revealing important stories rarely, if ever, covered in the establishment press, read this book!"

—DAN KOVALIK, author of *Cancel This Book* and *The Plot to Overthrow Venezuela*

"Media titans and politicians are finding new ways to censor independent journalism under the banner of combating 'fake news' and 'foreign propaganda.' For truth-tellers and researchers facing this new assault, Project Censored and its annual book represent a vitally important tool, highlighting the crucial issues to know and struggles to follow."

—ABBY MARTIN, *The Empire Files*

"Today's fake news becomes tomorrow's fake history. If journalism is the rough draft of history, [Project Censored] goes a long way to getting the record right the first time, stopping fake news in its tracks and ensuring that we have fewer Untold Histories in the future."

—PETER KUZNICK and OLIVER STONE, co-authors of *The Untold History of the United States* book and documentary series

"For more than forty years, Project Censored has been our watchdog on the establishment media, casting its eye on how the information that we receive—and don't receive—shapes our democracy. We need it more than ever today!"

—CHRISTOPHER FINAN, executive director, National Coalition Against Censorship

"A crucial contribution to the hope for a more just and democratic society."

—NOAM CHOMSKY

"[Project Censored] is a clarion call for truth telling."

—DANIEL ELLSBERG, *The Pentagon Papers*

"Project Censored brings to light some of the most important stories of the year that you never saw or heard about. This is your chance to find out what got buried."

—DIANE RAVITCH, author of *Slaying Goliath: The Passionate Resistance to Privatization and the Fight to Save America's Public Schools*

"Project Censored is a national treasure in American life.... *Censored* gives new meaning to the notion that critical citizens are at the core of a strong democracy and that informed resistance is not an option but a necessity."

—HENRY A. GIROUX, author of *American Nightmare*

PROJECT CENSORED'S

STATE OF THE FREE PRESS 2022
The Top Censored Stories and Media Analysis of 2020–21

EDITED BY **Andy Lee Roth** AND **Mickey Huff**
WITH **Project Censored**

FOREWORD BY **Danielle McLean**

ILLUSTRATED BY **Anson Stevens-Bollen**

Fair Oaks, CA • New York

The Censored Press
PO Box 1177
Fair Oaks, CA 95628
www.censoredpress.org

Seven Stories Press
140 Watts Street
New York, NY 10013
www.sevenstories.com

ISBN 978-1-64421-117-5 (paperback)
ISBN 978-1-64421-118-2 (electronic)
ISSN 1074-5998

College professors and high school and middle school teachers
may order free examination copies of Seven Stories Press titles.
viisit https://www.sevenstories.com/pg/resources-academics
or email academics@sevenstories.com.

9 8 7 6 5 4 3 2 1

Printed in the USA

Book design by Jon Gilbert

DEDICATION

To Glen Ford
November 5, 1949 – July 21, 2021

Radical independent journalist
Co-founder and executive editor of Black Agenda Report
Lifelong truth-teller

Contents

Foreword

DANIELLE MCLEAN

At their best, journalism and those who practice it have kept the powerful honest, held elected officials accountable for their actions and abuses of power, and revealed the complex causes of and solutions for societal ills such as poverty, housing insecurity, inequality, and public health crises.

But the state of the free press is in turmoil.

Yes, anti-democratic world leaders and their oligarch cronies vilify the media while trying to shield the public from truth and maintain a grip on power. But perhaps the biggest threat to the free press in the United States comes from inside it: the hedge funds such as Alden Global Capital and the corporate boards of other large media conglomerates that run so many newsrooms.

Since the new millennium, print publications have struggled to monetize a transition from paid advertisements and subscriptions to free internet stories adorned with ads that bring in a fraction of the revenue. For years, too many news organizations tried to chase whatever advertising dollars they could through clickbait headlines and stories that failed to find an audience or deliver high-quality journalism. Meanwhile, internet giants like Facebook and Google leeched news outlets' hard work by capitalizing off news articles posted online and not offering fair compensation to publishers in return.[1] The pandemic only worsened the situation.

According to an analysis by the Pew Research Center, newsroom employment declined 23 percent between 2008 and 2019.[2] That includes many behind-the-scenes staff as well as thousands of investigative, policy, city hall, and statehouse reporters, video operators and editors, copy-editors, and photographers. The pandemic has decimated newsrooms even further, as the Poynter Institute has been documenting with constant updates about staff layoffs and furloughs.[3] And huge media companies that own large collections of local and daily newspapers continue to consolidate into corporate giants or sell off their assets to hedge funds that are more than happy to cut newsrooms to the bare bone, sucking out whatever profit they can.

The dust still hasn't settled from all this devastation, and nationwide local newspapers have been forced to close or slash their staffs to near nothing. Large swathes of the country are now served by one or no local news-papers—replaced by all of the misinformation, lies, and propaganda that are so easily disseminated online.[4]

The reporters who remain are working harder than ever to cover more than they ever have, sometimes with man-dates to produce a certain number of stories, videos, and social media posts per day. Many get paid low wages while working long hours to meet their quotas and cover their beats with little time to really dig into complex issues. In uncertain economic times they are also regarded as expendable, and let go with scary regularity and no con-sideration for their personal struggles.

These conditions have forced reporters, often from underrepresented communities and lower socioeconomic backgrounds, out of the industry all too soon, terminating what could have been long and excellent careers. Making a bad situation worse, those reporters are often the ones best suited to understanding how laws, policies, and decisions by powerful corporations affect certain communities disproportionately. It's no wonder that trust in traditional media is at an all-time low.[5]

According to the Society of Professional Journalists's Code of Ethics, reporters should "be vigilant and courageous about holding those with power accountable" and give "voice to the voiceless."[6] They should serve as watchdogs over public affairs and the government and make sure the public's business is conducted in the open. They should also boldly "tell the story of the diversity and magnitude of the human experience" and seek "sources whose voices we seldom hear." The conditions that reporters are forced to endure today tremendously complicate that task.

Project Censored's *State of the Free Press 2022* shines a spotlight on critical issues investigated by reporters who succeeded in providing essential watchdog journalism despite the odds against them. The book recounts important stories focused on systems, governments, and corporations that harm the less powerful—stories which often go unnoticed by the establishment press. It's the kind of work news organizations must do to give democracy a chance.

We are fortunate that many nonprofit and alternative newsrooms throughout the country help to revitalize the news deserts that otherwise expand with each new merger or closure. However, those newsrooms can only do so much with minimal financial backing. Whether through new sources of public funding or philanthropy, reforms to antitrust laws, regulations that force Facebook and Google to properly compensate the publishers they profit off of, or something not yet envisioned, newsrooms need our support.

In recent years some national news outlets have ramped up support for investigative teams that have done groundbreaking watchdog journalism. At a time when so few job opportunities for watchdog journalists exist, their work is more crucial than ever, and they should be commended. Yet, as isolated instances bucking the trend of an entire industry in decline, these teams can only do so much.

Sadly, too many of the media's scarce resources are devoted to amplifying the voices of the country's most powerful government officials and corporate executives, uncritically publicizing their opinions and short-term goals instead of exploring the collective impacts that their decisions might have on society and its most vulnerable members.

This needs to change. Our industry needs to change.

We need to stop chasing ratings and meaningless clickbait headlines, stop treating politics like celebrity gossip and elections like popularity polls, demand change from the corporate boards and hedge funds that run news outlets without caring about the free press, and turn our focus toward the kind of journalism that our society deserves. We need more of the kind of journalism you'll find in this book.

DANIELLE MCLEAN is a senior editor at Smart Cities Dive, a national news outlet that provides in-depth journalism tracking the most impactful news and trends shaping cities and municipalities. She is also the chairperson of the Society of Professional Journalists's Ethics Committee. She previously served as chairperson of SPJ's Freedom of Information Committee.

Danielle is a former staff reporter at the *Chronicle of Higher Education*, where she covered federal and state higher ed policies. She is also a former investigative reporter at the *Bangor Daily News* and later ThinkProgress, writing about voter suppression, corruption, housing, poverty, and the impacts of federal and state policies, among a host of other issues. Her report on missing and murdered Indigenous women at ThinkProgress was selected as the top story in Project Censored's *State of the Free Press 2021*.

Notes

1. Jill Goldsmith, "NY Rep. Jerry Nadler Blasts Facebook, Google for Stealing News & Destroying Journalism Jobs at Antitrust Hearing," Deadline, July 29, 2020.
2. Elizabeth Grieco, "U.S. Newspapers Have Shed Half of Their Newsroom Employees since 2008," Pew Research Center, April 20, 2020.
3. Kristen Hare, "Here are the Newsroom Layoffs, Furloughs and Closures That Happened during the Coronavirus Pandemic," Poynter Institute, April 26, 2021, updated May 27, 2021.
4. Penelope Muse Abernathy, "The Expanding News Desert," Hussman School of Journalism and Media, University of North Carolina, 2020.
5. Felix Salmon, "Media Trust Hits New Low," Axios, January 21, 2021.
6. "SPJ Code of Ethics," Society of Professional Journalists, September 6, 2014.

A Return to News Normalcy?

MICKEY HUFF AND ANDY LEE ROTH

THE NEW "NORMAL"?

The year 2021 was deeply challenging, in the United States and throughout the world. By June 2021 the Johns Hopkins University Coronavirus Research Center reported more than 3.8 million deaths due to the global COVID-19 pandemic, including more deaths in the first half of 2021 than in all of 2020, with an estimated 600,000 fatalities in the United States since the start of the pandemic.[1] Survivors struggled with the new normal of widespread unemployment and quarantine restrictions, including lockdowns, masking, and social distancing. For some relatively fortunate people, the ongoing pandemic entailed adapting to new, remote routines for work and schooling, though even for the most fortunate the continuous threat of danger and indefinite isolation could exact a heavy toll on mental health.

Against the grim backdrop of the pandemic, 2021 began in the United States with the failed insurrection attempt on January 6th in Washington, DC. That day a mob of Donald Trump's supporters, motivated by the belief that Democrats had "stolen" the 2020 presidential election, violently occupied the US Capitol in an attempt to disrupt congressional certification of Joe Biden as the new president.[2]

As the United States experienced, in the midst of the pandemic, one of its most contentious presidential elections, the political class floundered in attempts to mitigate the unfolding tragedies of the mounting sick and dead, all while mass unrest and protests for social justice and racial equality exploded following the police murder of an unarmed Black American, George Floyd, in Minneapolis, Minnesota. At the same time, the gap between haves and have nots widened as the wealth of billionaires soared and unemployment rates for the masses spiraled off the charts.

While many Americans were trying to cope, there was also a sense of hope as many anticipated the election of Joe Biden and Kamala Harris as the signal of a significant change of power in Washington. In the course of the past year, government agencies at every level sought to keep the economy afloat and quell growing fears, pointing to the possibility that the pandemic would soon be under control. From the federal Coronavirus Aid, Relief, and Economic Security (CARES) Act to state and local efforts to provide food, shelter, and mental health care, major economic stimulus efforts were enacted to offset some of the negative impacts of the pandemic.

In that sense, Americans were channeling another tumultuous period of history—one from a hundred years ago, after World War I, when the United States faced another raging pandemic and economic recession. The United States then had experienced a crackdown on civil liberties and free speech in the form of Espionage and Sedition Acts; racial tensions flared during the Red Summer of 1919 as violence erupted from Chicago to Tulsa; Prohibition was the law of the land; and the first wave of US feminism ended with the passage of the 19th Amendment. People yearned for a return to "normalcy," as then–presidential hopeful Warren G. Harding proclaimed.[3]

The desire for simpler times, however, was more a phantom than a reality, as millions of Americans ultimately had to adjust to an ever- and fast-changing world. As in any period of crisis and change, citizens turned to the media not only to make sense of a chaotic world around them, but also for guidance, reassurance, and even some respite. In the 1920s, Americans tuned in to commercial radio broadcasts and combed through increasingly popular and widely available magazines, much the way that today they sign on to social media and other popular online platforms. Whether a century ago or this past year—as this book's cover by Anson Stevens-Bollen suggests, with Lady Liberty trying to turn back the clock to allegedly simpler times—Americans were eager to hear about a return to normalcy, even if such news would prove untrue, or useful only for its placebo effect. Nevertheless, large changes were afoot then, and are now, for the people of America and throughout the media landscape.

HOW US JOURNALISM HAS CHANGED SINCE PROJECT CENSORED'S FOUNDING

The media have changed significantly since Carl Jensen established Project Censored in 1976. In principle, journalism continues to serve as one crucial foundation for democratic self-government. But, from the advent of 24/7 cable news outlets in the 1980s to more recent developments involving the internet and social media, reporters and editors' daily working conditions—not to mention the economic pressures on news organizations—could scarcely have changed more drastically.

Americans today access news via internet-based feeds and handheld devices that would have seemed like the stuff of science fiction in 1976. However, as technological access to news has increased, Americans' trust in and understanding of journalism appear to have decreased.[4] Especially in the past decade, corporate media outlets have become increasingly hyper-partisan, sowing division to ramp up ratings rather than reporting in the general public interest.[5] Consequently, many Americans now seem to trust their own preferred news sources, but not those that they associate with people "on the other side" of an increasingly acrimonious political divide.[6] How did this happen? And what can be done about it?

Media Deregulation

In 1983, Ben Bagdikian published *The Media Monopoly*, his classic analysis of how the consolidation of media ownership would threaten the diversity of media content, especially as commercial interests took precedence over journalistic values.[7] Within a few years, the Federal Communications Commission (FCC) dealt a debilitating blow to media diversity when it voted to repeal the fairness doctrine, which had required broadcast networks to provide the public with balanced coverage of contrasting views on important issues. President Ronald Reagan vetoed a congressional bill that would have preempted the FCC's decision by writing the fairness doctrine into law.[8]

The 1996 passage of the Telecommunications Act ushered in a new wave of media conglomeration. Highlighted as the #1 story in the 1996 *Censored* yearbook, the Telecommunications Act moved federal media regulation "in the wrong direction, toward greater concentration and fewer choices for consumers, all under the guise of 'greater competition,'" consumer advocate Ralph Nader observed.[9] Taken together, the repeal of the fairness doctrine and the passage of the Telecommunications Act accelerated the corporate consolidation and silencing of diverse viewpoints that Bagdikian had predicted.

Censorship by Proxy

The impacts of the internet and the increasing influence of social media on journalism cannot be overstated. "Google may not be a country, but it is a superpower," Timothy Garton Ash has noted.[10] Though Google, Facebook, Twitter, and other Big Tech corporations lack the formal legal authority of sovereign states, "their capacity to enable or limit freedom of information and expression is greater than that of most states."[11] The new media giants—including Alphabet (which owns Google and YouTube), Facebook (which also owns Instagram), Twitter, Apple, and Microsoft—function as the arbiters of public issues and legitimate discourse, despite assertions by their leaders that they are tech platforms, not publishers or media companies.[12] Despite denying their roles, these tech giants are "the new gatekeepers," and their proprietary algorithms "determine which news stories circulate widely, raising serious concerns about transparency and accountability in determinations of newsworthiness."[13]

A January 2021 court ruling raises pointed questions about the limits on our cherished constitutional protection of free expression set by privately-owned, for-profit media platforms. That month, a federal judge dismissed a class-action lawsuit by LGBT YouTube content creators, which claimed that YouTube had violated their First Amendment rights by censoring their content and demonetizing their channels. US District Court Magistrate Virginia DeMarchi ruled that, as "private entities," Google and YouTube were not bound by the First Amendment.[14] But in this digitally connected era, the distinction between government entities and private ones may not be so clear, raising the possibility of government censorship by proxy.

Today's Big Tech gatekeepers trace their technological roots back to the Cold War of the 1950s and, specifically, the Defense Department's Defense Advanced Research Projects Agency (DARPA). Charged with developing technology to promote national security, DARPA played a crucial role in the development of computer networking that made the internet and related innovations, from the Global Positioning System (GPS) to drones, a reality. Many of the US-based global tech companies have benefited from federal funding for research and development and tax breaks, not to mention lucrative government contracts on projects involving national security and surveillance.[15] The result is a new twist on President Dwight D. Eisenhower's warning, sixty years ago, about the threats to democracy posed by the "military–industrial complex" and burgeoning government surveillance.[16]

These tech companies' unparalleled control over communication makes them a valuable proxy for government agencies struggling with political and legal obstacles to censorship. In this digital era, the biggest private tech companies can engage in what we term "censorship by proxy," restricting freedom of expression in ways that the government cannot, in the interest of both parties.[17]

Physical Threats

If media deregulation and censorship by proxy constitute subsurface, tectonic shifts in the US media landscape, then attacks on reporters and other direct assaults on the integrity of journalism stand as more obviously concerning developments. In late 2018, Reporters Without Borders (RSF) listed the United States among the world's most dangerous nations for journalists—the first time the United States ranked in the top five.[18] By 2021, the United States ranked only 44th out of 180 countries in RSF's annual World Press Freedom Index.[19]

Especially since the onset of protests against structural racism that arose following the police murder of George Floyd on May 25, 2020, US journalists have faced a sharp increase in attacks. According to the U.S. Press Freedom Tracker, the past year brought with it "unprecedented violence" against journalists, who across the United States were assaulted, arrested, or had their equipment damaged "in numbers never before documented."[20] Between May 26, 2020 and May 25, 2021, the U.S. Press Freedom Tracker documented 415 assaults on journalists, 153 arrests, and 105 cases of damage inflicted upon their equipment.[21] During that period, as they covered the Black Lives Matter movement, journalists and other media workers "faced near-unrelenting assaults"—more than 85 percent of which were perpetrated by law enforcement.[22]

Chilling Threats

Alongside physical assaults, US journalists have also been subjected to chilling threats by government agencies. In

Spring 2021, for example, journalists covering protests in Brooklyn Center, Minnesota and Portland, Oregon were detained by law enforcement officials who photographed reporters and their IDs or press credentials.[23] Minnesota law enforcement officials suggested that the photos were necessary to "expedite the identification process," but press freedom outlets registered concern that agencies, including the Minneapolis Police Department, have used facial recognition services, such as Clearview AI, to monitor and target individuals, including protestors.[24]

In May 2021 the *Washington Post* reported that, under the Trump administration, the Department of Justice (DOJ) had "secretly obtained" the phone records for three of the *Post*'s national security reporters, each of whom had reported on Russia's attempted meddling in the 2016 election. The *Post*'s report noted that it is "rare for the Justice Department to use subpoenas to get records of reporters in leak investigations," and that press organizations and First Amendment advocates "decried the government practice of seizing journalists' records in an effort to identify the sources of leaks, saying it unjustly chills critical newsgathering."[25]

The Biden administration initially supported the DOJ's maneuvers, but a month later reversed its position after additional information came to light about similar invasive actions directed at a reporter from CNN as well as four reporters at the *New York Times*. The DOJ had even placed a gag order on *Times* executives, preventing them from revealing the secret legal maneuvers to the public or anyone in the newsroom.[26] White House press secretary Jen Psaki announced that "the issuing of subpoenas for the records of reporters in leak investigations is not consistent with the President's policy direction to the Department."[27] The DOJ subsequently said it would no longer legally compel journalists to reveal source information in leak investigations.[28]

Freedom of the Press Foundation executive director Trevor Timm called this policy shift "a potential sea change for press freedom rights in the United States," but added that the Justice Department "must now write this categorical bar of journalist surveillance into its official 'media guidelines,' and Congress should also immediately enshrine the rules into law to ensure no administration can abuse its power again."[29] By taking these steps, the Biden administration could "stem the tide of more than ten years of erosion of press freedom," Timm concluded.

Time will tell whether the Biden administration fulfills these hopes, or whether it follows in the footsteps of the Obama and Trump administrations by continuing to prosecute government officials and other whistleblowers who disclose secrets to journalists.[30]

We present *State of the Free Press* in the context of ongoing developments in the COVID-19 pandemic and the nation's long-overdue reckoning with systemic racial inequality, as well as against the backdrop of media deregulation, censorship by proxy, and chilling threats, including physical violence, against journalists themselves. We hope that at least some of the weight of these concerns may be offset by the diversity of considered perspectives, fearless truth-telling, and bold civic solutions included in this volume.

INSIDE *STATE OF THE FREE PRESS 2022*

Chapter 1 presents the 25 most important but underreported news stories of 2020–2021. Each of the stories has been "censored" in the broad sense established by Project Censored founder Carl Jensen, who defined censorship as "the suppression of information, whether purposeful or not, by any method—including bias, omission, underreporting or self-censorship—that prevents the public from fully knowing what is happening in its society."[31] From investigative reports on prescription drug costs becoming a leading cause of death in the United States (this year's #1 story) and racial bias in police use of dogs (#9), to a historic wave of wildcat strikes (#3) and microplastic contamination of seafood (#5), during 2020–2021 independent journalists and news outlets provided vital reporting on fundamental public issues that corporate news media either marginalized or buried.

Noting the "dogged persistence of gaps in corporate news coverage of certain taboo topics," the authors of Chapter 2, on Déjà Vu News, revisit five Top 25 stories from previous years to update subsequent developments in those stories and to evaluate to what extent they remain "censored" by corporate news outlets. Shealeigh Voitl, Griffin Curran, Rachael Schwanebeck, and Steve Macek review—and, in some cases, reassess—the Project's previous coverage of private prison companies and anti-immigration legislation; spurious campus free-speech legislation promoted by right-wing funders; police "use of force" policies alleged to reduce civilian deaths; the FBI labeling racial justice activists as "Black Identity Extremists"; and a proposal by Indigenous groups to create the world's largest protected wildlife reserve in the Amazon.

Too often, and at too high a cost, corporate media titillate the public with Junk Food News, the term Carl Jensen coined to identify sensationalized trivia that often displaces quality news reporting on more significant public issues. In Chapter 3, Jen Lyons, Sierra Kaul, Marcelle Levine Swinburne, Vikki Vasquez, Gavin Kelley, and Mickey Huff review a host of Junk Food News stories from this past pandemic year that attest to the continued relevance of Jensen's concept. Surveying corporate media coverage of TikTok's "Gorilla Glue Girl," pop star Cardi B's latest controversial chart-topping song, and Oprah's interview with disenchanted British royal couple Meghan Markle and Prince Harry, the chapter's authors show how a fascination with "humilitainment" obscured more substantive reporting on topics including humanitarian crises in Yemen and Ethiopia, the wave of female unemployment propelled by COVID-19, and legislation to restrict voting rights.

In 2002, Peter Phillips coined the term "News Abuse" to refer to media outlets' minimization, exaggeration, or obscuring of key elements of stories, amounting to false representation by their omissions of the truth. In Chapter 4, Robin Andersen examines some of the most flagrant recent examples of News Abuse, providing an in-depth analysis of how one form of media bias—false balance—has distorted establishment coverage of some of 2020–2021's most significant stories, including the nationwide Black Lives Matter protests spurred by the police killing of George Floyd, claims by Donald Trump and his supporters that Democrats "stole" the 2020 presidential election, the ensuing January 6th insurrection attempt that resulted in the violent occupation of the US Capitol, and Republican efforts to restrict voting rights. Andersen shows in specific detail how establishment news outlets' insistence on presenting "both sides" of opposing viewpoints as equal, despite glaring evidence to the contrary, serves as a fundamental form of News Abuse.

Finally, in welcome contrast to the preceding chapters on Junk Food News and News Abuse, Chapter 5, on Media Democracy in Action, highlights six exemplars of critical media literacy, free press principles, and civic engagement. The chapter features the voices and the good work of Michelle Rodino-Colocino and Brian Dolber, co-editors of a new book on the double-edged role of media in the new "gig" economy; John K. Wilson of Academe Blog, assessing Big Tech's threats to higher education; Michael Gordon of the Propwatch Project, an accessible and authoritative online primer in propaganda techniques of all kinds; Sonali Kolhatkar, recounting the rewards and pitfalls of pursuing independent investigative journalism as a calling; Rachael Jolley, a journalism instructor in the United Kingdom, relating her experiences teaching budding investigative reporters to consider classic and contemporary detectives from novels and TV as models of inquiry; and Alison Trope and DJ Johnson of the Critical Media Project, an online resource housed at the University of Southern California's Annenberg School of Communication and Journalism, that explores media constructions of social identity and shows how media systems not only uphold systems of power but can also be used to upend them.

REMEDIES FOR A MORE
ROBUST FREE PRESS

The past year has made it clear that access to accurate, trustworthy news can be a matter of life or death, as indicated by reporting on the pandemic (see, e.g., story #13 in Chapter 1) as well as the claims of election fraud, promoted by Donald Trump, QAnon, and others, which precipitated the January 6th Capitol riot that left five dead and more than one hundred people injured (see Chapter 4).

When we hear calls for a return to normalcy, we need to ask, "Return to what?" and "Whose 'normal'?" Do we yearn for a return to neoliberal, top-down control with widening wealth gaps, social unrest, continued destruction of the environment, and divisive media and propaganda?[32] Or do we want a genuinely new normal based on democratic principles of inclusion and equality, both of which require a vigilant and truly free press?

Decades ago, when there were only three major television networks, America's top journalists used to sign off their broadcasts with statements that did little to encourage critical analysis of the day's news and how the networks reported it. In the 1950s, pioneering CBS anchor Edward R. Murrow ended his broadcasts by wishing his audience "good night, and good luck." A generation later, CBS's Walter Cronkite regularly signed off by asserting, "And that's the way it is." Given the challenges enumerated in this introduction, we need more than salutary phrases that promote passive acceptance of what passes for the news. We need the perspective and the tools to ask of our news sources, "Is that the way it is?"

It is a genuine challenge to convince people to consider

news they are disinclined to trust for *ideological* reasons, even when such reporting is based on well-founded *evidence*.[33] To foster that attitude toward news, we need critical media literacy education and a more robust and diverse independent press committed to journalistic ethics and reporting in the public interest.

The Society of Professional Journalists (SPJ) reminds us that journalists should seek truth and report it, minimize harm, act independently, and be accountable and transparent.[34] As Danielle McLean, chair of the SPJ's Ethics Committee, notes in the foreword to this volume, "We need to stop chasing ratings and meaningless click-bait headlines, stop treating politics like celebrity gossip and elections like popularity polls, demand change from the corporate boards and hedge funds that run news outlets without caring about the free press, and turn our focus toward the kind of journalism that our society deserves." But McLean's suggested remedy for today's media malaise goes further, noting, "At their best, journalism and those who practice it have kept the powerful honest, held elected officials accountable for their actions and abuses of power, and revealed the complex causes of and solutions for societal ills such as poverty, housing insecurity, inequality, and public health crises."

In the same spirit, Ralph Nader, who warned against the threats posed by the Telecommunications Act back in 1996, continues to fight for press freedoms and investigative reporting in the public interest, most recently with his initiative Reporters' Alert: Fresh Ideas for Journalists, which provides working leads for journalists by highlighting underreported news stories.[35] Other long-standing organizations such as the Freedom of the Press

Foundation support bold reporting by offering guides and training on security and privacy risks, knowledge crucial to the protection of journalists in dangerous times.[36] The Electronic Frontier Foundation's project on Surveillance Self-Defense goes still further, supplying practical tools to promote as much security as possible for online communications.[37] A truly free press is only possible when journalists and sources are free from the threat of violence, arrest, surveillance, or retaliation from the people and institutions they scrutinize, making safety and privacy no less paramount to healthy media than the truthfulness and substantiality of the stories reported.

A further important step toward reviving trust in news media would be the creation of a nonprofit, publicly funded media system, reframing journalism as a public utility and promoting it as a common good, rather than a societal luxury that only matters to select subgroups of the public. Such a step would necessarily entail confronting widespread prejudices against journalism. As Victor Pickard and Timothy Neff noted in a June 2021 *Columbia Journalism Review* article, although Americans seem united in the belief that "democracy requires a free and functional press," they don't seem interested in funding it.[38] Pickard and Neff observed how anemic financial support for news media is in the United States compared with other major democratic countries, noting that "if the US spent just 0.02 percent of its GDP, it would generate $4.5 billion for public media infrastructure that could serve local communities' information needs." Getting newsrooms out from under the management of hedge funds, tech billionaires, and other corporate conglomerates and into the hands of citizen-activists providing oversight for the proper reporting and representation of crucial community issues would be game-changing to the practice and consumption of journalism, promoting real trust and engagement in news through the active participation of the people it serves.

Finally, we need to accelerate efforts to teach critical media literacy to all Americans, from early education into adulthood. The work of organizations such as the Critical Media Project, the Propwatch Project, and Project Censored provide crucial resources to achieve this goal; but, as with Pickard and Neff's vital proposals for public media funding, supporting critical media literacy education at a national scale requires substantial financial support, independent of corporate sources that would inevitably compromise its critical rigor.

The importance of free speech and expression embodied in a free press protected by the First Amendment are foundational to democracy and our entire way of life. We deviate from them at our peril. In our push to return to normalcy, we must seriously deliberate over what freedom of expression really looks and sounds like in practice, which currently existing institutions provide for it, and how we can transform the ones that don't. As journalism is under threat from corporate consolidation, Big Tech censorship, governmental surveillance, police violence, and distrust from a divided public, it is up to us to stand up for reporting that matters, to protest against hyper-partisan misrepresentation and untruths, to demand de-monopolization, regulation, and security for our communication platforms, to envision new systems to support the news media we need, and to fight back against unjust and oppressive measures that privilege the powerful while spying on and punishing watchdogs, whistleblowers, and truth-tellers.

Business as usual won't save journalism, just as clickbait and skewed stories won't suffice to heal the wounds of the pandemic or the impoverishment and neglect that led to it hitting some of us so unequally and so hard. The future of journalism depends upon our active engagement as citizens, no less than the future of democracy depends upon a truly independent, ethical, and uncompromising free press—reporting not for the profits of the few, but selflessly in the true interest of the undivided public.

Mickey Huff, Fair Oaks, CA
Andy Lee Roth, Winthrop, WA
June 2021

Notes

1. Coronavirus Resource Center, Johns Hopkins University & Medicine, undated [accessed June 15, 2021]. For establishment news coverage of the Johns Hopkins data, see, e.g., Jon Kamp, Jason Douglas, and Juan Forero, "Covid-19 Deaths This Year Have Already Eclipsed 2020's Toll," *Wall Street Journal*, June 10, 2021; and Arielle Mitropoulos, "US Surpasses Grim Milestone with 600,000 Lives Lost to COVID-19," ABC News, June 15, 2021.
2. See Robin Andersen's "False Balance in Media Coverage Undermines Democracy: News Abuse in 2020–2021," Chapter 4 in this volume, for thorough analysis of the media coverage of the January 6th insurrection.
3. William Deverell, "Warren Harding Tried to Return America to 'Normalcy' after WWI and the 1918 Pandemic. It Failed," *Smithsonian Magazine*, May 19, 2020.
4. See, e.g., Andy Lee Roth, "Should This Article be Trusted?" *YES! Magazine*, December 21, 2020.
5. See Nolan Higdon and Mickey Huff, *United States of Distraction: Media Manipulation in Post-Truth America (and what we can do about it)* (San Francisco: City Lights Books, 2019).
6. John Gramlich, "What Makes a News Story Trustworthy? Americans Point to the Outlet That Publishes It, Sources Cited," Pew Research Center, June 9, 2021; and Jeffrey Gottfried, Mason Walker, and Amy Mitchell, "Americans See Skepticism of News Media as Healthy, Say

Public Trust in the Institution Can Improve," Pew Research Center, August 31, 2020.

7.	Ben Bagdikian, *The Media Monopoly* (New York: Beacon Press, 1983).
8.	Kenneth B. Noble, "Reagan Vetoes Measure to Affirm Fairness Policy for Broadcasters," *New York Times*, June 21, 1987.
9.	Justin Twergo, "Telecommunications Deregulation: Closing Up America's 'Marketplace of Ideas,'" *Censored: The News That Didn't Make the News—and Why, 20th Anniversary Ed.*, eds. Carl Jensen and Project Censored (New York: Seven Stories Press, 1996), 50–51, 51.
10.	Timothy Garton Ash, *Free Speech: Ten Principles for a Connected World* (London: Atlantic Books, 2016), 87.
11.	Ibid.
12.	See, e.g., Sam Levin, "Is Facebook a Publisher? In Public It Says No, but in Court It Says Yes," *The Guardian*, July 3, 2018.
13.	Andy Lee Roth, "The New Gatekeepers: How Proprietary Algorithms Increasingly Determine the News We See," The Markaz Review, March 15, 2021.
14.	Wendy Davis, "Judges Sides with YouTube in 'Censorship' Suit by LGBT Content Creators," MediaPost, January 11, 2021.
15.	Yasha Levine, *Surveillance Valley: The Secret Military History of the Internet* (New York: PublicAffairs, 2018).
16.	See, e.g., Shahid Buttar, "Ike's Dystopian Dream, and How It Came True," in *Censored 2017: Fortieth Anniversary Edition*, eds. Mickey Huff and Andy Lee Roth with Project Censored (New York: Seven Stories Press, 2016), 341–67.
17.	"The Long Sili-CON: Power & Censorship in the Digital Era," The Real News Network and Project Censored, May 5, 2021.
18.	"Worldwide Round-Up of Journalists Killed, Detained, Held Hostage, or Missing in 2018," Reporters Without Borders, undated [accessed June 15, 2021], 8, 10.
19.	"2021 World Press Freedom Index," Reporters Without Borders, undated [accessed June 15, 2021].
20.	"1 Year of Unprecedented Violence Against Journalists," U.S. Press Freedom Tracker, undated [accessed June 15, 2021]. The U.S. Press Freedom Tracker, which rigorously documents press freedom violations in the United States, is the joint effort of more than two dozen press freedom groups, including the Freedom of the Press Foundation, the Committee to Protect Journalists, the Knight First Amendment Institute at Columbia University, Reporters Without Borders, the Index on Censorship, and the Association of Alternative News Media.
21.	Ibid.
22.	"Between the Bookends: 1 Year of Press Freedom Violations," U.S. Press Freedom Tracker, May 24, 2021.
23.	"Law Enforcement Agencies Photograph Journalists and Their IDs as They Cover Protests," U.S. Press Freedom Tracker, March 12, 2021.
24.	Grayson Clary, "Why were Minnesota Police Photographing Journalists?" Reporters Committee for Freedom of the Press, April 25, 2021.
25.	Devlin Barrett, "Trump Justice Department Secretly Obtained Post Reporters' Phone Records," *Washington Post*, May 7, 2021.

26. Parker Higgins, "Biden Administration Defends Trump's Indefensible Surveillance of Reporters," Freedom of the Press Foundation, May 11, 2021; Parker Higgins, "Surveillance of CNN Reporter Underscores Urgency of Justice Department Ban on Journalist Spying," Freedom of the Press Foundation, May 21, 2021; and "US Justice Dept Got Gag Order on NY Times Execs in Fight Over Email Logs—NYT," Reuters, June 5, 2021.

27. Jen Psaki, "Statement by Press Secretary Jen Psaki on the Department of Justice Leak Investigation Policy," White House, June 5, 2021.

28. Associated Press, "DOJ Says It Will No Longer Seize Reporters' Records in Investigating Leaks," NPR, June 5, 2021.

29. "In a Sea Change for Press Freedom, Biden Administration Vows Not to Spy on Reporters Doing Their Job," Freedom of the Press Foundation, June 5, 2021.

30. Steve Macek and Andy Lee Roth, "How the Biden Administration Can Help Rejuvenate Journalism after Four Years of Carnage," Common Dreams, December 14, 2020.

31. Carl Jensen, "Project Censored: Raking Muck, Raising Hell," in *Censored: The News That Didn't Make the News—and Why*, ed. Carl Jensen (Chapel Hill, North Carolina: Shelburne Press, 1993), 1–14, 7.

32. Nolan Higdon and Mickey Huff, "Ripe for Fascism: A Post-Coup d'Trump Autopsy of American Democracy," *CounterPunch*, January 14, 2021.

33. See, e.g., Steve Macek and Andy Lee Roth, "It's True That Corporate Media is Biased—But Not in the Ways Right-Wingers Say," Truthout, November 27, 2020.

34. "SPJ Code of Ethics," Society of Professional Journalists, September 6, 2014.

35. Ralph Nader, "Reporters' Alert: Fresh Ideas for Journalists," Reporters' Alert, March 5, 2021 – May 7, 2021 [accessed June 15, 2021].

36. "Guides & Training," Freedom of the Press Foundation, undated [accessed June 15, 2021].

37. "Surveillance Self-Defense," Electronic Frontier Foundation, undated [accessed June 15, 2021].

38. Victor Pickard and Timothy Neff, "Strengthen Our Democracy by Funding Public Media," *Columbia Journalism Review*, June 2, 2021. For more on the case for public journalism, see Veronica Vasquez and Mickey Huff, "Revive Journalism with a Stimulus Package and Public Option," in *State of the Free Press 2021*, eds. Mickey Huff and Andy Lee Roth with Project Censored (New York: Seven Stories Press, 2020), 62–65.

CHAPTER 1

The Top *Censored* Stories and Media Analysis of 2020–21

Compiled and edited by STEVE MACEK,
ANALISA CHUDZIK, and ANDY LEE ROTH

INTRODUCTION: WHAT THE TOP 25 STORY LIST IS, AND WHAT IT IS NOT

The past year has been notable for its epochal, traumatic, and (hopefully) once-in-a-lifetime news stories: a pandemic that has so far killed nearly four million people worldwide and shut down commerce, travel, and global trade for months on end; a spate of police murders of Black and Brown people here at home that sparked a massive movement for racial justice; a US presidential election in which the losing incumbent refused to concede and resorted to misinformation and desperate legal maneuvers in order to preserve his grip on power; and a mass of armed right-wing protestors—including many members or veterans of the armed forces or the police—who stormed the US Capitol building in a desperate bid to keep their preferred, authoritarian candidate in office. CNN, ABC, Fox News, NPR, *USA Today*, the *New York Times*, and the *Washington Post* all breathlessly reported on these shocking developments, as hundreds of millions of people around the country and the world followed every tweet, headline, and news alert.

Yet for all the momentous news such outlets broke in

2020, the establishment press missed, minimized, or misframed at least as many important stories as they covered exhaustively and accurately. That is why Project Censored continues to monitor and identify the vital, sometimes earth-shaking news stories that get ignored or underreported each year by the corporate media.

So, what exactly are the defining characteristics of a Project Censored Top 25 story?

Throughout 2020–2021, 209 students at ten colleges and universities all across the United States worked with faculty mentors to find, research, and synopsize consequential news stories reported on by smaller, independent, often not-for-profit news outlets but passed over or underreported by the large, for-profit journalistic organizations that dominate the national media landscape. These Validated Independent News stories were then submitted to Project Censored, researched and fact-checked further, and, provided they met our rigorous standards, were submitted to our judges for evaluation.

In order to be included on the ballot for the Top 25 list, stories must be genuine examples of news reporting, not press releases, academic journal articles, or public relations materials designed to advance the agenda of a particular cause or movement. They must take the form of news articles, not editorials, opinion pieces, or political propaganda. They must be transparently sourced and grounded in facts gathered from reputable and identifiable sources, not based on mere speculation. The stories must also embody cardinal news values such as prominence, social impact, and timeliness.

Decisions about which stories to include on the Top 25 list and where to rank them are not made by one or two individual editors but rather reflect the collective effort and judgment of hundreds of student researchers, dozens of faculty evaluators, and the expert assessments of the Project's panel of international judges.

Perhaps most importantly, Project Censored spares no effort in verifying that the stories we include on our list meet our definition of "censored stories," often conducting three or more rounds of exhaustive database research to try to identify any potential corporate news coverage of the news items we spotlight each year.

In What Sense are These "Censored" Stories?

In the past, critics of Project Censored have complained that the stories included in our annual list are not "censored" at all, because they have been covered by "dozens of publications," albeit smaller, independent ones, or because occasionally stories that appear on the list have received attention from "at least one major mainstream newspaper, magazine, [or] television news program."[1]

Such criticisms badly miss the point of Project Censored's work and gloss over the deficits, biases, and blind spots in corporate media performance that the Project exposes.

When we say that an item on our Top 25 list has been "censored," we are not claiming that it has been completely and irrevocably repressed by the government or some other powerful institution (e.g., a political party, the military, big business, organized crime, an influential religious leader, etc.).

Censorship in this specific sense is known in First Amendment law as "prior restraint," the effort to *pre-*

vent publication or publicization of ideas or expression. In recent years, US courts have allowed very wide latitude for expression in the media of offensive, potentially harmful, or even false statements, and have consistently struck down efforts by officials to prevent newsworthy information from ever seeing the light of day. In its landmark ruling in the "Pentagon Papers" case of 1971, the US Supreme Court rejected President Richard Nixon's attempt to use his executive power to prevent the *New York Times* and the *Washington Post* from running stories based on top-secret documents about the Vietnam War provided to the newspapers by whistleblower Daniel Ellsberg.[2] More recently, a June 2020 lawsuit brought by the Justice Department against Donald Trump's former national security adviser John Bolton in an effort to halt publication of his book *The Room Where It Happened*, in which Bolton details Trump's lies and self-serving policy decisions during his presidency, only succeeded in drawing more attention to the tract (although, interestingly, a court case about whether the federal government can seize profits from the book was only finally dropped by the Justice Department in June 2021).[3]

In America circa 2021, it is next to impossible for government officials to get legal approval for censorship as it has been classically defined (although, as story #2 on the Top 25 list explains, libel laws in the United Kingdom are far more generous to would-be censors than they are in the United States). And, as Mickey Huff and Andy Lee Roth note in the introduction to this volume, sometimes the police and other officials interfere with journalists' reporting without asking courts for permission first—by arresting journalists covering protests, confiscating their equipment, or preventing them from recording acts of police violence.

More generally, independent news stories that Project Censored highlights as "censored" stories are subject to *partial* or *incomplete* corporate news coverage, as we recognize that the effect of underreporting or misreporting may ultimately be just as detrimental as nonreporting. After all, the blockade of establishment news coverage need not be total in order for an issue to remain unknown to all but a small segment of the public that actively seeks reporting on that topic.[4]

Important Facts and Perspectives Omitted

When we claim the stories in our Top 25 list are "censored," we mean not that such stories have been *completely silenced* but that the corporate news media have not given them the attention and detailed exploration to which their significance, social impact, and relevance to current political and cultural debates properly entitles them. These are stories that have been unfairly marginalized or superficially glossed rather than discussed in detail. Moreover, sometimes the way corporate media report these stories frames discordant facts or dissenting perspectives as matters of opinion, or omits key facts and crucial contextual elements that are vital to a full understanding of the issues these stories (ought to) raise.

Consider, for instance, story #3 on this year's Top 25: "Historic Wave of Wildcat Strikes for Workers' Rights." Since the onset of the pandemic, tens of thousands of American workers—service workers, drivers, health workers, teachers, and others—have taken part in more than a thousand short, impromptu, unauthorized work stoppages. Despite the fact that the United States has long had one of the least unionized, least politically active working-class populations in the advanced industrialized world, all of sudden previously docile workers have begun walking off the job in droves to demand better safety precautions against the dreaded COVID-19 virus, to insist on danger pay, or to protest against racial injustice. In fact, this recent burst of labor unrest may go down in history as the largest wave of wildcat strikes since the early 1970s.[5] As Project Censored's overview of the coverage of the story makes clear, local and specialized corporate news outlets often did *mention* or *make note* of individual labor actions (although some one-day strikes were simply ignored). Still, these strikes were hardly ever covered systematically, in-depth, or given follow-up coverage. The only wildcat strike last year that attracted any sustained commercial media attention was the National Basketball Association players' refusal to play in the aftermath of the police shooting of Black motorist Jacob Blake. More importantly, the corporate media's isolated, shallow coverage of work stoppages *not* involving professional athletes failed to note that these hundreds of short-lived collective acts of defiance added up to a significant and nearly unprecedented trend. Without being situated in the context of the ongoing national wave of wildcat strikes, reports about short work stoppages here and there could make the individual actions seem trivial. As we observe below, it is especially significant that most substantial treatment of the pandemic-driven explosion of grassroots labor insurgency in the agenda-setting *New York Times* was featured in op-eds, not news reports.

Discordant News Framed as "Opinion"

This year's Top 25 list demonstrates how commonplace it is for news that challenges the political and economic status quo to be relegated to the opinion pages of establishment newspapers and news sites or to be labeled as "commentary" in the broadcast media. Story #6, about Canary Mission maligning pro-Palestinian activists, is a case in point. The recent activities of this scandal-mongering website devoted to demonizing Israel's critics have been carefully chronicled by independent media like *The Nation*, the *Guardian*, and the Intercept, but the lone analysis of the site in the establishment press was a 2019 guest editorial in the *New York Times* about Canary Mission's McCarthyite tactics by civil rights advocate Michelle Alexander.[6]

Similarly, story #11, about the seed monopolies maintained by giant agribusiness conglomerates, was the focus of a *New York Times* op-ed by chef Dan Barber but has not been the focus of actual news reporting by any of the big corporate news organizations in the past year.[7] And story #14, about how factory farming creates a perfect breeding ground for new diseases that can easily spread to humans, was covered most thoroughly by small, independent investigative news outfits, while, apart from a substantial report on the topic published by Vox, the only corporate coverage of note was again an op-ed, in the *Los Angeles Times*.[8]

Isolated Corporate Coverage

This year's list does also include several stories that were the subject of extensive, meticulous, and extremely well-researched articles in a single major corporate newspaper or magazine but that never got picked up or investigated further by any other major news organization. For instance, story #19, about Europe's hunger for biomass fuel made from American forests, was the subject of a truly exemplary *New York Times* article, but no other corporate news outlet so much as ran an op-ed on the issue.[9] *The Atlantic* reprinted an article from Hakai Magazine, a Canadian ecological web journal, about the dire consequences of the darkening of coastal waters, story #23 on this year's list, but no other corporate news outlet paid any attention to the topic whatsoever.[10]

Blockaded Issues

Finally, some of the stories among this year's Top 25 have in fact been completely ignored by the corporate news media. Story #2, which concerns the dangers and legal harassment facing journalists investigating global financial corruption, has received some attention from the corporate news media *outside* the United States but none at all domestically. YouTube's wholesale demonetizing of progressive channels and video makers, story #17 on the 2020–2021 list, has been utterly overlooked by US corporate media, even as they have run several stories about the video sharing service's deplatforming of right-wing pundits and politicians. As noted in previous yearbooks, the Project's annual Top 25 story list can be "understood as an ongoing empirical investigation of the corporate news media's blind spots and lacunae, its third rails and 'no go' zones."[11]

From Critical Thinking to Critical Action

The summaries included in this chapter are not intended as replacements for the original reports on which they are based. Rather, they are intended to highlight each story's key points and crucial facts. Ideally, the brief summaries presented here will motivate readers to seek out and read the original reports filed by the independent journalists and news outlets that the Project's Top 25 list features. We hope that the information included in this year's Top 25 list will not only enhance your understanding of our divided and increasingly unequal world, but will also spur you to action on some of the pressing public issues brought to light by the exemplary journalism this chapter celebrates.

ACKNOWLEDGMENTS: Hedaia Anayah, Geoff Davidian, Sierra Kaul, Gavin Kelley, Marcelle Levine Swinburne, and Troy Patton provided research assistance during the final vetting of this year's top *Censored* stories.

A NOTE ON RESEARCH AND EVALUATION OF *CENSORED* NEWS STORIES

How do we at Project Censored identify and evaluate independent news stories, and how do we know that the Top 25 stories that we bring forward each year are not only relevant and significant but also trustworthy? The answer is that every candidate news story undergoes rigorous review, which takes place in multiple stages during each annual cycle. Although adapted to take advantage of both the Project's expanding affiliates program and current technologies, the vetting process is quite similar to the one Project Censored founder Carl Jensen established more than forty years ago.

Candidate stories are initially identified by Project Censored professors and students, or are nominated by members of the general public, who bring them to the Project's attention.[12] Together, faculty and students vet each candidate story in terms of its importance, timeliness, quality of sources, and corporate news coverage. If it fails on any one of these criteria, the story is deemed inappropriate and is excluded from further consideration.

Once Project Censored receives the candidate story, we undertake a second round of judgment, using the same criteria and updating the review to include any subsequent, competing corporate coverage. We post stories that pass this round of review on the Project's website as Validated Independent News stories (VINs).[13]

In early spring, we present all VINs in the current cycle to the faculty and students at all of our affiliate campuses, and to our panel of expert judges, who cast votes to winnow the candidate stories from several hundred to 25.

Once the Top 25 list has been determined, Project Censored student interns begin another intensive review of each story using LexisNexis and ProQuest databases. Additional faculty and students contribute to this final stage of review.

The Top 25 finalists are then sent to our panel of judges, who vote to rank them in numerical order. At the same time, these experts—including media studies professors, professional journalists and editors, and a former commissioner of the Federal Communications Commission—offer their insights on the stories' strengths and weaknesses.[14]

Thus, by the time a story appears in the pages of *State of the Free Press*, it has undergone at least five distinct rounds of review and evaluation.

Although the stories that Project Censored brings forward may be socially and politically controversial—and sometimes even psychologically challenging—we are confident that each is the result of serious journalistic effort, and therefore deserves greater public attention.

THE TOP *CENSORED* STORIES AND MEDIA
ANALYSIS OF 2020–21

Prescription Drug Costs Set to Become a Leading Cause of Death for Elderly Americans

Kenny Stancil, "High Drug Prices Could Result in Premature Deaths of More Than 1.1 Million Seniors in Next Decade: Analysis," Common Dreams, November 23, 2020.

Student Researcher: Silvia Morales (Sonoma State University)

Faculty Evaluator: Peter Phillips (Sonoma State University)

More than 1.1 million seniors in the federal government's Medicare program could die prematurely over the next decade because they will be unable to afford the high prices of their prescription medications, according to a November 2020 study issued by the West Health Policy Center, a nonprofit and nonpartisan policy research group, and Xcenda, the research arm of Amerisource-Bergen, a drug distributor.[15] As Kenny Stancil reported for Common Dreams, West Health projects that, with the continuation of current drug pricing trends, "cost-related nonadherence" will become "a leading cause of death in the U.S., ahead of diabetes, influenza, pneumonia, and kidney disease" by 2030.[16]

According to the West Health/Xcenda study, the rising cost of prescription medicines will lead to an estimated 112,000 premature deaths annually, due to elderly Americans being unable to afford necessary medications, a situation referred to as "cost-related nonadherence."[17] Explaining that "medication adherence" is a term used to describe how well patients follow healthcare professionals' instructions for taking medications, the study stated, "unaffordable drug prices can significantly impair medication adherence." As medicines become increasingly expensive, patients skip doses, ration prescriptions, or quit treatment altogether. According to the president of the West Health Policy Center, Timothy Lash, "One of the biggest contributors to poor health, hospital admissions, higher healthcare costs and preventable death is patients failing to take their medications as prescribed."[18]

A separate study, published in March 2020 by *JAMA*, one of the leading peer-reviewed medical journals, found that list prices on branded pharmaceutical products in the United States increased by 159 percent from 2007 to 2018.[19] The high cost of medicine will raise Medicare expenses by an estimated $17.7 billion each year from 2021 to 2031, the West Health/Xcenda study reported.[20] Established in 1965, Medicare is the national health insurance program that serves as the primary provider for Americans aged 65 and older.

The West Health/Xcenda study examined the impact of cost-related nonadherence on the general Medicare population, with a focus on five medical conditions that "significantly affect seniors and for which effective pharmaceutical treatments are available," including several types of heart disease, chronic kidney disease, and type 2 diabetes.[21]

Medicare beneficiaries are responsible for 25 percent

of a prescription drug's cost, until their expenses reach the out-of-pocket maximum. For this reason, "even with Medicare insurance, what seniors pay is linked to a drug's price," and patients are likely to experience "a significant increase" in their prescription costs as drug companies continue to raise list prices, according to the West Health/Xcenda study.[22] A June 2021 AARP study found that, between 2019 and 2020, the retail prices for 260 widely-used brand name prescription drugs increased by 2.9 percent, more than twice the general inflation rate of 1.3 percent.[23] AARP reported that, "[f]or the average older American taking 4.7 prescription drugs per month, the annual cost of therapy would have been more than $31,000 for 2020"—a figure that exceeded the median annual income for individual Medicare beneficiaries in 2019 ($29,650).

Stancil's Common Dreams report reviewed policy changes that could lower the cost of prescription drugs and "curb the power of Big Pharma, resulting in far fewer avoidable deaths." The West Health/Xcenda study recommended that limits on drug price increases and empowering Medicare to negotiate directly with drug companies on behalf of patients could prevent 93,900 deaths per year and reduce Medicare spending by $475.9 billion by 2030.[24] As a model for policymakers, the study pointed specifically to the Elijah E. Cummings Lower Drug Costs Now Act (H.R. 3), which had been passed by House Democrats in December 2019 but was stalled in the Senate by Republican majority leader Mitch McConnell at the time of the Common Dreams report. Since then, the newly elected president, Joe Biden, has declined to include Medicare negotiation in his $1.8

trillion American Families Plan proposal, but House Democrats, led by Energy and Commerce Committee chairman Frank Pallone Jr. (D-NJ), have reintroduced the Elijah E. Cummings Lower Drug Costs Now Act.[25]

Soaring prescription drug costs have been widely reported by corporate news outlets. Corporate coverage typically highlights the rising costs of the most expensive branded medications, as exemplified by a January 2021 CBS News report.[26] In April 2019, the *New York Times* reported that Americans had "borrowed an estimated $88 billion over the last year to pay for health care," according to a survey conducted by West Health and Gallup.[27] But corporate news outlets appear to have entirely ignored the subsequent West Health/Xcenda study on the consequences of rising drug prices for elderly Americans enrolled in Medicare. In May 2021, Rep. Peter Welch, a Democrat from Vermont, and David Mitchell, the founder of Patients For Affordable Drugs, co-authored an opinion piece for The Hill, advocating for H.R. 3, the Elijah E. Cummings Lower Drug Costs Now Act, and cited figures about preventable deaths from the West Health/Xcenda study.[28]

The public's understanding of the debate surrounding H.R. 3 and other proposed legislation designed to control inflation in prescription drug prices ought to be informed by accurate information about the grim repercussions of continuing the status quo. Sadly, the corporate media have failed to provide the public with such information for far too long, and the consequences could turn out to be deadly for millions of seniors.

Journalists Investigating Financial Crimes Threatened by Global Elites

Spencer Woodman, "Threats, Violence, Trolling, and Frivolous Lawsuits Used to Silence Journalists Investigating Financial Crimes, Survey Finds," International Consortium of Investigative Journalists, November 2, 2020.

Michael W. Hudson, Dean Starkman, Simon Bowers et al., "Global Banks Defy U.S. Crackdowns by Serving Oligarchs, Criminals and Terrorists," International Consortium of Investigative Journalists, September 20, 2020, updated December 22, 2020.

Nick Cohen, "Are Our Courts a Playground for Bullies? Just Ask Catherine Belton," *The Guardian*, May 8, 2021.

Student Researcher: Zach McNanna (North Central College)

Faculty Evaluator: Steve Macek (North Central College)

In November 2020 the Foreign Policy Centre (FPC) released "Unsafe for Scrutiny," a report about the threats faced by journalists investigating the financial misconduct that lets 'dirty money' flow through the world's most powerful banks.[29] As Spencer Woodman detailed in an article for the International Consortium of Investigative Journalists (ICIJ), the report reveals that global elites have been abusing their intimidating legal and financial powers by targeting reporters with defamation lawsuits, "cease and desist" letters, social media smear campaigns, trolling, verbal harassment, and even occasionally physical violence. Yet, as Woodman underscored, the report concluded that legal threats "are chief among the types of harassment facing journalists conducting financial investigations." The harassment faced by investigative journalists looking into financial crimes has a chilling effect on reporting about corruption and, ultimately, infringes the public's right to know about the money laundering, bribery, theft of public funds, and other illicit acts carried out (or facilitated) by wealthy banks, government officials, and corporate leaders.

Sponsored in part by the Justice for Journalists Foundation, the FPC's study was based on a survey of investigative reporters from all around the world, many of whom had worked on cross-border financial crime investigations such as the multi-year investigations into the financial records leaked in the Panama Papers or the FinCEN Files. Responses from 63 investigative journalists working in 41 countries indicated that a vast majority

---

The harassment faced by investigative journalists looking into financial crimes has a chilling effect on reporting about corruption and, ultimately, infringes the public's right to know about the money laundering, bribery, theft of public funds, and other illicit acts carried out (or facilitated) by wealthy banks, government officials, and corporate leaders.

---

had faced threats and harassment during their investigations into financial crimes. Susan Coughtrie, project director at the Foreign Policy Centre, told Woodman that the large-scale transnational investigations conducted by these reporters exposed "explosive insights into how political and business elites, as well as organised crime groups, all over the world get away with financial crime and corruption."

The report found that wealthy individuals and corporations involved in financial corruption often resort to legal action against underfunded investigative journalists as a tactic to thwart their research into corruption. These frivolous suits, known as "strategic lawsuits against public participation," or SLAPPs, are said to "create a similar chilling effect on media freedom to more overt violence or attack," according to the FPC's study.[30] More than 70 percent of respondents to the FPC survey reported being subjected to threats of legal action against them. The report also noted that these legal threats are often communicated in secret, in letters from lawyers marked "private and confidential" intended to intimidate journalists into shielding the action from public view.[31] One journalist working full-time in Africa who responded to the survey explained that "[t]hreats of legal action, especially in the UK[,] where court processes themselves are often prohibitively expensive, has forced me to be increasingly vigilant in terms of sustaining the facts and claims in a story."[32]

According to Woodman, the United Kingdom, with its plaintiff-friendly defamation laws, "was, by far, the most frequent country of origin for legal threats, FPC found." Unlike Canada, Australia, and certain US states, the United Kingdom has not passed anti-SLAPP legislation, making its courts an attractive venue for elites seeking to use the law to bully journalists into silence.

In a May 8, 2021 column in the *Guardian* that mentioned the FPC report, Nick Cohen discussed how the United Kingdom's costly court system has turned it into "the censorship capital of the democratic world." As evidence, he pointed to the case of a former Moscow correspondent for the *Financial Times*, Catherine Belton. In April 2020, Belton published *Putin's People: How the KGB Took Back Russia and Then Took On the West*, a book that traces how Vladimir Putin and his inner circle consolidated their grip on political power in Moscow and looted much of the country's wealth in the process.[33] As Cohen explained, in response, a host of Putin's super-wealthy associates are now bombarding Belton with one lawsuit after another. According to Cohen, "Rosneft, the Kremlin-dominated oil producer (market capitalisation circa $75bn) whose chief executive, president and chairman, Igor Sechin, began his rise to power as Vladimir Putin's secretary in the 1990s, has lodged an action for libel." Belton is likewise being sued by Roman Abramovich, the billionaire owner of Chelsea Football Club, for what he claims are "false and defamatory" statements in the book. The owner of Russia's largest private bank, Mikhail Fridman, and at least two other Russian oligarchs are also bringing libel suits against Belton over *Putin's People*.

The Foreign Policy Centre report additionally found that the intimidation and harassment faced by investigative journalists like Belton often goes well beyond lawsuits or legal threats. As Woodman explained in his article on the study, "60% of respondents working in sub-Saharan Africa [...] and 50% of respondents from North Africa and the Middle East region reported threats of physical attack." Moreover, the report revealed that a significant number of financial corruption reporters have experienced on- and off-line surveillance, hacking of their social media accounts, questioning by authorities, denial of journalistic credentials, and blacklisting.[34]

Tragically, powerful individuals being investigated for corruption have sometimes turned to murder to prevent further probing into their illicit acts. The fatal October 16, 2017 car bombing of Daphne Caruana Galizia, a journalist who reported on the Panama Papers and corruption in Malta, struck fear into the hearts of many journalists working to expose rampant financial misconduct. In February 2018, Slovak investigative journalist Ján Kuciak, who was investigating tax fraud and embezzlement among Slovak businessmen, was shot to death in a village not far from Bratislava, a city in which he'd recently investigated suspicious real estate transactions. According to FPC's report, an additional thirty reporters from Brazil, Russia, India, Ukraine, Mexico, and other countries who were researching financial corruption have been murdered since 2017.[35]

While a number of larger corporate news outlets such as the BBC, BuzzFeed, Reuters, and the *Wall Street Journal* have publicized the findings of investigative journalists digging into wrongdoing by the world's most powerful banks and wealthy individuals, virtually no corporate media attention has been given to the threats faced by journalists doing the digging.[36] In addition to Woodman's ICIJ article and Cohen's column, the "Unsafe for Scrutiny" report was the focus of a November 2, 2020 article in the *Guardian* and a brief November 6, 2020 report on Voice of America.[37] OpenDemocracy, the UK-based independent, nonprofit news site, also published a short commentary on the report.[38] To date, however, no major commercial newspaper or broadcast outlet in the United States has so much as mentioned the FPC's report.

Threats to journalists are not only detrimental to individual reporters, they also undermine freedom of the press and jeopardize the health of democratic polities that rely on that freedom to keep corruption from spreading like wildfire. This story deserves far more attention than it has received.

Historic Wave of Wildcat Strikes for Workers' Rights

"COVID-19 Strike Wave Interactive Map," Payday Report, March 2020, updated continuously.

Michael Sainato, "Strikes Erupt as US Essential Workers Demand Protection Amid Pandemic," *The Guardian*, May 19, 2020.

Mike Elk, "700 CA. Hospital Workers Strike—UNC May Strike Over Reopening—Sheet Metal Strike in Missouri," Payday Report, July 23, 2020.

Mike Elk, "How Black & Brown Workers are Redefining Strikes in the Digital COVID Age," Payday Report, July 8, 2020.

Student Researcher: Cem Ismail Addemir (North Central College)

Faculty Evaluator: Steve Macek (North Central College)

After the United States went into lockdown in spring 2020, millions of people were designated 'essential workers'—individuals who were expected to continue laboring at their jobs as meatpackers, teachers, janitors, delivery drivers, nurses, or grocery store clerks, at the potential cost of their lives. In response, thousands of wildcat strikes erupted to challenge dangerous working conditions and confront chronically low wages for these essential positions. This wave of wildcat strikes has continued and reached remarkable levels in the United States, as documented by Mike Elk from the labor news website Payday Report. Elk created a continuously updated COVID-19 Strike Wave Interactive Map, which had identified 1,100 wildcat strikes as of March 24, 2021, many of which the corporate media have chosen to ignore.

Traditionally, workers who strike belong to unions and only go on strike after discussing the possibility within their local (and sometimes national) unions and then taking a vote. Wildcat strikes are a different matter; they occur when workers without unions, or without explicit approval by the unions that do represent them, collectively stop working. Most wildcat strikes last for only a few days, though they often result in employers making some concessions to workers' demands.

Throughout our unprecedented national health crisis, employers have relentlessly pushed to cut workplace costs. Many unauthorized work stoppages throughout the nation have been over appalling actions by employers who put workers at risk; some of the many outrageous actions by employers that essential workers were expected to simply accept included skimping on protective gear that could prevent workers from contracting the coronavirus, and attempting to cut workers' ability to receive healthcare. In one instance, as Mike Elk of Payday Report detailed in a July 23, 2020 article, seven hundred healthcare workers in Santa Rosa, California went on strike because their hospital lacked sufficient personal protective equipment to keep employees safe, and management warned employees that their insurance fees would be doubled if they wanted continued coverage for their families. Another example that Elk covered in the same article took place in St. Joseph, Missouri, where 120 sheet metal workers went on strike due to management's repeated attempts to cut their healthcare benefits during the pandemic. As Michael Sainato from the *Guardian* reported, the Trump administration failed to issue federal mandates that employers take specific steps to keep workers safe from COVID-19, allowing employers to implement the government's health and safety guidance as they pleased.

In some cases, workers have engaged in wildcat work stoppages to advance long-standing demands for higher wages, leveraging their increased bargaining power during the pandemic to wrest pay concessions from employers. In May 2020, workers at fifty McDonald's, Burger King, Starbucks, and other fast food restaurants and coffee shops throughout the state of Florida staged a day-long strike for higher pay and better protective equipment.[39] Similarly, in April 2021, employees at Peet's Coffee & Tea locations in the Chicago area staged a coordinated work stoppage together with the Fight for $15 campaign to demand workplace protections and quarantine pay.[40]

Another important and underreported force driving the massive wave of wildcat strikes this past year has been Black and Brown workers using digital technologies to organize collective actions as a way to press some of the demands for racial justice raised by Black Lives Matter and George Floyd protestors. As Mike Elk explained in a July 8, 2020 article for Payday Report, in June 2020 "the U.S. saw more than 600 strikes or work stoppages by workers in solidarity with the Black Lives Matter movement.... Payday [Report] estimates that the strike and work stoppages total [that the Strike Wave Interactive Map has identified] is likely a severe underestimation as many non-union Black and Brown workers are now calling out en masse to attend Black Lives Matter protests without it ever being reported in the press or on social media." Elk observed that many Black and Brown workers believe white labor leaders fail to understand organizing strategies that are nontraditional, such as using social media platforms to create a viral movement: "Scores of Black and Brown workers say that this failure is yet another indicator of how the overwhelming[ly] white leadership of organized labor struggles to understand the organizing of Black and Brown workers."

Corporate media have largely avoided reporting on the burgeoning wildcat protests in the United States. While local and regional newspapers and broadcast news outlets have reported on particular local actions, corporate news coverage has failed to report the strike wave *as* a wave, at no time connecting the dots of all the individual, seemingly isolated work stoppages and walkouts to create a picture of the overarching trend. Thus, the one-day strikes by fast food and coffee shop workers discussed above were covered only by national restaurant trade publications and local news outlets. No national corporate newspapers or broadcast news operations bothered to report on these unprecedented coordinated actions.

It is telling that the most in-depth discussion of the COVID-19 strike wave in the nation's newspaper of record, the *New York Times*, was not a news report at all but an opinion piece, published March 30, 2020, by Steven Greenhouse, arguing that businesses' refusal to provide workers with gloves, masks, and other protections against the virus had "set off a burst of walkouts, sickouts and wildcat strikes."[41] A few other *New York Times* articles made fleeting references to wildcat strikes, including one that briefly noted several impromptu strikes at Amazon warehouses.[42] Outlets such as *USA Today*, the *Washington Post*, and Fox News have yet to run a single story on the wildcat strikes sweeping the nation. Overall, the establishment media's scattered, scant coverage has rendered invisible the remarkable work of the working-class Black and Brown activists who are largely responsible for this wave of protests.

The sole exception to the corporate media's blackout on the year-long strike wave occurred during a brief period in August 2020 when Vox, the *New Yorker*, the *New York Times*, the *Washington Post*, and CNN all suddenly decided to cover wildcat strikes, but only of one particular kind—specifically, those involving highly-paid athletes on pro basketball and baseball teams. The players walked out against the terms of their contracts to protest the shooting of Jacob Blake by Wisconsin police, and the corporate media coverage of US strikes swiftly ended once the players returned later that same week.[43]

"Climate Debtor" Nations Have "Colonized" the Atmosphere

Sarah Lazare, "'Colonizing the Atmosphere': How Rich, Western Nations Drive the Climate Crisis," *In These Times*, September 14, 2020.

Student Researcher: Sarah Uysal (Diablo Valley College)

Faculty Evaluator: Mickey Huff (Diablo Valley College)

In April 2021, President Joe Biden's "Leaders Summit on Climate" brought together more than forty national leaders to address global carbon emissions. At the virtual summit, Biden outlined his administration's goals to reduce US carbon emissions by 50–52 percent of the nation's 2005 levels by 2030, and Vice President Kamala Harris, who introduced Biden, told summit attendees, "As a global community, it is imperative that we act quickly and together to confront this crisis." The president's summit was widely reported by corporate news media, and coverage frequently included the vice president's call for global responsibility.[44]

By contrast, a September 2020 study, which examined long-term carbon dioxide emissions data to assess national responsibilities for the climate crisis, contradicted Harris's sunny thoughts about a global community but received scant news coverage from establishment outlets.

As Sarah Lazare reported for *In These Times*, "An analysis published in the September issue of *The Lancet Planetary Health* shines new light on the outsized role of the United States, European Union and the Global North in creating a climate crisis that, while felt everywhere, is disproportionately harming the Global South." The *Lancet* study, conducted by Jason Hickel, an economic anthropologist, found that the world's richest, most industrialized nations—including the United States, Canada, members of the European Union, Israel, Australia, New Zealand, and Japan—are responsible for 92 percent of carbon dioxide emissions, while the Global South is responsible for only 8 percent.[45]

As Hickel's *Lancet* study stated, "To date, there has been no robust attempt to quantify national responsibility for the ecological, social, and economic damages caused by excess global CO_2 emissions."[46] Previous research had not taken into account both the scale of national emissions and countries' populations.

As Hickel told *In These Times*, his research began from the premises that "the atmosphere is a common resource" and that "all people should have equal access" to a fair share of it. Hickel calculated each nation's fair share of a sustainable global carbon budget in conjunction with an analysis of "territorial emissions from 1850 to 1969, and consumption-based emissions from 1970 to 2015." Using this data, he then assessed "the extent to which each country has overshot or undershot its fair share." His report refers to the countries that have overshot their fair share of emissions as "climate debtors" and those that have undershot their fair share as "climate creditors."

The biggest climate debtors include the United States (responsible for 40 percent of global overshoots), Russia and Germany (8 percent each), the United Kingdom (7 percent), and Japan (5 percent). By contrast, the world's leading climate creditors to date include India (accounting for 34 percent of global "undershoots"), China (11 percent), Bangladesh (5 percent), Indonesia (5 percent), and Nigeria (4 percent).[47]

The results, Hickel told *In These Times*, show that "the countries of the Global North have 'stolen' a big chunk of the atmospheric fair-shares of poorer countries, and on top of that are responsible for the vast majority of excess emissions." These countries have "effectively colonized the global atmospheric commons for the sake of their own industrial growth," Hickel determined. His *Lancet* article elaborated on this process of atmospheric colonization: "Just as many of these countries have relied on the appropriation of labour and resources from the Global South for their own economic growth, they have also relied on the appropriation of global atmospheric commons, with consequences that harm the Global South disproportionately."[48] Therefore, he concludes, nations that operate as climate debtors should be responsible for damages sustained by undershooting countries.

Corporate news outlets appear to have entirely ignored the findings of Jason Hickel's *Lancet* study. Among independent outlets, Common Dreams republished Lazare's *In These Times* article, and *Foreign Policy* published an article by Hickel regarding the study.[49] In assessing President Biden's pledge to reduce US carbon emissions significantly by 2030, *Jacobin* magazine cited Hickel's 2020 *Lancet* report, noting that, by his calculation, the United States had already by 2020 overshot its fair share of global carbon emissions by 40 percent.[50] *The New York Times* quoted Hickel in an April 2021 opinion piece on Biden's virtual summit on climate change, but only as a foil to the enthusiastic endorsement of a former UN climate official, and without offering any context for Hickel's criticism.[51]

Although it may be imperative to act "quickly and together" to reduce carbon emissions, as Vice President Harris asserted at the April 2021 climate summit, corporate media have failed to cover Hickel's cutting-edge research, which demonstrates that the United States and other would-be leaders in addressing climate change are in fact, as the world's worst climate debtors, disproportionately responsible for climate breakdown.

5 Microplastics and Toxic Chemicals Increasingly Prevalent in World's Oceans

Robby Berman, "Study Found Plastic in Every Seafood Sample It Analyzed," Medical News Today, August 29, 2020.

Graham Readfearn, "More Than 14m Tonnes of Plastic Believed to be at the Bottom of the Ocean," *The Guardian*, October 5, 2020.

Daniel Ross, "More Traces of Cancer-Causing PFAS in Arctic Raise Alarm over Global Spread," Truthout, October 18, 2020.

Sharon Lerner, "PFAS Chemical Associated with Severe COVID-19," The Intercept, December 7, 2020.

Student Researchers: Eduardo Amador, Kolby Cordova, and Natalia Fuentes (Sonoma State University)

Faculty and Community Evaluators: Peter Phillips (Sonoma State University) and Polette Gonzalez

According to a pair of recent scientific studies, microplastics and a class of toxic chemicals known as polyfluoroalkyl substances (or PFAS) are becoming increasingly prevalent in the world's oceans and have begun to contaminate the global seafood supply.

According to a July 2020 study published in the scholarly journal *Environmental Science & Technology*, PFAS—a family of potentially harmful chemicals used in a range of products including carpets, furniture, clothing, food packaging, and nonstick coatings—have now been found in the Arctic Ocean.[52] This discovery worries scientists because it means that PFAS can reach any body of water anywhere in the world and that such chemicals are likely present in our water supply. Meanwhile, researchers at the QUEX Institute, a partnership between the University of Exeter and the University of Queensland, have found microplastics in crabs, oysters, prawns, squid, and sardines sold as seafood in Australian markets, findings also first published in *Environmental Science & Technology* and covered by Medical News Today in August 2020.[53] As Robby Berman reported for Medical News Today, the new findings suggest that microplastics—small pieces of plastic, less than five millimeters in length (about the size of a sesame seed) that are a consequence of plastic pollution—have "invaded the food chain to a greater extent than previously documented."

The presence of PFAS in the Arctic Ocean is concerning for many reasons. As Daniel Ross reported in an October 2020 article for Truthout, PFAS chemical exposure is known to have serious impacts on human health as a cause of cancer, liver damage, thyroid problems, and increased risk of asthma. People with elevated levels of PFAS chemicals are twice as likely to develop a severe form of COVID-19 since these chemicals are endocrine disruptors.[54]

Because the Arctic Ocean is so remote from human population centers, exactly how these chemicals may have reached these waters is also a deeply concerning question. As Ross pointed out in the Truthout article, "Emerging research suggests that one important pathway is through the air and in rainwater" rather than through ocean circulation. Discovering the pathways through which these "forever chemicals" are contaminating isolated areas is important for regulators as they attempt to remove these chemicals from the environment. Atmospheric spread may make removal considerably more difficult.

Like PFAS compounds being found in Arctic waters, the discovery of microplastics in popular forms of seafood is truly alarming.

Microplastics are less than five millimeters in length, and nanoplastics are less than one hundred nanometers in length. According to the QUEX study, their small size allows these microplastics to spread through "airborne particles, machinery, equipment, and textiles, handling, and [...] from fish transport."[55] The research team at Exeter and Queensland found microplastics present in all of the seafood samples they studied, with polyvinyl chloride being found in every case. The study's lead author, Francisca Ribeiro, told Medical News Today that, for an average serving, a seafood eater could be exposed to "approximately 0.7 milligrams (mg) of plastic" when ingesting oysters or squid, and "up to 30 mg of plastic" when eating sardines. For comparison, note that a grain of rice weighs approximately 30 mg.

As Medical News Today reported in its August 29, 2020 article on the study, approximately 17 percent of the protein that humans consume worldwide is seafood. The findings suggest that "people who regularly eat seafood are also regularly eating plastic." According to Tamara Galloway, a researcher from Exeter University who is one of the study's co-authors, "We do not fully understand the risks to human health of ingesting plastic, but this new method [used in the study for detecting selected plastics] will make it easier for us to find out."

In October 2020 the *Guardian* reported that at least 14 million tons of microplastics are likely sitting on the ocean floor—"more than 30 times as much plastic at the bottom of the world's ocean than there is floating at the surface," according to an estimate based on new research, Graham Readfearn reported.

As the *Guardian* report noted, "Stemming the tide of plastic entering the world's waterways and ocean has emerged as a major international challenge." In September 2020, leaders from more than seventy countries signed a voluntary pledge to reverse biodiversity loss which included, as a goal, stopping plastic entering the ocean by 2050. The United States, Brazil, China, Russia, India, and Australia did not sign that pledge.[56]

Media coverage of both the study on microplastics in

seafood and the research on PFAS in the Arctic Ocean has predominantly come from independent news sources as well as journals and websites aimed at members of the scientific community. Of the articles covering the presence of PFAS in Arctic waters, many simply summarize the findings of the research. However, Truthout and *Chemical & Engineering News* each took their coverage further by including professional opinions on the significance of the study and addressing remedies to the problem.[57]

Lack of corporate news attention could stem from the idea that the research findings are nothing new or simply confirm what many have previously assumed. However, the significance of these PFAS pollutants potentially being airborne deserves greater recognition because this poses greater challenges for abatement efforts. The Exeter and Queensland researchers' findings about micro- and nano-plastics in seafood likewise require publicizing despite the findings confirming certain earlier assumptions, because the evidence they present could prove crucial in mobilizing political will to address an issue that is barely visible and that few people recognize as a serious problem. Outside of coverage by the *Guardian*, no major news outlet has paid attention to the topic of microplastics in seafood.[58]

Canary Mission Blacklists Pro-Palestinian Activists, Chilling Free Speech Rights

Murtaza Hussain, "The Real Cancel Culture: Pro-Israel Blacklists," The Intercept, October 4, 2020.

Lexi McMenamin, "Protecting Pro-Palestine Activists Can Feel Almost Impossible—but These Students Succeeded," *The Nation*, March 16, 2021.

Student Researcher: Miranda Morgan (Sonoma State University)

Faculty Evaluator: Allison Ford (Sonoma State University)

Pro-Palestinian activism—including the global Boycott, Divestment and Sanctions (BDS) movement that works to peacefully pressure Israel to obey international law and respect Palestinians' human rights—has become a contentious testing ground for activists' rights and free-speech policies, especially on US college and university campuses.

For an October 2020 article published by the Intercept, Murtaza Hussain interviewed a handful of pro-Palestinian activists who have been targeted by Canary Mission, an anonymously-run website, established in 2015, that seeks to publicly discredit critics of Israel as "terrorists" and "anti-Semites." As Hussain wrote, "Canary Mission is difficult to describe as anything other than a blacklist." One activist told the Intercept that Canary Mission has proven "very powerful in silencing people and making them think free speech is not their right. It instills a powerful sense of fear and paranoia."

Although conservatives decry the development of "cancel culture" and alleged progressive intolerance, "when it comes to Israel-Palestine, full-blown authoritarian coercion, like the blacklisting carried out by Canary Mission, is already well entrenched," Hussain wrote. Both US and Israeli government agencies have used information from Canary Mission to question pro-Palestinian student activists, according to previous reports.[59]

For many otherwise unknown activists, a Canary Mission profile is their most visible online presence. "It's the first thing that comes up when you Google my name, the claim that I'm a terrorist supporter and an extremist," one former activist on Palestinian issues told the Intercept. The activists Hussain interviewed—some of whom asked to remain anonymous "for fear of suffering further consequences from speaking out"—described how Canary Mission's blacklist affected their employment opportunities, immigration status, freedom to travel, and mental health.

Although conservatives decry the development of "cancel culture" and alleged progressive intolerance, "when it comes to Israel-Palestine, full-blown authoritarian coercion, like the blacklisting carried out by Canary Mission, is already well entrenched."

—Murtaza Hussain

Beyond Canary Mission, a variety of pro-Israel organizations that seek to suppress pro-Palestinian activism have pursued litigation against chapters of Students for Justice in Palestine (SJP) at the University of California, Los Angeles (UCLA), University of Massachusetts Amherst, Columbia University, San Francisco State University, and the City University of New York, Lexi McMenamin reported in March 2021 for *The Nation*.

McMenamin's article spotlighted a complaint filed by David Abrams, director of the Zionist Advocacy Center, against UCLA, demanding that the university release the names of speakers who participated in the 2018 National Students for Justice in Palestine conference, which UCLA's SJP chapter hosted. The student organizers of the UCLA event had coordinated with university officials "to preserve the anonymity of speakers, in order to prevent them from being put on no-fly-lists, potentially denied entry to other countries, or contacted by the FBI over their organizing work," *The Nation* reported. For his part, Abrams sought release of the anonymous speaker's names, which he claimed as information that should be available to him under the California Public Records Act, so that he could use them to "investigate terrorism."

In March 2021 a California judge denied Abrams's petition, noting that disclosure of the SJP speakers' names "would violate their rights to freedom of association, anonymous speech, and privacy."

Furthermore, in May 2021 a federal judge ruled that the state of Georgia cannot compel groups or individuals who contract with public entities to disavow support for the BDS movement against Israel.[60] As Project Censored has previously reported, Abby Martin, a journalist and an advocate of BDS, brought suit against the state of Georgia and officials at Georgia Southern University after she was barred from speaking at a critical media literacy conference hosted by the university, for refusing to pledge that she would not boycott Israel.[61] In his ruling, US District Court Judge Mark Cohen wrote that the state law "places an unconstitutional incidental burden on speech" and was "more offensive to the First Amendment" than comparable statutes previously ruled unconstitutional by the US Supreme Court, because the Georgia statute "burdens speech exclusively for those who hold particular political beliefs."[62]

Heightened violence in Israel/Palestine in May 2021 has focused attention on powerful pro-Israel media biases in US news coverage,[63] but Canary Mission and legal efforts to suppress pro-Palestinian activism have nonetheless received minimal corporate news coverage. In January 2019 the *New York Times* featured an opinion piece by Michelle Alexander that compared Canary Mission to the McCarthyite tactics used during the Cold War against suspected Communists;[64] and two news articles in the *Times*, dating back to 2018, made passing mention of Canary Mission, as a "shadowy organization."[65] In February 2019 the *Washington Post* published an opinion article, by Mairav Zonszein, which mentioned Canary Mission, alongside the American Israel Public Affairs Committee (AIPAC), StandWithUs, and Christians United for Israel, as "parts of the pro-Israel lobby" asserting that support for the BDS movement is anti-Semitic.[66] Aside from this coverage, major establishment news outlets have provided no substantive reports on the role played by Canary Mission and other pro-Israel organizations in stifling the First Amendment rights of pro-Palestinian activists.

Google's Union-Busting Methods Revealed

Lauren Kaori Gurley, "'Lazy,' 'Money-Oriented,' 'Single Mother': How Union-Busting Firms Compile Dossiers on Employees," Motherboard (Vice), January 5, 2021.

Student Researcher: Cem Ismail Addemir (North Central College)

Faculty Evaluator: Steve Macek (North Central College)

Leaked files from IRI Consultants, a union avoidance firm, obtained by Vice's Motherboard show the disturbing lengths to which companies will go in order to derail workplace organizing. The leaked records include a spreadsheet of anecdotal personal information the company had gathered about the employees of one client, Conifer Health Solutions, who hired IRI Consultants to thwart a union drive at two hospitals the company owns in Seattle. The document included data about employees' private lives, including descriptions of workers as "lazy," "impressionable," "money oriented," and "a single mother." IRI Consultants was hired by Google in 2019 at a time when a growing number of the tech giant's workers were pushing for unionization.

IRI Consultants is one of many union-busting firms that help businesses prevent workplace organizing by intimidating workers, tracking employee behavior, and engaging in workplace anti-union propaganda. The war against workplace organizing in the United States through intimidation and surveillance dates back to the 1870s and the origins of the American labor movement. In response to strikes and other labor agitation, the National Labor Relations Act of 1935 was passed by Congress, making it illegal for employers to spy on employees and guaranteeing workers the ability to organize and engage in collective bargaining. Nevertheless, companies like Google attempt to circumvent the law by hiring union avoidance firms like IRI Consultants as independent contractors to engage in surveillance and intimidation on their behalf.

As Lauren Kaori Gurley reported for Motherboard, "[E]mployers in the United States spend roughly $340 million on union avoidance consultants each year." These union avoidance consultants usually move from one business to the next, giving advice to management and holding anti-union "educational" meetings.

The leaked documents Motherboard obtained demonstrate IRI Consultants's detailed profiling of workers. The documents show that the firm collected incredibly detailed information on 83 Seattle hospital employees, including their "personality, temperament, motivations, ethnicity, family background, spouses' employment, finances, health issues, work ethic, job performance, disciplinary history, and involvement in union activity in the lead-up to a union election." IRI Consultants assigned each worker surveilled a rating on a scale from one to five, with ones deemed to be the most pro-union and fives believed to be the most pro-company, based on the information IRI Consultants gathered. It then used the metric to target individual workers in an effort to sway them to vote "no" during union certification elections.

Google has adamantly denied allegations that it engaged in personal data collection on employees to prevent their organizing, arguing that it enlisted consulting firms for a host of reasons and not for the purposes of union-busting. However, such claims are highly dubious given that Google hired IRI Consultants, which specializes in union avoidance, at precisely the moment when its employees were attempting to organize a union. January 2021 saw the creation of one of the first tech company unions, the Alphabet Workers Union, that represents workers at Google. The union has responded to Google's denial that it collected personal data by telling Motherboard that "Google claims to value privacy, then expends resources on consultants like IRI who are intent on collecting worker data in order to manipulate employees to work against their best interests."

Google is not the only Big Tech company to enlist union avoidance consultants in recent years. In fall 2020 and spring 2021, employees at Amazon's massive fulfillment center in Bessemer, Alabama launched a much-publicized unionization effort. As John Logan detailed in a lengthy article for LaborOnline, Amazon responded to the Bessemer drive by spending at least $3,200 per day on anti-union consultants Russ Brown and Rebecca Smith and by bringing in a second union-busting consulting firm, Labor Information Services.[67] The company also hired Morgan Lewis, one of the largest law firms in the country specializing in union avoidance. Ultimately, Bessemer employees voted 1,798 to 738 against joining the Retail, Wholesale and Department Store Union, a crushing defeat for organizers and an apparent vindication of Amazon's anti-union maneuvers.[68]

There has been some establishment press coverage of large corporations hiring union-avoidance firms to undermine workplace organizing, mostly focusing on tech giants like Google and Amazon. In November and December 2019, both the *New York Times* and the *Washington Post* noted that Google had hired IRI Consultants.[69] The cover story in the February 23, 2020

New York Times Magazine, entitled "The Great Google Revolt," was devoted to unionization efforts at Alphabet and other Silicon Valley companies, and mentioned in passing the tech giants' use of anti-union consultants.[70] However, there has been no corporate news coverage whatsoever of the sensational leaks that Motherboard released in January, and there has been very little in-depth corporate media reporting on the use of union-busting consultants in general.

Indeed, the only other coverage of the Motherboard leaks was a brief January 8, 2021 post on the independent, grassroots labor news site Payday Report.[71] In August 2020, The Conversation published an article by labor educator John Logan about how "a handful of little-known law and consulting firms do much of the dirty work that keeps companies and other organizations union-free," which mentioned Google's use of IRI Consultants and discussed the tactics of such consulting firms in general. The documents leaked to Motherboard confirm and greatly elaborate upon what labor organizers and educators have suspected of the specific tactics the union-busting firms employ.[72]

Pfizer Bullies South American Governments over COVID-19 Vaccine

Madlen Davies, Rosa Furneaux, Iván Ruiz, and Jill Langlois, "'Held to Ransom': Pfizer Demands Governments Gamble with State Assets to Secure Vaccine Deal," Bureau of Investigative Journalism, February 23, 2021.

Sarah Lazare, "Pfizer Helped Create the Global Patent Rules. Now It's Using Them to Undercut Access to the Covid Vaccine," *In These Times*, December 17, 2020.

Student Researchers: Ryan Jackson, Mohammad Haider, and John Deery (Queens College, City University of New York)

Faculty Evaluator: Roopali Mukherjee (Queens College, City University of New York)

Pfizer, whose global reputation as one of the world's leading pharmaceutical companies has been bolstered by its development of a COVID-19 vaccine, has a record of exerting undue influence on low- and middle-income nations and international organizations to pursue its intellectual property rights and financial interests at the expense of global efforts to ensure that poor countries are able to access the company's vaccine, according to independent news reports from the Bureau of Investigative Journalism and *In These Times*.

In February 2021, Madlen Davies, Rosa Furneaux, Iván Ruiz, and Jill Langlois of the Bureau of Investigative Journalism (BIJ) reported that Pfizer has essentially held Latin American governments to ransom for access to its lifesaving COVID-19 vaccine. In negotiations with Argentina and Brazil, Pfizer demanded that the nations offer sovereign assets—such as federal bank reserves, military bases, and embassy buildings—as collateral for any liability resulting from future legal cases. Officials from several Latin American countries spoke with the BIJ on condition of anonymity, due to confidentiality agreements that Pfizer has required. One national official who participated in negotiations with Pfizer described its demands as "high-level bullying" that "held to ransom" the government attempting to access life-saving vaccines. Consequently, legal experts expressed concern that Pfizer's demands "amount to an abuse of power," the BIJ reported.

Some protections against liability are conventional for pharmaceutical companies that administer vaccines during an epidemic—but those protections do not typically indemnify a company for fraud, gross negligence, mismanagement, or failure to follow good manufacturing practices, as Pfizer has demanded in its deals with a number of Latin American nations. Shortly after the Argentinian Ministry of Health began negotiations with Pfizer Argentina in June 2020, the nation's Congress had to enact a new law in order to meet Pfizer's demands for indemnity. The Argentinian government believed that, at the least, Pfizer ought to be accountable for acts of negligence on its part in the delivery and distribution of the vaccine, but, instead of offering any compromise, Pfizer "demanded more and more," according to one government negotiator. That was when Pfizer called for Argentina to put up sovereign assets as collateral. Argentina broke off negotiations with Pfizer, leaving the nation's leaders at that time without a vaccine supply for its people.

Overall, Pfizer has negotiated with more than one hundred countries and has supply agreements with nine Latin American and Caribbean countries—Chile, Colombia, Costa Rica, Dominican Republic, Ecuador, Mexico, Panama, Peru, and Uruguay. "The terms of those deals are unknown," the BIJ reported.

In December 2020, just after the United States approved Pfizer's COVID-19 vaccine for emergency use, *In These Times*'s Sarah Lazare filed a detailed report on the history of the pharmaceutical giant's opposition to expanding vaccine access to poor countries. From the mid-1980s to the early 1990s, Lazare wrote, Pfizer "played a critical role in establishing the very [World Trade Organization] intellectual property rules that it is now invoking to argue against freeing up vaccine supplies for poor countries." Dating back to the General Agreement on Tariffs and Trade negotiations between 1986 and 1993, which led to the 1995 establishment of the World Trade Organization, Pfizer promoted the idea that "international trade should be contingent on strong intellectual property rules," Lazare wrote. Countries that opted not to comply with US intellectual property rules would be cast as engaging in "piracy." This trade-based approach to intellectual property served to protect Pfizer's bottom line, by reinforcing the monopoly power of the pharmaceutical company and other US industries.

"It is difficult to think of a clearer case for suspending intellectual property laws than a global pandemic," Lazare wrote. But Pfizer is "not alone" in opposing any pause on intellectual property rules. Pharma trade groups and other companies—including Moderna, which has developed another leading COVID-19 vaccine—have "come out in full force" against proposals to relax, even temporarily, the "stringent" intellectual property rules that restrict access to the vaccine, Lazare reported. As a result, a map of global poverty and a map of countries lacking vaccine access would reveal "a virtual one-to-one match," she noted. This, she concluded, "is a logical outcome for a system designed from the onset to reinforce long-existing power structures informed by an entrenched legacy of colonialism." That system leaves "majority black and brown countries [...] to suffer and die while wealthy Global North countries far exceed their needed capacity."

A May 2021 *In These Times* report noted that, despite President Biden's April pledge to donate 60 million doses of the AstraZeneca vaccine to countries in need once the Food and Drug Administration completes its review of AstraZeneca's vaccine, there will still be a shortfall of vaccines in nations such as Argentina, as intellectual property restrictions prevent the countries from manufacturing their own vaccine supplies. "[C]onvincing Big Pharma to directly share its medical tools and technologies in the Global South by suspending these patent rights" would do "far more" than Biden's promise of donated vaccine doses to protect people from the pandemic's deadly consequences, *In These Times* reported.[73]

Pfizer's dealings in South America are not exactly secret, yet corporate media outlets have either failed or refused to cover Pfizer's demands on countries such as Argentina. In December 2020, CNBC published an article about how US citizens would be unable to sue Pfizer or Moderna if their COVID vaccines produced severe side effects.[74] CNBC's coverage explained how both companies received legal immunity from the United States, but made no mention of the methods Pfizer has employed to compel even stronger legal immunity from South American countries. As of May 2021, there has been no corporate media coverage of Pfizer's actual dealings in South America or how the pharmaceutical giant helped establish the global intellectual property standards it now invokes to protect its control over access to the vaccine.

Big Pharma has a long, underreported track record of leaving developing nations' medical needs unfulfilled, as Project Censored has previously documented.[75]

Police Use Dogs as Instruments of Violence, Targeting People of Color

Bryn Stole and Grace Toohey, "The City Where Police Unleash Dogs on Black Teens," The Marshall Project, February 12, 2021.

Abbie VanSickle and Challen Stephens, "Police Use Painful Dog Bites to Make People Obey," The Marshall Project, December 14, 2020.

Abbie VanSickle, Challen Stephens, Ryan Martin, Dana Brozost-Kelleher, and Andrew Fan, "When Police Violence is a Dog Bite," The Marshall Project, October 2, 2020.

Ashley Remkus, "We Spent a Year Investigating Police Dogs. Here are Six Takeaways," The Marshall Project, October 2, 2020.

Student Researchers: Ian M. Williams and Jason Medrano (North Central College)

Faculty Evaluator: Steve Macek (North Central College)

An investigation conducted by several independent news outlets coordinated by the Marshall Project lays bare mounting evidence of extensive and disproportionate deployment of police dogs against people of color.

"It felt like I was being eaten," recounted Joseph Malott, a 22-year-old Black student who was mauled by a police dog moments after deflecting a tear gas canister, away from himself and allegedly toward officers, in June 2020 during a Black Lives Matter protest in California. Later that night, Malott became one of the approximately 3,600 Americans per year sent to the emergency room for severe bite injuries sustained during altercations with police

K-9s. Although men and women of just about every age and ethnicity in all fifty states have been subjected to violent K-9 incidents, a series of 13 linked reports, titled "Mauled: When Police Dogs are Weapons," produced by AL.com, *IndyStar*, the Invisible Institute, and the Marshall Project, suggests Black men have been inordinately targeted.[76]

According to Bryn Stole and Grace Toohey's February 2021 report, the rate of police K-9 bites in Baton Rouge, Louisiana, a majority-Black city of 220,000 residents, averages more than double that of the next-ranked city,

---

"Police dogs have a highly charged history in the United States, especially in the South, where they were used against enslaved people and, in the 1960s, civil rights protesters."

—The Marshall Project

Indianapolis; and nearly *one-third* of the police dog bites are inflicted on teenage men, most of whom are Black. Overall, between 2017 and 2019, Baton Rouge police dogs bit at least 146 people. Fifty-three of those people were 17 years old or younger. A majority of the dog-bite victims were Black, and most of them were unarmed and suspected by police of nonviolent crimes such as driving a stolen vehicle or burglary.

Stole and Toohey recounted the stories of two Black teens, neither suspected of violent or serious crimes, who were hunted and mauled by Baton Rouge police K-9s in June and October of 2019 after attempting to run or bike away from officers. Lester (a minor whose last name was not revealed to protect his anonymity) and Charles Carey, respectively 14 and 17 years old when attacked, will grow up with physical and mental scars from the attacks they sustained. As Abbie VanSickle, Challen Stephens, Ryan Martin, Dana Brozost-Kelleher, and Andrew Fan reported in October 2020, medical researchers have found that police dog attacks are "more like shark attacks than nips from a family pet" due to the aggressive training police dogs undergo. The Baton Rouge Police Department gives K-9 officers nonspecific leeway to release dogs based on officers' assessments of "the severity of the crime" and whether "the suspect poses an immediate threat," Stole and Toohey reported in February 2021.

As the October 2020 report by VanSickle and her colleagues noted, "Police dogs have a highly charged history in the United States, especially in the South, where they were used against enslaved people and, in the 1960s, civil rights protesters."

Though the Black Lives Matter movement has significantly raised public awareness of police using disproportionate force against people of color, police K-9 violence has received strikingly little attention from corporate news media. One might expect horrific stories, including cases in which "[a] woman's scalp was torn in California; a man's vocal cords were damaged in Colorado; [and] an Arizona man's face was ripped off," as Ashley Remkus reported in an October 2020 installment of the "Mauled" investigation, to be undeniably newsworthy. Nevertheless, corporate coverage has been limited. To its credit, the *Washington Post* published a front-page story on the topic, in November 2020, which cited the Marshall Project's reporting.[77] In October 2020, *USA Today* published an article on police dogs and excessive force, authored by the Marshall Project's Maurice Chammah and Abbie VanSickle, the same day that it was published by the Marshall Project.[78] An August 2020 NBC News report covered the Salt Lake City Police Department's suspension of its police K-9 program, after video circulated of a police dog biting a Black man who was kneeling on the ground with his hands held up.[79] Otherwise, coverage appears to have been limited to local news outlets.[80]

In April 2021, Harvard University's Shorenstein Center on Media, Politics and Public Policy announced that the Marshall Project's "Mauled: When Police Dogs are Weapons" investigation had been selected as a finalist for the Center's 2021 Goldsmith Prize for Investigative Reporting.[81]

 ## 10 Activists Call Out Legacy of Racism and Sexism in Forced Sterilization

Alexandra Minna Stern, "Forced Sterilization Policies in the US Targeted Minorities and Those with Disabilities—and Lasted into the 21st Century," The Conversation, August 26, 2020.

Ray Levy Uyeda, "How Organizers are Fighting an American Legacy of Forced Sterilization," *YES! Magazine*, February 8, 2021.

Student Researcher: Morgan Nichols (Saint Michael's College)

Faculty Evaluator: Rob Williams (Saint Michael's College)

During the 20th century, at least 60,000 Americans in some 32 states were sterilized without their consent.

The majority of individuals subjected to forced sterilization at the hands of the government have been people of color, inmates of jails, prisons, or institutions for people with mental illness or disabilities, and members of other marginalized and disempowered groups. As reports from The Conversation and *YES! Magazine* have documented, forced sterilization continues in the United States today. Organizations such as Project South, California Latinas for Reproductive Justice, and the Sterilization and Social Justice Lab are actively working to document the extent of this underreported problem—and to bring an end to it.

"All forced sterilization campaigns, regardless of their time or place, have one thing in common. They involve dehumanizing a particular subset of the population deemed less worthy of reproduction and family formation."
—Alexandra Minna Stern

A February 8, 2021 article by Ray Levy Uyeda in *YES! Magazine* highlighted the experience of Kelli Dillon, who was an inmate in a California prison in 2001 when she underwent a procedure to remove a potentially cancerous growth. During that procedure, Dillon's surgeon also performed a hysterectomy she did not authorize. Dillon's experience is far from unique. In 2001 alone, 148 women in California prisons underwent tubal ligation or total hysterectomies without their knowledge, and between 1997 and 2010 some 1,400 California women prisoners underwent unwanted sterilizations.

Levy Uyeda's *YES! Magazine* article also reported on more recent allegations of forced sterilizations sanctioned by US officials, including charges that between October and December of 2019 an immigration detention center in Georgia "had forcibly sterilized at least five women in the custody" of Immigration and Customs Enforcement (ICE).[82]

Forced sterilization campaigns "merge perceptions of disability with racism, xenophobia and sexism—resulting in the disproportionate sterilization of minority groups," Alexandra Minna Stern reported for The Conversation. Some sources report anywhere from 100,000 to 150,000 women have been victims of these campaigns in the United States alone.

The United States has a long and sordid history of forced sterilization. This barbaric practice was deemed constitutional in a 1927 Supreme Court decision, *Buck v. Bell*, which paved the way for a century of nonconsensual sterilization. This case involved a young woman, Carrie Buck, who had been classified by a Virginia state institution as "feeble-minded" and "promiscuous" and deemed therefore unfit to raise a child. As a result, she was sterilized without her knowledge or consent during a separate procedure. Although Buck's family may have suffered from various mental illnesses and poverty, Buck herself did not suffer from mental illness—she was merely living in poverty. But, due to her family's history and economic status, the Supreme Court ruled that sterilization without her consent was necessary and justified. With *Buck v. Bell* as precedent, doctors were permitted to sterilize countless Black Americans during the Jim Crow and Civil Rights eras, and the practice grew so common in the South it came to be known as a "Mississippi Appendectomy." Although most states now have laws against forced sterilization, the 1927 Supreme Court decision has never been overturned.

As University of Michigan professor Alexandra Minna Stern wrote in an August 26, 2020 commentary for The Conversation, "All forced sterilization campaigns, regardless of their time or place, have one thing in common. They involve dehumanizing a particular subset of the population deemed less worthy of reproduction and family formation." Stern directs the Sterilization and Social Justice Lab, an interdisciplinary research group that "explore[s] patterns and experiences of eugenics and sterilization in the 20th century using mixed methods from the social sciences, humanities, and public health."[83] Other organizations, including Project South and California Latinas for Reproductive Justice, are beginning to petition for laws that would ban forced sterilization in prisons, according to Ray Levy Uyeda's *YES! Magazine* report.

The history of eugenics has been thoroughly researched and criticized by scholars and human rights activists, but coverage by the corporate media of the US practice of forced sterilization throughout the 20th century and into the 21st has tended to be limited and narrowly focused. After allegations surfaced that ICE had sterilized detainees without their consent, there was some corporate news coverage. For example, the *Washington Post* published a September 2020 article about these allegations in the context of the history of forced sterilization in the United States but omitted any mention of the activists resisting the practice.[84] September 2020 articles from CNN and the *Boston Globe* also took the same limited approach.[85] In February 2021 the *Los Angeles Times* carried a damning op-ed by Alexandra Minna Stern about the newspaper's role in promoting eugenics and sterilizations in the 1930s and 1940s.[86] However, the specific focus of Stern's *Los Angeles Times* editorial could suggest to some readers that sterilization is an issue confined to the past, and not a current, pressing concern.

Project South, California Latinas for Reproductive Justice, and the Sterilization and Social Justice Lab all work to document and raise awareness of forced sterilizations, seek compensation for victims, and fight to ensure that these procedures are never forced upon an individual without their knowledge and consent again. But corporate news coverage of the work of these organizations has been virtually nonexistent. Some establishment press articles on the topic of forced sterilization include comments from members of these organizations to provide context on the issue, but few spotlight the groups' tireless organizing and record of accomplishments. Exceptions to this include articles from both *Marie Claire* magazine and Refinery29, a website targeted at younger women.[87] However, for the past year the vast majority of articles recognizing the work of these groups have originated from independent news sources.

It is only as of July 2021, as this book goes to print, that the trend finally seems to be changing, with the Associated Press and other establishment news outlets reporting that California is preparing to approve reparations of up to $25,000 per person to women who had been sterilized without consent in public hospitals and other state institutions because the government had deemed them unfit to have children.[88] The Associated Press and *Washington Post* articles on the topic briefly mention the work of the Sterilization and Social Justice Lab, and the *Post* quotes Alexandra Minna Stern; the *New York Times* and *Guardian* pieces quote Alexandra Minna Stern without mentioning her connection to the Sterilization and Social Justice Lab; and the Associated Press, *Washington Post*, Reuters, ABC7 (Los Angeles), and the *Guardian* quote a representative of California Latinas for Reproductive Justice, with the *Los Angeles Times* featuring the organization's programs director on a podcast.

Seed Sovereignty Movements Challenge Corporate Monopolies

Charli Shield, "Seed Monopolies: Who Controls the World's Food Supply?" DW (Deutsche Welle), April 8, 2021.

Student Researcher: Taylor Greene (San Francisco State University)

Faculty Evaluator: Kenn Burrows (San Francisco State University)

Throughout the world, seed sovereignty activists are reclaiming the right to plant, in resistance to seed laws that threaten food security by criminalizing farmers for using diverse crops, Charli Shield reported for DW (Deutsche Welle) in April 2021.

Although establishment news outlets have covered how corporate producers of genetically modified seeds, such as Bayer and Corteva, benefit from patents that provide exclusive ownership rights, Shield's report highlighted another, more obscure but nonetheless powerful, way that corporations and international agriculture agreements benefit Big Ag at the expense of ordinary farmers and biodiversity. Under the auspices of intellectual property statutes known as "plant variety protection," other, non-GMO plant varieties can be "strictly controlled," Shield reported.

According to guidance from the World Trade Organization, all of the world's nations are expected to establish legislation to protect different plant varieties. Many countries now fulfill this expectation by joining the International Union for the Protection of New Varieties of Plants (UPOV), which limits the production, sale, and exchange of seeds—in principle, to encourage innovation by allowing breeders to profit from temporary monopolies, according to UPOV and its agribusiness backers such as Bayer.

The catch is that, to qualify for UPOV protections, commercial seeds must be genetically distinct, uniform, and stable; "Most ordinary seeds are none of these things," Shield wrote. Instead, the varieties that ordinary farmers have developed and handed down for generations are "genetically diverse and continually evolving." In fact, under some nations' plant variety protections, traditional farmers' varieties "can't be certified as seeds at all." To compound the threats to traditional agriculture and biodiversity, many countries now enforce seed marketing laws that restrict the sale—or even the sharing—of non-certified seeds, leaving farmers with only one legal option: buying seeds from Big Ag.

As a result, Shield reported, "[a] huge wealth of locally adapted crops is being replaced by standardized varieties."

"We're looking at this as neocolonialism destroying our livelihoods and our environment," Mariam Mayet, director of the African Centre for Biodiversity in South

Africa, told DW. Countries are not legally obligated to join UPOV, but the United States, Canada, members of the European Union, and other nations are encouraging "neocolonial agriculture" by pressuring countries such as Zimbabwe and India to join.

Mayet is one of numerous leaders throughout the world who seek to preserve the autonomy of indigenous agriculture—which she calls "the bedrock to ensure ecological integrity"—by developing what DW described as "seed networks that allow farmers and communities to bypass the corporate agribusiness giants and manage seeds on their own terms." From the Alliance for Sustainable and Holistic Agriculture in India, and the Third World Network in Southeast Asia, to Let's Liberate Diversity! in Europe, and the Open Source Seed Initiative based in the United States, a global seed sovereignty movement now challenges the "staggering monopolies" that otherwise "dominate the global food supply," DW reported.

According to the United Nations Food and Agriculture Organization, 75 percent of the world's crop varieties disappeared between the years 1900 and 2000. By reclaiming the right to plant, the seed sovereignty movement helps protect food security in a time of climate change. "The more uniform our genetic pool is, the more vulnerable we are to all sorts of environmental stresses, and we know that with climate change there will be more of these stresses," said Karine Peschard, a researcher at the Graduate Institute of International and Development Studies in Geneva. Encouraging a wide range of different crops ensures genetic diversity, which in turn provides resilience to climate change.

"Seeds are ultimately what feed us and the animals we

eat," Jack Kloppenburg, a sociologist at the University of Wisconsin–Madison and a participant in the Open Source Seed Initiative, told DW. "Control over seeds is, in many ways, control over the food supply. The question of who produces new plant varieties is absolutely critical for the future of all of us."

The global movement for seed sovereignty has been largely overlooked by corporate news media. The only mention of "seed sovereignty" found during review of this story was an article about home gardening and seed saving during the pandemic, published by the *New York Times*.[89] Bayer's global influence has been the subject of establishment news coverage, particularly after its 2018 acquisition of Monsanto. A 2019 *Washington Post* article noted that, as the 2020 presidential campaign developed, monopolies, including agribusiness mergers such as Bayer-Monsanto, were emerging "as major issues for Democrats."[90] *The Post*'s coverage, however, focused on the domestic politics of the Democratic primaries, without any mention of global struggles over restrictive plant variety protections or threats to agricultural diversity.

The Open Source Seed Initiative was the subject of one recent, noteworthy feature: In June 2019 the *New York Times* published an article by Dan Barber, a professional chef and co-founder of a seed company. Noting that "seed oligarchies" are a "new thing," Barber observed that Big Seed—Corteva, ChemChina, Bayer, and BASF—keeps "doubling down on a system of monocultures and mass distribution."[91] Barber's important article advocated for seeds "not as software, but as living systems" and "the source of a new food revolution," though his article focused on the United States and mentioned plant variety protection certificates only in passing. *The Times* featured his report as a (lavishly illustrated) opinion piece, rather than front-page news.

Top 25 stories in the 2001 and 2008 editions of the *Censored* yearbook covered antecedents to the current seed sovereignty movement.[92]

 Grave Threats to Amazon Rainforest from Domestic Industries and Global Capital

Mauricio Angelo, "Complicity in Destruction III: How Global Corporations Enable Violations of Indigenous Peoples' Rights in the Brazilian Amazon," Amazon Watch, 2020.

Harry Cockburn, "Climate Crisis: Amazon to Reach Critical Tipping Point 'by 2064'," Study Suggests," *The Independent*, January 4, 2021.

Student Researcher: Richard Gonzalez (Sonoma State University)

Faculty Evaluator: José Javier Hernández Ayala (Sonoma State University)

A 2020 report from Amazon Watch, entitled "Complicity in Destruction III," shows how global corporations contribute to Indigenous rights abuses in the Brazilian Amazon. The report identifies threats including deforestation, land grabbing, and illegal fires, which, taken together, severely threaten the rights and survival of Brazil's Indigenous people. Specifically, companies in three sectors of industry—mining, agribusiness, and energy—are "directly or indirectly involved in conflicts affecting Indigenous peoples and their territories." This "commodity-driven destruction" makes the Brazilian Amazon "an epicenter of the planet's spiraling human rights and environmental crisis," according to the report.

The extensively documented report provides case studies from each of the three industrial sectors threatening Indigenous populations. For instance, mining operations overseen by Vale—a Brazilian company that operates in more than thirty countries and is the world's second-largest producer of iron ore and nickel—have created many conflicts with the local Indigenous people, and Vale stands accused of contaminating the Cateté River, the main source of water on Xikrin Indigenous land. Vale's principal investors include BlackRock, Capital Research Global Investors, and Vanguard, all US-based companies that together hold more than 11 billion dollars' worth of shares in Vale. And Vale is just one example of the industrial exploitation of the Amazon that is impacting Brazil's Indigenous people.

In addition to Brazilian industry, the report also identifies six of the world's top investment companies—BlackRock, Citigroup, JPMorgan Chase, Vanguard, Bank of America, and Dimensional Fund Advisors—as enablers of corporate wrongdoing in Amazonia. From 2017 to 2020, these six financial firms contributed more than 18 billion dollars to nine of the eleven destructive companies profiled in the report. "The human rights and environmental abuses documented in this report would not be possible without the extensive investments of international financial leaders," the report's authors wrote.

Amazon Watch issued its report in partnership with the Association of Brazil's Indigenous Peoples (APIB), a coalition that consists of eight regional Indigenous organizations.

Noting that it is imperative for Brazilian companies and their international investors and trading partners to "forge and adhere to policies that respect Indigenous rights and the environment," the Amazon Watch report also highlighted the APIB's 18-point set of recommendations for companies operating in Brazil, importers of Brazilian products, financial institutions investing in these operations, and governments and policymakers responsible for oversight of the private sector. These recommendations include:

- Adopting a zero-tolerance policy for any acts of violence against environmental or land defenders in areas where a company operates;

- Committing to zero deforestation policies and guaranteeing respect for Indigenous and human rights, with verifiable targets and public progress reports; and

- Creating or strengthening internal control and monitoring mechanisms to ensure that no investments occur in areas involving environmental destruction, human rights violations, or conflicts on Indigenous lands.

The report concludes that the devastation of the Amazon rainforest in Brazil "cannot be simply understood as a Brazilian issue, but rather one that is actively enabled by global markets." Therefore, "[o]nly a truly global effort can meet the challenges of this pivotal moment."

In December 2020 the peer-reviewed scholarly journal *Environment* published a study conducted by Robert Toovey Walker predicting that by the year 2064 the Amazon rainforest, the world's largest tropical rainforest, will reach a "tipping point."⁹³ Due to a combination of droughts driven by global climate change and deforestation, once that tipping point is reached, Walker reported, the Amazon's tree canopy will no longer be able to recover, and the rainforest will be "permanently invaded by flammable grasses and shrubs."

Major US news outlets, including the *New York Times* and *Time,* have provided extensive coverage of the destruction of the Brazilian Amazon rainforest, but this coverage has mostly focused on specific problems within Brazil, such as the policies of Brazilian president Jair Bolsonaro, and less on the global markets and international investors that drive the destruction.⁹⁴ As of June 2021, the establishment press in the United States does not appear to have covered Amazon Watch's 2020 "Complicity in Destruction" report. However, the news division of the Canadian CTV Television Network ran a brief story on the report on October 27, 2020 which noted that "[m]any of the companies named denied the accusations."⁹⁵ Independent environmental news website Mongabay published an extensive write-up of the report on November 5, 2020.⁹⁶

 Corporate Media Sideline Health Experts during Pandemic

Julie Hollar, "In Pandemic, Sunday Shows Centered Official Voices, Sidelined Independent Health Experts," Fairness & Accuracy In Reporting (FAIR), May 22, 2020.

Student Researcher: Madisen Ritter (Indian River State College)

Faculty Evaluator: Elliot D. Cohen (Indian River State College)

As COVID-19 spread rapidly across the United States, so too did unclear (and sometimes contradictory) information about it. Establishment media outlets had the crucial task of clarifying information and providing factual evidence about the disease to support the statements being made to the American public by government officials. However, as Julie Hollar reported in an article posted on the Fairness & Accuracy In Reporting (FAIR) website in May 2020, many prominent commercial TV news networks failed to provide this essential service by excluding the voices of independent health officials in their coverage of, and discussion panels about, the pandemic. The networks' disregard for health experts and public interest advocates raises serious ethical concerns, as it exacerbated the risks posed by the spread of COVID-19 to the health and well-being of those watching.

Renowned media watchdog FAIR analyzed the Sunday schedule of programs for five major media networks—NBC, CBS, ABC, CNN, and Fox News—during April 2020 to determine how many health experts and public interest groups were featured on each network's programs. Of all 121 featured guests, only 26 were health experts; most of the rest were current or former government appointees. The number of independent public health experts featured also varied depending upon the network; for instance, health experts made up 14 percent of the guests featured on CBS and NBC, but 0 percent of the guests on CNN.

FAIR's research uncovered other disparities in guests' backgrounds. Among elected officials or political appointees featured as guests, Republicans dominated Democrats 41 to 34. This is hardly a surprise. As Hollar points out, "FAIR and others have shown that Republicans historically dominate on Sunday shows regardless of which party is in power."

There were other significant disparities as well. The programs that FAIR examined included only three foreign officials across all five networks. Further, while the five major TV networks provided platforms for the CEO of Bank of America, two Federal Reserve bank presidents, and billionaire businessmen Bill Gates, Barry Diller, and Mark Cuban, FAIR "found not a single mention of the cancel rent movement or the widespread struggles people are facing to pay for housing, or of the labor strikes against Amazon to protest unsafe conditions." Additionally, men (70 percent of guests) were featured far more than women (30 percent of guests).

As of June 2021, no corporate media outlets had reported on FAIR's study. Two independent media outlets—Nation of Change and EgbertoWillies.com—republished Julie Hollar's original article.[97]

US Factory Farming a Breeding Ground for Next Pandemic

Jessica Moss, "The Next Pandemic May be Bred on US Farms," WhoWhatWhy, March 11, 2021.

Student Researcher: Emily Utsig (Indian River State College)

Faculty Evaluator: Elliot D. Cohen (Indian River State College)

As the impacts of COVID-19 continue to deepen, experts say global pandemic prevention programs should also focus on the United States, where intensive agricultural practices are breeding grounds for disease, according to a March 2021 report by WhoWhatWhy.

"The threat boils down to American excess," Jessica Moss wrote. Over the past fifty years, meat production has increased about 260 percent, mostly in the form of so-called factory farms or confined animal feeding operations (CAFOs) that fulfill the US and global demand for producing cheap and plentiful animal protein. As Moss reported, 99 percent of US meat comes from factory farms where "[p]oor conditions and stress on the animals means that disease can emerge on the farms and spread through the herd at lightning speed—like COVID-19 in a nightclub."

Factory farming operations confine animals in tight, packed indoor pens. "Overcrowding not only threatens to 'amplify' disease in animals, it also hastens mutation, increasing the likelihood of a jump from animals to human beings," Moss wrote. According to Michael Greger, the author of *Bird Flu: A Virus of Our Own Hatching*, the export of US factory farming methods has contributed to the new bird flu viruses that have developed in Asia since the 1990s. These new viruses are "tied to industrial-ization—the 'Tysonization'—of our poultry production," Greger said, referencing Tyson Foods, a US-based cor-poration that is one of the world's largest processors and marketers of chicken, beef, and pork.

A July 2020 United Nations (UN) report, "Preventing the Next Pandemic: Zoonotic Diseases and How to Break the Chain of Transmission," warned that further infec-tious disease outbreaks could occur if governments do not take active measures to prevent animal diseases from crossing into the human population. (A "zoonotic disease" is an illness transmitted from animal sources to humans.) The UN report specifically listed "increasing demand for animal protein" and "unsustainable agricultural intensification" as the first two of seven major human drivers of "zoonotic disease emergence."[98] The UN assessment recommended ten policy options to reduce the risk of future zoonotic outbreaks, including phasing out "unsustainable" agricultural processes and strengthening the health of animals involved in food production.

As WhoWhatWhy reported, many factory farm operations try to prevent disease by treating animals with antibiotics, which also facilitate fast growth. The problem, Moss wrote, is that "excessive use of these medicines helps microbes develop drug-resistant pathogens—a phenomenon known as antimicrobial resistance." Michael Martin, a professor of epidemiology at the University of California, San Francisco and president of the organization Physicians Against Red Meat, told WhoWhatWhy, "If you wanted to find a way to promote antibiotic resistance in bacteria, you almost would not be able to find a better way to do it than concentrat[ing] animals together and feeding them antibiotics on a regular basis." Under such conditions, the demand for meat is itself a driver of disease, Moss's report concluded.

In December 2014 a study commissioned by the UK government estimated that 700,000 people die each year due to antibiotic-resistant microbes; and in October 2020 the World Health Organization identified antimicrobial resistance as one of the top ten threats to global health.[99]

"It is a human failing that we predict, but we do not prepare," Inger Andersen, executive director of the United Nations Environment Programme, observed in July 2020 when she spoke at the launch of the United Nations's "Preventing the Next Pandemic" report. To avoid future pandemics, Andersen stated, we must recognize that human health, animal health, and planetary health are "inextricably linked."[100]

Corporate news coverage has been limited on the links between factory farming and the risks posed by antibiotic resistance and disease transmission from animals to humans. The Project's extensive review found no significant corporate news coverage of the UN report on zoonotic diseases.[101] Instead, when corporate news media have covered factory farming, their stories have focused, even during the COVID-19 pandemic, on the role of industrialized farming in contributing to the climate crisis.[102]

In November 2020 the *Los Angeles Times* published an article entitled "Want to Avoid Pandemics? Eliminate Factory Farming" by Wendy Orent, an author of books on Lyme disease and plague—though the newspaper positioned Orent's historical overview of links between livestock farming and the transmission of animal diseases to humans as an opinion piece.[103] *Wired* reported in September 2019 that antibiotic resistance in livestock poses significant threats to human health.[104] In August 2020, Vox published "The Meat We Eat is a Pandemic Risk, Too," by Sigal Samuel. Samuel's report on links between factory farming and disease deserves recognition for addressing the critical question of how to build food systems that avoid the pitfalls of industrialized livestock farming.[105] Vice also published a report on the topic in December 2020.[106]

Project Censored has previously reported on threats posed by antibiotic resistance.[107]

Thousands of 5G Satellites Pose Risk of Future Space Wars

John Keller, "What 5G Means to the Military," *Military & Aerospace Electronics*, December 2, 2020.

Karl Grossman, "The Perils of Military 5G," *CounterPunch*, March 15, 2021.

Kit Klarenberg, "Battle for the Galaxy: New Paper Reveals How UK is Making Extensive Plans for War in Space," RT, March 25, 2021.

Student Researcher: Amber Yang (Sonoma State University)

Faculty Evaluator: Kenn Burrows (San Francisco State University)

The prospect of *Star Wars*–esque battles in space has become much more likely with the rollout of fifth generation (5G) wireless technology, powered by tens of thousands of satellites approved by the Federal Communications Commission and on track to be launched into space without significant public oversight.

Despite demands from the public, including anti-war activists in particular, for a 5G moratorium, the media push for 5G has been enormous—with constant advertising by Verizon and other telecommunications giants, a news blackout on critical discussions of the technology's possible health and environmental impacts, and censorship on social media platforms of those questioning 5G tech.[108]

5G wireless technology is a major factor in the weaponization of space. On October 8, 2020 the Department of Defense (DOD) announced $600 million in awards to advance its 5G capabilities, claiming that 5G technology has the potential to transform the military, because 5G's high-speed connectivity would significantly enhance the ease and speed of sharing data from video, voice, sensors, targeting, reconnaissance, and even the sights on infantry weapons.[109] Experimentation will take place at five US military sites, representing the largest 5G tests for dual-use applications—applications employed for both military and civilian purposes—in the world.

As John Keller explained in a December 2020 article for *Military & Aerospace Electronics*, the "ubiquitous high-speed data connectivity" promised by 5G will enable the US military to make use of "swarming unmanned vehicles," "smart hypersonic weapons with re-targeting on-the-fly," and "unmanned aircraft that can fly alongside passenger aircraft in commercial airspace." It will also give the Pentagon "instant situational awareness anywhere on Earth."

In March 2021, Kit Klarenberg reported for RT that the UK government is also planning for the eventuality of space warfare. In order to position the British military for "dominance" in space, the UK government intends to "launch a National Space Operations Centre, develop an 'intelligence, surveillance and reconnaissance satellite constellation' and create a 'Space Academy' to train the country's new army of 'space specialists.'"

Many critics have voiced concerns about the consequences of the militarization of space. A March 2021 *CounterPunch* piece by Karl Grossman quoted Bruce Gagnon, coordinator of the Global Network Against Weapons and Nuclear Power in Space, who warned that the "[l]aunches of tens of thousands of 5G satellites will ensure that every person on Earth will have a satellite over their head 24/7. Imagine the surveillance and targeting capabilities that would become available." According to Gagnon, "The DOD and NASA are awarding hundreds of billions of dollars to the likes of Elon Musk of SpaceX and other private launch corporations to hoist the 5G satellites into the heavens."

Other corporations—including OneWeb, Telesat, Omnispace, Lynk, Facebook, and Amazon—also plan to launch and operate large constellations of satellites in low orbit around the Earth.[110] Gagnon predicts that congestion in the orbital paths of all these satellites "will become a point of conflict in the near future as other nations become agitated that the U.S. is grabbing most of the parking spaces in the increasingly contested orbits."

Nor are these the only complaints critics of the drive to militarize space have raised. Other issues include worries about the effect of burning rocket fuel on climate change, satellite collisions generating space debris, increased surveillance and data mining, and the use of child labor in the mining of the rare minerals needed to make satellite and 5G infrastructure.[111]

Heedless of these dangers and concerns, governments and the telecommunications industry continue to propagate wireless technologies and infrastructure, helped along by captive regulatory agencies and legislative efforts to silence public debate. At the same time, media campaigns and apps designed to addict the public—and especially children—have been effective in generating consumer enthusiasm for the new technology.

Gagnon told *CounterPunch* that "[t]here is presently no national or international regulation over the use of space. [...] It is up to all of us to speak out and demand that NASA, the Federal Communications Commission, the United Nations and the Pentagon quickly undertake a process of fair regulation of space operations." Short of such immediate action, Gagnon warns that we will soon face a cascade of companies competing over space traffic, military confrontations, "deadly collisions"—"and even war in space."

5G technology and its connection to the militarization of space has not been covered in any meaningful way by the corporate media. *Foreign Policy* ran a May 2021 editorial by an astrophysicist and an expert in diplomacy about space junk and other problems caused by the unregulated use of space.[112] A July 2020 *New York Times* article noted that the "new Cold War" between the United States and China includes rivalry in outer space.[113] Although the militarization of space—and especially the efforts being made by US adversaries like Russia and China to project military power into space—has been discussed by the *New York Times*, the *Washington Post*, and other corporate news outlets, the important role of 5G in this militarization has only been reported by independent publications like *CounterPunch* or military-focused news outlets like *Military & Aerospace Electronics* and Defense One.[114]

Project Censored has previously covered growing health concerns regarding 5G technology.[115]

Femicide Census Connects UK Killings with Global Wave of Violence against Women

Julia Long, Emily Wertans, Keshia Harper et al., "UK Femicides 2009–2018," Femicide Census, November 25, 2020.

Karen Ingala Smith, "Coronavirus Doesn't Cause Men's Violence Against Women," KarenIngalaSmith.com, April 15, 2020.

Karen Ingala Smith, "2020," KarenIngalaSmith.com, April 14, 2020, updated January 9, 2021.

Karen Ingala Smith, "2021," KarenIngalaSmith.com, February 8, 2021, updated June 7, 2021.

Yvonne Roberts, "'If I'm Not in on Friday, I Might be Dead': Chilling Facts about UK Femicide," *The Guardian*, November 22, 2020.

Student Researcher: Arden Kurhayez (North Central College)

Faculty Evaluator: Steve Macek (North Central College)

Fatal violence against women across the world is increasing. A November 2020 report from the UK-based nonprofit Femicide Census spanning nearly a decade found that, on average, "a woman was killed by a male partner or ex-partner every four days," with that number increasing to every three days when the focus is expanded to include killings outside romantic relationships. Due to a lack of accumulated data, the Femicide Census reports that these killings are typically treated as isolated incidents by law enforcement and legislators despite being "identified globally as a leading cause of premature death for women."

According to the Femicide Census, 62 percent of the 1,425 women killed by men from 2009 to 2018 in the United Kingdom were killed at the hands of a current or former intimate partner, and the remaining 38 percent were either killed by a family member, a friend, or someone they had just met. Of the 888 women killed by intimate partners, 38 percent were killed within the first month of separating from their partner, 89 percent within the first year of separating or attempting to separate, and 5 percent were killed three or more years later. Fifty-nine percent of the femicides perpetrated by family members or current or former partners had a known history of abuse, and one-third of those murdered women had disclosed the abuse to police.

As Yvonne Roberts observed in her November 2020 *Guardian* article on the staggering statistics from the Femicide Census, these seemingly isolated killings are part of a bigger public health crisis—one that is likely even larger than reported, as the Femicide Census only considers killings that have been legally proven as having been committed by a man. The "Counting Dead Women" section of the UK website KarenIngalaSmith.com, created by Femicide Census co-founder Karen Ingala Smith, keeps a record of every killing—noting suspected killings as well—and reported at least 107 cases in 2020, and 74 so far in 2021 (as of June). However, "research [...] is limited and unconnected" across the world, so data on femicides outside of the United Kingdom is not included.

The United States has its own version of the census, known as Women Count USA, which was started in 2017 by Dawn Wilcox.[116] Women Count USA has collated incomplete but nevertheless essential information about violence against women and girls in the United States dating back to the mid-1900s.

The organization UN Women has described this global wave of domestic violence against women as a shadow pandemic within the COVID-19 pandemic.[117] Despite this warning, most corporate news coverage continues to fail to acknowledge the scope of femicide and gender-based violence throughout the world. Instead, coverage tends to spend more time on individual cases of abuse or on the stories of individual victims. The existing coverage on femicide provided by the corporate media also all too often excludes instances that occur in the United States or in advanced industrialized European nations like the United Kingdom. Corporate broadcast news outlets like CNN, ABC, and NBC have covered protests about violence against women in Turkey and Mexico, usually dwelling on politics and policy, rather than examining the issue holistically or exploring the systematic nature of the problem.[118]

The lack of coverage is especially an issue when it comes to femicide that occurs in the United States. It is clear from the work of Women Count USA that instances of femicide are indeed growing domestically. Despite this, corporate news continues to gloss over the extent of the epidemic of gender-based violence in this country. In the limited existing coverage, writers tend to frame the issue as an international one that seemingly does not impact the United States. One notable exception to this is an August 2020 article from Teen Vogue that focused on the increasing rates of femicide in the United States and spotlighted the work of Women Count USA.[119]

 ## New Wave of Independent News Sources Demonetized by Google-Owned YouTube

Caitlin Johnstone, "YouTube Financially Deplatforms Swath of Indie Media," Consortium News, February 5, 2021.

Student Researchers: Trinity Marshall, Allison Okeley, and Mackenzie Bardol (Saint Mary's College, Notre Dame)

Faculty Evaluator: Helen K. Ho (Saint Mary's College, Notre Dame)

In February 2021 independent news sources such as Progressive Soapbox, The Convo Couch, Franc Analysis, and Hannah Reloaded were demonetized by YouTube, the latest instance of YouTube penalizing independent and alternative voices by removing entire channels or videos with no explanation, raising concerns over censorship on the platform. YouTube told the creators that their channels contained videos that violated YouTube's community guidelines, yet failed to inform them or comment on which content was in violation.

The demonetized videos and channels were made ineligible to receive advertising revenue, and some lost out on a share of subscription revenue from YouTube Premium as well.

With an unclear appeal process, it is unknown how long the accounts will remain deactivated. As Caitlin Johnstone explained in her February 5, 2021 article for Consortium News, "These accounts could remain demonetized for months, or forever, without any clear explanation at all."

> **"The general population is herded onto huge monopolistic social media platforms offering democratization of information where your voice can be heard, and then those platforms proceed to censor an increasing amount of political speech."**
>
> —Caitlin Johnstone

Other punitive measures from YouTube range from putting heavy restrictions on accounts to completely banning entire channels. After receiving YouTube's notification, Progressive Soapbox tweeted, "You guys have destroyed my channel without legit explanation as to why. [. . .] [F]rankly there is literally zero 'harmful' content on my channel." Another victim of demonetization, comedian Graham Elwood, tweeted, "Nope. No superchats, no ad revenue, no YouTube premium money. Thanks Stalin I mean google."[120]

Ford Fischer, a freelance video journalist who has filmed US political demonstrations like the notorious Unite the

Right rally, tweeted, "Last time you demonetized my channel, I spoke out for seven months. [...] Please don't do this again." According to a June 7, 2019 article in The Verge, Fischer's channel, a channel run by a history teacher, and a video uploaded by the Southern Poverty Law Center were just a few of the scores of videos taken down shortly after YouTube made an announcement that it was implementing stronger measures against "videos alleging that a group is superior in order to justify discrimination, segregation or exclusion based on qualities like age, gender, race, caste, religion, sexual orientation or veteran status."[121] Among the videos of Fischer's that were banned were one featuring footage of white supremacist speaker Mike Enoch talking at an event in the lead-up to the Unite the Right rally and another about "pro-Israel and pro-Palestine groups coming together to debate a holocaust denier."

YouTube is a unique platform for independent voices, and this latest round of demonetization not only censors those voices but also, due to the resulting lack of funding, puts these smaller outlets under considerable financial distress.

As Johnstone pointed out in her article, "This has been a continually escalating trend for years. The general population is herded onto huge monopolistic social media platforms offering democratization of information where your voice can be heard, and then those platforms proceed to censor an increasing amount of political speech."

A few corporate media outlets have mentioned similar deplatforming stories involving either YouTube's demonetization of right-wing channels for disseminating hate speech or its suppression of specific videos as indecent or age-inappropriate. For instance, on October 27, 2020, the

Hollywood Reporter published an article by Ashley Cullins about a group of 15 conservative YouTubers—with a combined audience of 4.5 million subscribers—who filed a lawsuit against the platform for deleting their channels.[122] A widely circulated Fox News story from March 2021 criticized restrictions YouTube placed on a Bella Thorne music video featuring a tame simulated sex scene.[123] Yet the Google-owned platform's demonetization and muzzling of left-wing and progressive YouTubers has largely gone unremarked in the establishment press.

"Collision of Crises" for Black and Brown Survivors of Sexual Violence during COVID-19

Shani Saxon, "COVID Causes Long-Term Harm for Sexual Violence Survivors of Color: Report," ColorLines, November 20, 2020.

Student Researcher: Lindsay Wilkinson (Salisbury University)

Faculty Evaluator: Shannon O'Sullivan (Salisbury University)

During the COVID-19 pandemic, women of color who are survivors of sexual violence have faced disproportionate hardships compared to white women survivors, Color-Lines's Shani Saxon reported in November 2020. Saxon's report focused on the findings of a study, "Measuring the Economic Impact of COVID-19 on Survivors of Color," conducted by the organizations "me too." and FreeFrom, which examined the "compounding socioeconomic effects" of structural racism and COVID-19 on survivors of sexual violence and intimate-partner violence. According to its authors, the report "represents a call to action and social investment in survivors' lives that cannot wait."[124]

The study's findings—based on survey responses from 737 participants, aged 18 years or older—revealed a "collision of crises," involving the intersection of systemic racial inequality with unemployment or unsafe work, food and housing insecurity, economic precarity, and lack of healthcare. Survivors of color, the study found, are especially at risk of facing "pronounced food and housing insecurity" during the pandemic, with financial insecurity "greatest among Black and Brown women survivors" (with white women having, on average, 5.76 times the financial resources of Black and Brown women). Moreover, the study noted that survivors who lack financial resources during the pandemic have been "at greater risk of returning to a harm-doer."[125]

Survivors of color reported that specific resources, including child support payments, student loan debt relief, and hazard pay for essential workers, were crucial to their health and safety. The study also made seven policy recommendations for addressing the impacts of COVID-19 on survivors of color. These recommendations included investments in housing, healthcare, childcare, and programs that enable survivors' financial freedom. For instance, the study's action plan calls for changing the federal definition of domestic violence to include economic abuse, creating paid and protective work leave for survivors of sexual or intimate-partner violence, and resources for "survivor-led initiatives to end sexual violence."[126]

Establishment news outlets such as the *Washington Post* and *Los Angeles Times* have covered racial and gender inequalities in the impact of the COVID-19 pandemic;[127]

but, at the time of this volume's publication, none appear to have reported on the study of the pandemic's economic impacts on women of color who are survivors of sexual or intimate-partner violence, which is the specific focus of Shani Saxon's ColorLines report.

The closest relevant coverage appears to have been a March 2021 *New York Times* article that explained how President Joe Biden's pandemic relief plan included millions of dollars for organizations dedicated to ending domestic abuse, as well as vouchers for survivors to help them find a safe place to rebuild their lives.[128] But the *Times*'s report failed to connect all of the dots, acknowledging that the pandemic "has disproportionately affected people of color" while describing domestic abuse as "a crisis that cuts across race, class and gender." Though the latter claim is true, it seems like a deceptively incomplete analysis in light of the findings reported by ColorLines.

19 European Demand for Biomass Energy Propels Destruction of US Forests

Danna Smith, "Europe Drives Destruction of US Forests in the Name of Fighting Climate Change," Truthout, September 21, 2020.

Student Researcher: Tai Lam (Sonoma State University)

Faculty Evaluator: Allison Ford (Sonoma State University)

Driven by demand in European Union countries, the southern United States is now the world's largest producer and exporter of the wood pellets used to produce biomass energy, Danna Smith reported for Truthout in September 2020. Despite popular beliefs that solar and wind power are its main sources of renewable energy, the European Union (EU) sources nearly 60 percent of its renewable energy from biomass. Championed as a renewable source of energy, biomass energy uses plants, wood, and waste materials as sources of heating or power. However, as Smith reported, in many European countries the carbon costs of imported wood are not considered. As a result, the true costs of biomass energy are not widely understood.

As Smith explained in her article, many European nations, including the United Kingdom, Netherlands, and Denmark, are increasingly relying on biomass electricity, with the unintended consequence of "speeding up carbon emissions, pollution and forest destruction." The shift has led many to see forests as fuel, encouraging the cutting of timber for the production of wood pellets.

The deforestation that began in Europe has now arrived in the United States, as the Natural Resources Defense Council (NRDC) documented in a June 2019 report, "Global Markets for Biomass Energy are Devastating U.S. Forests."[129] According to the NRDC report, Enviva, the world's largest wood pellet manufacturer, engages in logging practices that have ravaged "iconic" wetlands forests in the southwest United States to produce pellets that are shipped to utility companies such as Drax Power in the United Kingdom and Ørsted in Denmark.[130]

Anticipating this crisis, in January 2018, a group of 784 scientists warned the EU Parliament that cutting down forests for bioenergy increases carbon pollution.[131] Biomass energy releases more carbon per unit of energy generated than coal or gas release, they reported. The scientists also warned that logging degrades forests as a natural form of flood control.

The "voracious European demand" for wood pellets has put forests and communities in the southern United States at increased risk of toxic air pollution and catastrophic flooding, Smith reported. In recent years, the southern coastal plain that includes North and South Carolina, southern Georgia and Alabama, and northern Florida, has been subjected to "some of the most devastating and costly flooding events in the world," Smith reported, noting that these events have had "disproportionate impacts to low-income, rural communities of color."

Many of the communities most affected by the devastation are now fighting back. In North Carolina, for example, local leaders and residents coordinated to oppose plans by Enviva to expand production at three of its facilities in that state. In Alabama a similar coalition formed to oppose Enviva's plans to construct a new wood pellet production facility in Epes, Alabama, the first of four such plants the company hopes to establish in the state.[132]

In May 2020 the European Union announced that it would reassess its biomass policies as part of its broader biodiversity action plan. As Smith reported, this reassessment could lead to the discontinuation of the use of wood as a source of EU biomass energy, and it might also lead to more accurate accounting for carbon emissions from imported biomass sources.

This issue has received little in the way of recent corporate news coverage. Credit is due to the *New York Times* for publishing an in-depth April 19, 2021 article by Gabriel Popkin and Erin Schaff that explored the impact of wood pellet production for export to Europe on one community in North Carolina.[133] The article accurately described the forces driving Europe's demand for pellets and noted that "[m]any scientists have long been skeptical of biomass's climate benefits" because the policies European nations have adopted to combat climate change "fail to account for the carbon losses caused by cutting down trees to burn them." But even Popkin and Schaff's excellent article engaged in a bit of false balance by providing a platform for specious arguments from Enviva's in-house scientists about why burning pellets should be "considered carbon neutral." Sadly, Popkin and Schaff's article appears to be the lone substantive corporate media report on this topic since at least 2015.

By contrast, environmental news sites have devoted considerable space to analyzing the burgeoning wood pellet industry in the Southeast, the factors driving its growth, and the severe climatic repercussions of burning wood as an energy source. For instance, in July 2020, Saul Elbein wrote an in-depth account for environmental news outlet Mongabay of Enviva's wood pellet plants and their likely environmental consequences.[134] On February 15, 2021, Mongabay followed up Elbein's article with a report from Justin Catanoso about hundreds of scientists and economists calling on the countries of the world not to burn forests as fuel.[135] A few weeks later, Mongabay published an article by Catanoso about a move by the Netherlands to limit subsidies for "biomass-for-heat" plants.[136] It is worth noting that both Danna Smith's Truthout article and the Mongabay series predate Popkin and Schaff's *New York Times* piece, though the coverage provided by the independent outlets went unmentioned in the *Times*.

Proposed Domestic Terrorism Legislation Imperils Civil Liberties

Alex Emmons, "Capitol Hill Assault Revives Calls for Domestic Terrorism Law, but Civil Liberties Groups are Wary," The Intercept, January 10, 2021.

Student Researcher: Samuel Berry (Saint Michael's College)

Faculty Evaluator: Rob Williams (Saint Michael's College)

The violent insurrection of January 6th, 2021, when supporters of Donald Trump unlawfully occupied the US Capitol building, threatened members of Congress, and temporarily derailed certification of the presidential election, has prompted a new wave of federal anti-terrorism statues targeting domestic terrorism. As Alex Emmons of the Intercept and independent news commentators reported, the proposed legislation—including the Domestic Terrorism Prevention Act of 2021—is unnecessary, because existing laws already cover domestic terrorism, and dangerous, because new laws could be used to repress legitimate political protest and to target activists and religious or ethnic minorities.

The Intercept's Alex Emmons reported that the siege of the Capitol on January 6th was "the culmination of years of warnings" about the increasing threat of far-right extremism, including an October 2020 assessment by the Department of Homeland Security which identified "white supremacist extremists" as "the most persistent and lethal threat in the Homeland."[137]

Proponents of new domestic terrorism legislation include a group of former Justice Department officials, the Federal Bureau of Investigation Agents Association, and President Biden, but civil liberties groups are opposed, Emmons wrote, because "federal law enforcement already has powerful tools to investigate and prosecute acts of domestic terrorism without any new laws."

As Chip Gibbons noted in a report for *Jacobin*, the "vast security apparatus" established "in the name of 'national security'" after the September 11, 2001 terrorist attacks "completely failed to thwart a plot carried out in plain sight."[138] The problem now, much the same as it was twenty years ago, is not a lack of effective terrorism laws, but how they tend to be interpreted and applied.

A 2019 review by the Intercept found that Justice Department prosecutors "routinely declined to bring terrorism charges against right-wing extremists even when their alleged crimes meet the legal definition of domestic terrorism."[139] Out of 268 right-wing extremists prosecuted in federal courts since the 9/11 attacks for crimes that appear to meet the legal definition of domestic terrorism, the Intercept study found that Justice Department officials applied anti-terrorism laws against only 34 of them.

Noting that the label "terrorist" is "vulnerable to political exploitation," Faiza Patel, the co-director of the Brennan Center's Liberty and National Security Program, told the Intercept that, since 9/11, the Federal Bureau of Investigation (FBI) has "gained extraordinary authorities to investigate." For example, to open an "assessment"—the FBI's lowest level of investigation—requires no factual evidence, only an "authorized purpose" for law enforcement.[140]

"Given the fact that there are at least 50 statutes that count as domestic terrorism," Patel stated, "I feel confident [the FBI] could find an authorized purpose" to open an "assessment" on any group or individual.[141] The socialist news website Left Voice noted that federal agencies such as the FBI have historically used their law enforcement powers to infiltrate and break up the Communist Party in the 1950s and the Black Panther Party and the New Left in the 1960s and 1970s. Any new domestic terrorism measure, reporter Sou Mi wrote, would "give more power, funding, and resources to agencies like the FBI" and the National Security Agency, which have a long record of using their authority to "hunt down and neutralize the Left."[142]

Establishment news coverage of proposed domestic terrorism legislation has been limited, and mostly uncritical—framing the issue simply in terms of regular partisan dispute between Democrats and Republicans, or as a matter of forecasting the policy agenda of the newly inaugurated president, Joe Biden, and his administration.[143] When corporate news outlets have included more critical analyses, these perspectives have been categorized as opinion rather than as news.[144]

Conservative Christian Groups Spend Globally to Promote Anti-LGBTQ Campaigns

Matt Tracy, "Report Exposes Trump's Ties to Religious Right Global Anti-LGBTQ Campaigns," Gay City News, October 29, 2020.

Student Researcher: Tritan Hai To (Diablo Valley College)

Faculty Evaluator: Mickey Huff (Diablo Valley College)

Major Christian organizations, including the Billy Graham Evangelistic Association and the Fellowship Foundation, have together spent close to a quarter of a billion dollars over the past 13 years campaigning against

LGBTQ and abortion rights, according to a report by the United Kingdom–based political website openDemocracy.[145] Matt Tracy, Gay City News's editor in chief, wrote that the October 2020 report exposes "the depth of cash flowing from American Christian anti-LGBTQ and anti-abortion groups into dangerous campaigns against reproductive rights and queer rights across the globe." Even as the LGBTQ community has struggled to achieve equality in the United States, organizations representing the US Christian Right, such as Focus on the Family, have spent millions to promote prejudice against and persecution of LGBTQ people in Latin America, Asia, the Middle East, Africa, and Europe.

There has also been "an unmistakable focus on Africa, which many Christian groups have eyed in recent decades," Tracy noted. For example, the Fellowship Foundation is reported to have spent more than three-quarters of its anti-LGBTQ campaign funds in Africa, including support for Ugandan lawmaker David Bahati, the author of a notorious "Kill the Gays" bill from 2014.

Peter Tatchell, a well-known British gay activist, wrote to Gay City News describing this movement as "Christian imperialism," "menacing the well-being and human rights of millions of LGBTQ people."

Tracy's coverage also noted that, since Donald Trump became president in 2016, anti-LGBTQ groups have been "simultaneously juggling those foreign influence projects with efforts to lock up close ties" to Trump, and the report revealed "just how connected the president is to the far-right's agenda."

Corporate media coverage of far-right religious organizations funding efforts to promote homophobic, transphobic, and anti-abortion policies has been sparse, despite coverage of the openDemocracy report by the news agency Reuters, from which many establishment news outlets source stories.[146] A March 2020 NBC News report covered a study, conducted by the Southern Poverty Law Center, which found that anti-LGBTQ hate groups were on the rise in the United States, but NBC's report did not address the amount of money invested

---

Even as the LGBTQ community has struggled to achieve equality in the United States, organizations representing the US Christian Right, such as Focus on the Family, have spent millions to promote prejudice against and persecution of LGBTQ people in Latin America, Asia, the Middle East, Africa, and Europe.

---

abroad by religiously-motivated anti-LGBTQ groups.[147] In October 2020, *Time* magazine published a report based on the same openDemocracy study covered by Matt Tracy for Gay City News.[148] However, *Time*'s reporting of religious anti-LGBTQ organizations focused more on the connections these groups cultivated with the Trump administration, while making only passing reference to their massive spending on anti-LGBTQ campaigns in other nations.

Dataminr Introduces Racial Bias, Stereotypes in Policing of Social Media

Sam Biddle, "Twitter Surveillance Startup Targets Communities of Color for Police," The Intercept, October 21, 2020.

Student Researcher: Leslie Palacios (Diablo Valley College)

Faculty Evaluator: Mickey Huff (Diablo Valley College)

In an October 2020 article published by the Intercept, Sam Biddle reported on racial bias at Dataminr, a New York company that monitors Twitter for "suspicious behavior," which it reports to law enforcement agencies. According to Biddle's report, Dataminr's Twitter surveillance program "targets communities of color." Sources directly familiar with Dataminr's work told the Intercept that, in Biddle's words, Dataminr has "relied on prejudice-prone tropes and hunches to determine who, where, and what looks dangerous." Dataminr's "domain experts" lacked training, creating a powerful but untrustworthy monitoring system made in the image of their own prejudices and those of the law enforcement agents the system was intended to serve.

According to Dataminr's own marketing materials, the company's controversial First Alert program was created to notify "first responders to breaking events, enabling the fastest real-time response,"[149] but, as one source told the Intercept, "Dataminr and law enforcement were perpetuating each other's biases."

As Biddle reported, First Alert's monitoring staff "brought their prejudices and preconceptions along with their expertise." Sources directly related to Dataminr told the Intercept that they were instructed to search for evidence of crime in specific neighborhoods and streets where a majority of residents were people of color. Furthermore, the Intercept reported that, according to sources familiar with the program, Dataminr's anti-gang activity amounted to "white people, tasked with interpreting language from communities that [they] were not familiar with," coached by predominantly white former law enforcement officials who themselves "had no experience from these communities where gangs might be prevalent."

The tolls of policing people of color on social media include heightened levels of tension among those being policed and unnecessary or excessive use of force by authorities. Companies such as Dataminr show that the crisis of over-policing manifests not only in person, on the street, but also online. In a previous article for the Intercept from July 2020, Biddle wrote, "Dataminr relayed tweets and other social media content about the George Floyd and Black Lives Matter protests directly to police, apparently across the country," despite Twitter's official policy against "using Twitter data to derive or infer potentially sensitive characteristics about Twitter users."[150]

The Intercept contacted Lindsay McCallum, a spokesperson for Twitter, but she refused to discuss Dataminr's surveillance of protesters, most of whom were peaceful. Instead, Dataminr contends that its law enforcement service only "delivers breaking news alerts on emergency events, such as natural disasters, fires, explosions and shootings."[151]

Biddle's October 2020 report quoted Forrest Stuart, a sociologist heading the Stanford Ethnography Lab, who observed that Dataminr's use of Twitter to infer gang affiliation is "totally terrifying." Stuart said that research has established how often police officers lack the "cultural competencies and knowledge" required to understand the "behavioral and discursive practices, [and] aesthetic practices" of urban Black and Brown youth, but the "domain experts" employed by Dataminr lack "even the basic knowledge" that officers have regarding criminal behavior.

Almost all of the corporate media news coverage regarding Dataminr has been positive, highlighting the company's business partnerships and financial successes without addressing the charges of racial bias raised by Biddle's reports. In March 2021, for example, CNBC reported on the company's estimated value having risen to more than $4 billion, and its CEO's plans for a stock market launch in 2023.[152] In September 2020 the *Wall Street Journal* published an article about Dataminr and how it "provided alerts to police and other government clients that included Twitter handles of users discussing plans for protests or where activists were blocking streets" during Black Lives Matter protests, noting that Twitter's rules "prohibit partners from using its data for 'tracking, alerting or monitoring sensitive events,' specifically including protests and rallies."[153] Although the *Journal*'s report included concerns from privacy advocates about "what level of social-media monitoring qualifies as surveillance," it failed to address how Dataminr's service for law enforcement disproportionately targets communities of color. In July 2020, Mashable published a piece based on Biddle's July 2020 Intercept article about how Dataminr helped police track protestors at Black Lives Matter events following the killing of George Floyd.[154] Black Agenda Report republished Biddle's October 2020 Intercept article one week after its original publication.[155]

23 Coastal Darkening Threatens Ocean Food Chains

Doug Johnson, "The Environmental Threat You've Never Heard Of," Hakai Magazine, February 10, 2021.

Student Researcher: Victor Rodriguez (North Central College)

Faculty Evaluator: Steve Macek (North Central College)

Researchers at the University of Oldenburg in Germany have concluded that pollution-related darkening of coastal waters in the world's oceans poses a serious threat to ocean food chains.

Since 2016, researchers with the Coastal Ocean Darkening Project at the University of Oldenburg have been investigating how pollution and runoff alter the color and clarity of coastal waters and assessing the degree to which this darkening jeopardizes the health of ocean ecosystems. As Hakai Magazine reported in February 2021, the Project's research shows that coastal darkening has "the potential to cause huge problems for the ocean and its inhabitants."

Coastal darkening is usually the result of introducing organic matter, such as decaying plants or loose soil, into an aquatic environment. Sometimes heavy rains wash organic matter into oceans and rivers. But more frequently, organic matter is introduced into aquatic environments by human activity, such as boating or the application of fertilizers to farmland. When fertilizer is washed away and ends up in the oceans, it causes an algal bloom that creates a light-blocking layer on the water's surface. Boating causes silt to be kicked up, which can likewise obstruct light to the marine life beneath it.

Light-blocking layers of organic material affect sea

life in two ways. First, they prevent many types of sea life from gathering food. These impacts begin with phytoplankton that require light for photosynthesis, and extend up the food chain to impact other species that feed on plankton. As documented by researchers at the University of Oldenburg, a lack of light means a lack of food for small fish and other low-level consumers, which in turn means these low-level consumers have a reduced level of nutritional value for the organisms that feed on them. This drop in nutritional value in low-level consumers leads to reduced food quality and compromises coastal organisms' trophic efficiency—scientists' term for efficiency of energy transfer between different links in a food chain. At the same time, a lack of adequate light directly prevents many larger fish and other ocean predators from hunting their prey (although it should be noted that this lack of light actually benefits some organisms, such as jellyfish, that do not rely on light to hunt). On a large scale, these changes in ocean ecosystems could eventually lead to shortages of fish not only for humans, but also for other species that depend on them for sustenance.

The second main problem stemming from light-blocking organic material is that sunlight normally serves to break down toxic chemicals in the water. Decreased light compromises this process, resulting in higher contamination levels, which further damages oceanic food chains.

As of May 2021 there has been no coverage whatsoever by corporate media of coastal darkening. Hakai Magazine, a web journal focused on coastal science and societies, published the first news account of the phenomenon on February 10, 2021. Doug Johnson's Hakai article was reprinted four days later in *The Atlantic*.[156] Since then, environmental news outlet EcoWatch has published a short article on the problem based almost entirely on Johnson's reporting, and the Europe-based public affairs website Modern Diplomacy carried a brief commentary on the combined effect of sea level rises and coastal darkening that referenced the work of the Oldenburg University research team.[157]

 ## Juvenile Justice Reform Remains Elusive

Shani Saxon, "Juvenile Justice Advocates Call on Biden Administration to Prioritize Jailed Youth," ColorLines, February 4, 2021.

Student Researchers: Winnie O'Brien, Julia Sanchez, and Natalia Speedon (Saint Mary's College, Notre Dame)

Faculty Evaluator: Helen K. Ho (Saint Mary's College, Notre Dame)

Juvenile justice reform continues to be ignored throughout the United States, despite President Biden's campaign pledge to close youth prisons and establish a $100 million fund for youth and communities. Shani Saxon's interview for ColorLines with a juvenile justice advocate, Liz Ryan, highlights some of the underreported issues that incarcerated children face in the United States. As Saxon wrote, these issues are multiplied by the impacts of COVID-19.

According to the Children's Defense Fund's 2020 report, "76,000 children are prosecuted, sentenced or incarcerated as adults annually," with nearly ten times that number arrested nationally in a single year, and with children of color being "overcriminalized and overrepresented at every point—from arrests to post-adjudication placements."[158] Sixty-two percent of arrested children in the United States are white, but children of color are nearly twice as likely to be arrested in comparison to white children. Children of color make up approximately two-thirds of the population in the juvenile justice system, with 41 percent being Black and 21 percent being Hispanic.[159] These racial disparities continue into the adult criminal justice system as well, making it more likely that minority youth will continue to be criminalized later in life.

Political leaders often discuss mental and physical health issues—such as those arising from solitary confinement—in adult correctional facilities, yet have continued in these conversations to exclude the plights of incarcerated youth. As Ryan explained to Saxon, room confinement has increased due to COVID-19 procedures; similar to solitary confinement, room confinement impacts youths' mental health, maturation, and school progress.

In addition, the pandemic has made juvenile facilities a breeding ground for the virus due to often crowded and unsanitary conditions. Incarcerated youth "are not getting what they need inside" correctional facilities, Ryan told ColorLines.

There has been nearly no coverage regarding the need for reform in the juvenile justice system, and the topic evidently continues to be a low priority on the agendas of government officials and corporate news media. Coverage of youth juvenile facilities is mostly limited to local and regional news outlets, and focused on piecemeal changes in policy or the threat of COVID-19, rather than on reform of the system as a whole.[160]

Abusers Benefiting from International Anti-Abduction Treaty

Misha Valencia, "Treaty Created to Stop Child Abductions Could Now be Protecting Abusers," WhoWhatWhy, July 20, 2020.

Student Researchers: Meredith Chapple and Maricella Chavez (Saint Mary's College, Notre Dame)

Faculty Evaluator: Helen K. Ho (Saint Mary's College, Notre Dame)

The Hague Convention on Civil Aspects of International Child Abduction was created to protect children from being abducted and taken away from their home countries. But, as Misha Valencia observes in a July 20, 2020 WhoWhatWhy article, abusers are now using this treaty as a way to manipulate the courts and regain custody of their children.

An analysis of Hague cases and court decisions found "that an overwhelming number of 'abductors' were really mothers escaping abuse—and that the majority of them were forced to return their children" to abusive partners. Children's fear of abusive fathers, as well as mothers' claims of abuse, are often dismissed or not believed. According to psychotherapist Sarah Gundle, "[T]he intention of this treaty was to protect children, but, in reality, the legal system and the Hague Convention often fail to understand the principles of trauma and how they play out for abuse survivors and vulnerable children."

With 101 countries participating in this treaty, the repercussions of this problem are truly global. Article 13(b) of the Hague Convention allows for exceptions to be made, if a child's return home might expose them to physical or mental trauma. In instances of domestic violence, Gundle explains, "batterers frequently take their anger out on their children" when their spouse is no longer present. In 2020 the Hague Commission issued a "Guide to Good Practice" which emphasized the importance of Article 13(b) but failed to acknowledge that many survivors of abuse are too afraid to report abuse for fear of disbelief, embarrassment, or shame. Without a history of filing claims, mothers and children fleeing from abusive environments generally cannot meet a strict standard of proof for court cases. Studies show that abusers were able to argue that the victim is unfit for sole custody of their child in 70 percent of challenged custody cases, as pointed out by the American Judges Association.[161]

As of May 25, 2021, corporate news media coverage of international abductions has been limited in both quantity and depth of coverage. Existing corporate news reporting tends to focus on countries joining the treaty or on individual abduction cases as they relate to the news publications' country or locale. For instance, a *USA Today* piece from June 2019 examined a child custody battle between a mother in Ohio and a father residing in Italy.[162] A Cleveland.com article from February 25, 2020 covered the results of that case.[163] An August 2020 *New York Times* article by David Yaffe-Bellany, "The Three Abductions of N.," briefly mentioned the treaty.[164] The article's focus, however, was on examining how certain individuals and organizations have found a way to profit from abduction recoveries. Overall, the corporate media have not paid adequate attention to a flawed treaty that has sent hundreds of children around the world back into the custody of abusive parents.

Notes

1. Brooke Shelby Biggs, "The Unbearable Lameness of Project Censored," *Mother Jones*, April 11, 2000.
2. "Texts of the Supreme Court Decision, Opinions and Dissents in Times-Post Case," *New York Times*, July 1, 1971.
3. Charlie Savage, "Government Lawsuit Over John Bolton's Memoir May Proceed, Judge Rules," *New York Times*, October 1, 2020; and Michael S. Schmidt and Katie Benner, "Justice Dept. Ends Criminal Inquiry and Lawsuit on John Bolton's Book," *New York Times*, June 16, 2021.
4. "That a careful reader looking for a fact can sometimes find it with diligence and a skeptical eye tells us nothing about whether that fact received the attention and context it deserved, whether it was intelligible to the reader or effectively distorted or suppressed." Edward S. Herman and Noam Chomsky, *Manufacturing Consent: The Political Economy of the Mass Media* (New York: Pantheon Books, 2002 [1988]), lxiii.
5. For more on the often-overlooked labor upheaval of the late 1960s and early 1970s, see Kim Moody, *An Injury to All: The Decline of American Unionism* (New York and London: Verso, 1988), 83–95.
6. Michelle Alexander, "Time to Break the Silence on Palestine," *New York Times*, January 19, 2019.
7. Dan Barber, "Save Our Food. Free the Seed," *New York Times*, June 7, 2019.
8. Sigal Samuel, "The Meat We Eat is a Pandemic Risk, Too," Vox, August 20, 2020; and Wendy Orent, "Want to Avoid Pandemics? Eliminate Factory Farming," *Los Angeles Times*, November 30, 2020.
9. Gabriel Popkin and Erin Schaff, "There's a Booming Business in America's Forests. Some Aren't Happy about It," *New York Times*, April 19, 2021, updated April 23, 2021.
10. Doug Johnson and Hakai Magazine, "Coastal Darkening is a Hidden Environmental Nuisance," *The Atlantic*, February 14, 2021.
11. Andy Lee Roth, Introduction to "The Top *Censored* Stories and Media Analysis of 2016–17," in *Censored 2018: Press Freedoms in a "Post-Truth" World*, eds. Andy Lee Roth and Mickey Huff with Project Censored (New York: Seven Stories Press, 2017), 31–37, 33.
12. For information on how to nominate a story, see "How to Support Project Censored" at the back of this volume.
13. Validated Independent News stories are archived on the Project Censored website.
14. For a complete list of the Project's judges and their brief biographies, see the acknowledgments at the back of this volume.
15. "High Drug Prices and Patient Costs: Millions of Lives and Billions of Dollars Lost," Council for Informed Drug Spending Analysis, November 18, 2020.
16. See Aimee Brierly, "New Study Predicts More Than 1.1 Million Deaths among Medicare Recipients Due to the Inability to Afford Their Medications," West Health, November 19, 2020.
17. "High Drug Prices and Patient Costs," Council for Informed Drug Spending Analysis.

18. Brierly, "New Study Predicts More Than 1.1 Million Deaths."

19. Inmaculada Hernandez, Alvaro San-Juan-Rodriguez, Chester B. Good, and Walid F. Gellad, "Changes in List Prices, Net Prices, and Discounts for Branded Drugs in the US, 2007–2018," *JAMA: The Journal of the American Medical Association*, Vol. 323 No. 9 (March 3, 2020), 854–62.

20. "High Drug Prices and Patient Costs," Council for Informed Drug Spending Analysis.

21. Ibid.

22. Ibid.

23. Stephen W. Schondelmeyer and Leigh Purvis, "Trends in Retail Prices of Brand Name Prescription Drugs Widely Used by Older Americans, 2006 to 2020," AARP Public Policy Institute, June 2021, 1, 3.

24. "High Drug Prices and Patient Costs," Council for Informed Drug Spending Analysis.

25. Justine Coleman, "Pallone Commits to Using 'Whatever Vehicle I Can' to Pass Democrats' Drug Pricing Bill," The Hill, May 4, 2021.

26. Khristopher J. Brooks, "Big Drugmakers Just Raised Their Prices on 500 Prescription Drugs," CBS News, January 5, 2021.

27. Karen Zraick, "Americans Borrowed $88 Billion to Pay for Health Care Last Year, Survey Finds," *New York Times*, April 2, 2019.

28. Peter Welch and David Mitchell, "Allow Medicare to Negotiate on Behalf of Patients to Lower Drug Prices," The Hill, May 12, 2021.

29. Susan Coughtrie and Poppy Ogier, eds., "Unsafe for Scrutiny: Examining the Pressures Faced by Journalists Uncovering Financial Crime and Corruption around the World," Foreign Policy Centre, November 2, 2020.

30. Ibid., 46.

31. Ibid., 12.

32. Ibid., 24.

33. Catherine Belton, *Putin's People: How the KGB Took Back Russia and Then Took On the West* (London: William Collins, 2020).

34. Coughtrie and Ogier, "Unsafe for Scrutiny," 17.

35. Ibid., 11.

36. Some notable recent examples of corporate media coverage of money laundering and other international financial crimes include "FinCEN Files: All You Need to Know about the Documents Leak," BBC News, September 21, 2020; Jason Leopold, Anthony Cormier, John Templon et al., "The FinCEN Files," BuzzFeed, September 20, 2020; Alun John, Sumeet Chatterjee, and Lawrence White, "Global Banks Seek to Contain Damage over $2 Trillion of Suspicious Transfers," Reuters, September 20, 2020; and Ian Talley and Dylan Tokar, "Leaked Treasury Documents Prompt Fresh Call for Updated Anti-Money-Laundering Regulations," *Wall Street Journal*, September 21, 2020.

37. Juliette Garside, "English Law 'Abused by the Powerful to Threaten Foreign Journalists,'" *The Guardian*, November 2, 2020; and Jamie Dettmer, "Investigative Journalists Facing 'Vexatious' Lawsuits Aimed at Silencing Them," Voice of America, November 6, 2020.

38. Thomas Rowley, "UK Plays Leading Role in Legal Threats against Investigative Journalists, New Report Says," openDemocracy, November 2, 2020.

39. Olee Fowler, "Workers from McDonald's, Burger King, and More are Planning a State-Wide Strike," Eater Miami, May 6, 2020.

40. Ron Ruggless, "Workers Expand Protests at Chicago-Area Peet's Unit," Nation's Restaurant News, April 15, 2021.

41. Steven Greenhouse, "Is Your Grocery Delivery Worth a Worker's Life?" *New York Times*, March 30, 2020.

42. David Streitfeld, "As Amazon Rises, So Does the Opposition," *New York Times*, April 19, 2020, updated December 22, 2020.

43. Paul Frymer and Jacob M. Grumbach, "The NBA Strike is a Big Moment for Athlete Activism—and the Labor Movement in America," Vox, September 4, 2020; Vinson Cunningham, "The Exhilarating Jolt of the Milwaukee Bucks' Wildcat Strike," *New Yorker*, August 27, 2020; Derrick Bryson Taylor, "N.B.A. 'Boycott' or Strike: What's the Difference?" *New York Times*, August 27, 2020; Ben Strauss, "'Strike'?, 'Boycott'?, When Athletes Stopped Playing, the Arguments over Wording Began," *Washington Post*, August 28, 2020; and Jill Martin, Leah Asmelash, and David Close, "These Teams and Athletes Refused to Play in Protest of the Jacob Blake Shooting," CNN, August 28, 2020.

44. See, for example, Kate Sullivan and Kevin Liptak, "Biden Announces US Will Aim to Cut Carbon Emissions by as Much as 52% by 2030 at Virtual Climate Summit," CNN, April 23, 2021.

45. Jason Hickel, "Quantifying National Responsibility for Climate Breakdown: An Equality-Based Attribution Approach for Carbon Dioxide Emissions in Excess of the Planetary Boundary," *The Lancet Planetary Health*, Vol. 4 No. 9 (September 1, 2020), 399–404.

46. Ibid.

47. Ibid. Although China is within its fair share, Hickel told *In These Times* "we are all doomed" if China does not act quickly to reduce its emissions.

48. Hickel, "Quantifying National Responsibility."

49. Sarah Lazare, "'Colonizing the Atmosphere': How Rich, Western Nations Drive the Climate Crisis," Common Dreams, September 16, 2020; and Jason Hickel, "The World's Sustainable Development Goals Aren't Sustainable," *Foreign Policy*, September 30, 2020.

50. Rishika Pardikar, "Joe Biden's New Climate Pledge Isn't Fair or Ambitious," *Jacobin*, April 26, 2021.

51. Spencer Bokat-Lindell, "Debatable," *New York Times*, April 27, 2021. The article quoted former UN climate official Christiana Figueres, who described Biden's pledge as "an extraordinary step that should be commended." Bokat-Lindell then noted, "But to others, like the economic anthropologist Jason Hickel, the pledge is so 'morally and politically untenable' as to be almost insulting to the rest of the world."

52. Hanna Joerss, Zhiyong Xie, Charlotte C. Wagner et al., "Transport of Legacy Perfluoroalkyl Substances and the Replacement Compound HFPO-DA through the Atlantic Gateway to the Arctic Ocean—Is the Arctic a Sink or a Source?" *Environmental Science & Technology*, Vol. 54 No. 16 (July 29, 2020), 9958–67.

53. Francisca Ribeiro, Elvis D. Okoffo, Jake W. O'Brein et al., "Quantitative Analysis of Selected Plastics in High-Commercial-Value Australian Seafood by Pyrolysis Gas Chromatography Mass Spectrometry,"

Environmental Science & Technology, Vol. 54 No. 15 (July 9, 2020, updated October 5, 2020), 9408–417.

54. Sharon Lerner, "PFAS Chemical Associated with Severe COVID-19," The Intercept, December 7, 2020.

55. Ribeiro, Okoffo, O'Brien et al., "Quantitative Analysis of Selected Plastics," 9413.

56. Lisa Cox, "Australia Joins US, China and Russia in Refusing to Sign Leaders' Pledge on Biodiversity," *The Guardian*, September 28, 2020.

57. Katherine Bourzac, "CFC Replacements are a Source of Persistent Organic Pollution in the Arctic," *Chemical & Engineering News*, May 2, 2020.

58. Graham Readfearn, "It's on Our Plates and in Our Poo, but are Microplastics a Health Risk?" *The Guardian*, May 15, 2021.

59. See, for example, Alex Kane, "The FBI is Using Unvetted, Right-Wing Blacklists to Question Activists about Their Support for Palestine," The Intercept, June 24, 2018; and Noa Landau, "Official Documents Prove: Israel Bans Young Americans Based on Canary Mission Website," *Haaretz*, October 4, 2018, updated October 18, 2018.

60. Kevin Gosztola, "Journalist Abby Martin Had Free Speech Rights Violated by Georgia's Anti-BDS Law, Court Rules," Shadowproof, May 24, 2021.

61. Kathleen Doyle, Troy Patton, Rob Williams, and Mickey Huff, "Silenced in Savannah: Journalist Abby Martin Challenges Georgia's BDS 'Gag Law,'" in *State of the Free Press 2021*, eds. Mickey Huff and Andy Lee Roth with Project Censored (New York: Seven Stories Press, 2020), 102–104.

62. However, the judge also ruled that specific individual defendants named in Martin's lawsuit could not be held liable for their enforcement of the law. See *Abby Martin v. Steve Wrigley, Kyle Marrero, Bonnie Overstreet, Michel Blitch, and Sandra Lensch*, United States District Court, Northern District of Georgia, Atlanta Division, No. 1:20-CV-596-MHC, May 21, 2021.

63. For example, Gregory Shupak, "Israel/Palestine Coverage Presents False Equivalency between Occupied and Occupier," Fairness & Accuracy In Reporting (FAIR), May 18, 2021.

64. Michelle Alexander, "Time to Break the Silence on Palestine," *New York Times*, January 19, 2019.

65. Isabel Kershner, "Israeli Airport Detention of Prominent U.S. Jewish Journalist Prompts Uproar," *New York Times*, August 14, 2018; and Isabel Kershner, "U.S. Student, Barred from Israel Over Boycott, Goes to Court," *New York Times*, October 9, 2018.

66. Mairav Zonszein, "How U.S. Politicians Use Charges of Anti-Semitism as a Weapon," *Washington Post*, February 13, 2019.

67. John Logan, "How Amazon's Anti-Union Consultants are Trying to Crush the Labor Movement," LaborOnline, LAWCHA (The Labor and Working-Class History Association), March 22, 2021.

68. Suhauna Hussain and Jenny Jarvie, "Amazon Unionization Efforts Dealt a Blow by Alabama Vote," *Los Angeles Times*, April 9, 2021.

69. Noam Scheiber and Daisuke Wakabayashi, "Google Hires Firm Known for Anti-Union Efforts," *New York Times*, November 20, 2019; and Greg

Bensinger, "Another Fired Google Engineer Alleges Retaliation for Union Activity," *Washington Post*, December 17, 2019.

70. Noam Scheiber and Kate Conger, "The Great Google Revolt," *New York Times Magazine*, February 18, 2020.

71. Mike Elk, "Unions Mobilize for General Strike against Trump—UFCW Criticized for Inaction at Waterloo Tyson Plant—600 Mass Nurses Unionize," Payday Report, January 8, 2021.

72. John Logan, "The Labor-Busting Law Firms and Consultants That Keep Google, Amazon and Other Workplaces Union-Free," The Conversation, August 24, 2020.

73. Jacob Sugarman, "We're Living with the Consequences of Rich Nations' Vaccine Hoarding," *In These Times*, May 13, 2021.

74. MacKenzie Sigalos, "You Can't Sue Pfizer or Moderna If You Have Severe Covid Vaccine Side Effects. The Government Likely Won't Compensate You for Damages Either," CNBC, December 17, 2020, updated December 23, 2020.

75. Brandon Grayson and Susan Rahman, "Developing Countries' Medical Needs Unfulfilled by Big Pharma," in *Censored 2020: Through the Looking Glass*, eds. Andy Lee Roth and Mickey Huff with Project Censored (New York: Seven Stories Press, 2019), 45–46.

76. Abbie VanSickle, Maurice Chammah, Michelle Pitcher et al., "Mauled: When Police Dogs are Weapons," The Marshall Project, October 15, 2020. *USA Today* partnered with the Marshall Project, AL.com, *IndyStar*, and the Invisible Institute on two of the 13 reports in the "Mauled" series: See Maurice Chammah and Abbie VanSickle, "She Went Out for a Walk. Then Drogo the Police Dog Charged," The Marshall Project, October 15, 2020, also published as Maurice Chammah and Abbie VanSickle, "She Went Out for a Walk, Then Drogo the Police Dog Charged," *USA Today*, October 15, 2020; and "'A Dog Can be Trained to be Anti-Black': A New Film Highlights Historical Use of Canines against Black People," The Marshall Project, June 23, 2021.

77. Kimberly Kindy and Julie Tate, "These Brutal Police Dog Attacks were Captured on Video. Now Some Cities are Curtailing K-9 Use," *Washington Post*, November 29, 2020. *The Post* published a print version of the story on the front page of its November 30, 2020 edition with the title "Brutal Footage of K-9s is Canceling the 'Lassie Effect.'" On September 2, 2020, the *Washington Post* published an article, Tyler D. Parry's "Police Still Use Attack Dogs against Black Americans," that provided historical perspective on the racist aspects of contemporary police dog attacks, but this story only appeared on the *Post*'s website and not in print.

78. Chammah and VanSickle, "She Went Out for a Walk."

79. Tim Stelloh, "Salt Lake Police Suspend K9 Program after Video Shows Dog Biting Black Man with His Hands Up," NBC News, August 12, 2020.

80. See, for example, Danielle Leigh, Grace Manthey, and John Kelly, "Eyewitness News Investigation Finds Use of Police Dogs Causing Serious Injury, Death Even When Suspects Weren't Combative," ABC7 (Los Angeles), December 24, 2020; and WBRZ Staff, "BRPD Revising Policy for Chasing Juvenile Suspects with Police Dogs," WBRZ (ABC, Baton Rouge), February 12, 2021.

81. "Announcing the Winner of the 2021 Goldsmith Prize for Investigative Reporting," Shorenstein Center on Media, Politics and Public Policy, Harvard Kennedy School, April 13, 2021. The Goldsmith Prize was awarded to *another* Marshall Project investigation, "Mississippi's Dangerous and Dysfunctional Penal System."

82. On the Georgia cases, *YES! Magazine* cited original reporting by José Olivares and John Washington, "'He Just Empties You All Out': Whistleblower Reports High Number of Hysterectomies at ICE Detention Facility," The Intercept, September 15, 2020.

83. Brinker Ferguson, Sarah Gao, Gabriella Garcia et al., Sterilization and Social Justice Lab, 2021.

84. Steven Moore, "ICE is Accused of Sterilizing Detainees. That Echoes the U.S.'s Long History of Forced Sterilization," *Washington Post*, September 25, 2020, updated September 28, 2020.

85. Catherine E. Shoichet, "In a Horrifying History of Forced Sterilizations, Some Fear the US is Beginning a New Chapter," CNN, September 16, 2020; and Abdallah Fayyad, "America's Shameful History of Sterilizing Women," *Boston Globe*, September 18, 2020.

86. Alexandra Minna Stern, "How the Los Angeles Times Shilled for the Racist Eugenics Movement," *Los Angeles Times*, February 28, 2021.

87. Rachel Epstein, "Forced Sterilizations are America's Best-Kept Secret," *Marie Claire*, October 28, 2020; and Britni de la Cretaz, "It's Not Just Hysterectomies: The U.S. Has a Long, Shameful History of Forced Sterilizations," Refinery29, September 18, 2020.

88. Adam Beam, "California to Pay Victims of Forced, Coerced Sterilizations," Associated Press, July 7, 2021; Derek Hawkins, "California Once Forcibly Sterilized People by the Thousands. Now the Victims May Get Reparations," *Washington Post*, July 9, 2021; Amanda Morris, "'You Just Feel Like Nothing': California to Pay Sterilization Victims," *New York Times*, July 11, 2021, updated July 14, 2021; Daniel Trotta, "California to Compensate People Forcibly Sterilized under Eugenics," Reuters, July 13, 2021; Anabel Muñoz, "California Will Pay Reparations to Survivors of State-Sanctioned Forced, Involuntary Sterilizations," *Eyewitness News*, ABC7 (Los Angeles), July 13, 2021; CBSLA Staff, "Los Angeles County Supervisors Urge State Leaders to Pay Reparations to Local Victims of Forced Sterilization," CBSN (Los Angeles), July 14, 2021; Times Editorial Board, "Editorial: Paying $25,000 to Every Living Forced-Sterilization Victim is the Least California Can Do," *Los Angeles Times*, July 14, 2021; Gustavo Arellano, interview with Wendy Carrillo and Ena Suseth Valladares, "Podcast: Eugenics in Our Own Backyard," *The Times* podcast episode, *Los Angeles Times*, July 15, 2021; and Erin McCormick, "Survivors of California's Forced Sterilizations: 'It's Like My Life Wasn't Worth Anything,'" *The Guardian*, July 19, 2021.

89. Margaret Roach, "Enjoy Those Vegetables, but Don't Forget to Save Some Seeds," *New York Times*, August 5, 2020.

90. James Hohmann, "Monopolies, Mergers Emerge as Major Issues for Democrats," *Washington Post*, April 2, 2019, A16.

91. Dan Barber, "Save Our Food. Free the Seed," *New York Times*, June 7, 2019.

92. Tom Lough, Ambrosia Crumley, Karen Parlette, Adam Sullens, Kimberly Wilson, and Hope Shand, "Indigenous People Challenge Private Ownership and Patenting of Life," in *Censored 2001: 25th Anniversary Edition*, eds. Peter Phillips and Project Censored (New York: Seven Stories Press, 2001), 87–91; and Jonathan Stoumen, Michael Januleski, Phil Beard, Arun Shrivastava, and Vandana Shiva, "KIA: The US Neoliberal Invasion of India," in *Censored 2008: The Top 25 Censored Stories of 2006–07*, eds. Peter Phillips and Andrew Roth with Project Censored (New York: Seven Stories Press, 2007), 61–66.

93. Robert Toovey Walker, "Collision Course: Development Pushes Amazonia Toward Its Tipping Point," *Environment: Science and Policy for Sustainable Development*, Vol. 63, No. 1 (2021; published online December 23, 2020), 15–25.

94. Reuters, "Brazil Amazon Deforestation Hits 12-Year High under Bolsonaro," *New York Times*, November 30, 2020; and Matt Sandy, "The Amazon Rain Forest is Nearly Gone," *Time*, September 12, 2019.

95. AFP Staff, "U.S. Firms Fund Deforestation, Abuses in Amazon: Report," CTV News, October 27, 2020.

96. Sue Branford, Thais Borges, and Diego Rebouças, "Brazilian and International Banks Financing Global Deforestation: Reports," Mongabay, November 5, 2020.

97. Julie Hollar, "In Pandemic, Sunday Shows Centered Official Voices, Sidelined Independent Health Experts," Nation of Change, May 25, 2020; and Julie Hollar, "In Pandemic, Sunday Shows Centered Official Voices, Sidelined Independent Health Experts," EgbertoWillies.com, May 22, 2020.

98. Delia Grace Randolph, Johannes Refisch, Susan MacMillan et al., "Preventing the Next Pandemic: Zoonotic Diseases and How to Break the Chain of Transmission," United Nations Environment Programme and International Livestock Research Institute, 2020, 15.

99. "Antimicrobial Resistance: Tackling a Crisis for the Health and Wealth of Nations," Review on Antimicrobial Resistance (Jim O'Neill, chair), Wellcome Collection, December 2014; and "Antimicrobial Resistance," World Health Organization, October 13, 2020.

100. Inger Andersen and Jimmy Smith, "Inger Andersen (UNEP) and Jimmy Smith (ILRI) on the Launch of the Report, 'Preventing the Next Pandemic: Zoonotic Diseases and How to Break the Chain of Transmission,'" UN Web TV, United Nations, July 6, 2020; quotations at 4:01–4:24.

101. A May 2021 opinion article, written by Ezra Klein and published by the *New York Times*, did mention the report. See Ezra Klein, "Let's Launch a Moonshot for Meatless Meat," *New York Times*, April 24, 2021 online, and in the print edition on May 3, 2021, A22.

102. See, for example, Brad Plumer, "The Meat Business, a Big Contributor to Climate Change, Faces Major Tests," *New York Times*, April 17, 2020, updated April 22, 2020.

103. Wendy Orent, "Want to Avoid Pandemics? Eliminate Factory Farming," *Los Angeles Times*, November 30, 2020.

104. Maryn McKenna, "Farm Animals are the Next Big Antibiotic Resistance Threat," *Wired*, September 19, 2019.

105. Sigal Samuel, "The Meat We Eat is a Pandemic Risk, Too," Vox, August 20, 2020. Vox also produced a video and a podcast episode on the topic of Samuel's report: see Danush Parvaneh, "The Next Pandemic Could Come from Factory Farms," Vox, August 18, 2020; and Byrd Pinkerton, Sigal Samuel, and Amy Drozdowska, "Factory Farms are an Ideal Breeding Ground for the Next Pandemic," Vox, October 21, 2020, which includes Sigal Samuel's interview with Martha Nelson on "How to Prevent a Factory Farmed Pandemic," a *Future Perfect* podcast episode.

106. Valerie Kipnis and Joe Hill, "The Next Pandemic Could Come from an American Factory Farm," Vice, December 11, 2020.

107. Yadira Martinez, Bridgette McShea, Roxanne Ezzet, and Rob Williams, "Antibiotic Resistant 'Superbugs' Threaten Health and Foundations of Modern Medicine," in *Censored 2018: Press Freedoms in a 'Post-Truth' World*, eds. Andy Lee Roth and Mickey Huff with Project Censored (New York: Seven Stories Press, 2017), 54–57.

108. On social media censorship of criticism of 5G technology, see, for instance, Shona Ghosh, "Facebook Blocked 5G Conspiracy Groups with Thousands of Members after Users Celebrated the Destruction of Phone Masts," Business Insider, April 14, 2020.

109. "DOD Announces $600 Million for 5G Experimentation and Testing at Five Installations," U.S. Department of Defense, October 8, 2020.

110. Liam Tung, "Amazon's Big Internet Plan: 3,236 Satellites to Beam Faster, Cheaper Web to Millions," ZDNet, April 5, 2019; and Mike Dano, "Omnispace Raises $60M to Beam 5G from Space," Light Reading, February 2, 2021.

111. On Big Tech's alleged use of child labor, see, for instance, Matthew Lavietes, "Tesla, Apple among Firms Accused of Aiding Child Labor in Congo," Reuters, December 16, 2019.

112. W. Robert Pearson and Benjamin L. Schmitt, "The Crisis in Space," *Foreign Policy*, May 15, 2021.

113. Steven Lee Myers and Paul Mozur, "Caught in 'Ideological Spiral,' U.S. and China Drift toward Cold War," *New York Times*, July 14, 2020, updated July 23, 2020.

114. Brandi Vincent, "Pentagon Looks to Tap 5G in Space," Defense One, February 23, 2021.

115. Jamie Wells and Kenn Burrows, "New 5G Network Spurs Health Concerns," *Censored 2020: Through the Looking Glass*, eds. Andy Lee Roth and Mickey Huff with Project Censored (New York: Seven Stories Press, 2019), 50–53.

116. Dawn Wilcox, "Databases of Women and Girls Lost to Femicide," Women Count USA, undated, updated June 28, 2021.

117. "The Shadow Pandemic: Violence against Women during COVID-19," UN Women, undated [accessed June 28, 2021].

118. Beril Eski, "Turkey Femicides are Rising—with Erdogan Poised to Make the Violence Worse," NBC News, August 14, 2020; and Ella Torres, "More Than 380 Women Have been Killed in Mexico This Year. Activists Say a Cultural Change is Needed," ABC News, March 14, 2020.

119. Nidia Bautista, "Femicide is a Growing Issue in the United States," Teen Vogue, August 28, 2020.

120. Graham Elwood, Twitter post, February 3, 2021, 2:27 p.m.

121. Julia Alexander, "YouTube's New Policies are Catching Educators, Journalists, and Activists in the Crossfire," The Verge, June 7, 2019.

122. Ashley Cullins, "Google Sued Over Purged Conservative YouTube Channels," *Hollywood Reporter*, October 27, 2020.

123. Melissa Roberto, "Bella Thorne Slams Big Tech Companies after YouTube Restricts Music Video: 'It's Endangering American Freedom,'" Fox News, March 6, 2021.

124. Elena Ruíz, Yanet Ruvalcaba, Nora Berenstain, and Steph Fluegeman, "Measuring the Economic Impact of COVID-19 on Survivors of Color," me too./FreeFrom, 2020, 5.

125. Ibid., 8–9.

126. Ibid., 19–22.

127. See, for example, Dan Keating, Ariana Eunjung Cha, and Gabriel Florit, "'I Just Pray God Will Help Me': Racial, Ethnic Minorities Reel from Higher COVID-19 Death Rates," *Washington Post*, November 20, 2020; and Margot Roosevelt, "'I Don't Know How I Can Survive.' Women Have been Hit Hardest by COVID's Economic Toll," *Los Angeles Times*, May 7, 2021.

128. Melena Ryzik and Katie Benner, "Biden's Aid Package Funnels Millions to Victims of Domestic Abuse," *New York Times*, March 18, 2021.

129. "Global Markets for Biomass Energy are Devastating U.S. Forests," Natural Resources Defense Council, June 17, 2019.

130. Ibid., 3.

131. John Beddington, Steven Berry, Ken Caldeira et al., "Letter from Scientists to the EU Parliament Regards Forest Biomass," Partnership for Policy Integrity, January 14, 2018.

132. Emily Zucchino, "Alabama Groups Oppose Enviva's Epes Facility," Dogwood Alliance, October 29, 2019.

133. Gabriel Popkin and Erin Schaff, "There's a Booming Business in America's Forests. Some Aren't Happy about It," *New York Times*, April 19, 2021, updated April 23, 2021.

134. Saul Elbein, "Burning Down the House? Enviva's Giant U.S. Wood Pellet Plants Gear Up," Mongabay, July 29, 2020.

135. Justin Catanoso, "500+ Experts Call on World's Nations to Not Burn Forests to Make Energy," Mongabay, February 15, 2021.

136. Justin Catanoso, "Dutch to Limit Forest Biomass Subsidies, Possibly Signaling EU Sea Change," Mongabay, March 9, 2021.

137. "Homeland Threat Assessment," U.S. Department of Homeland Security, October 2020.

138. Chip Gibbons, "The Capitol Riot was Bad Enough. New Domestic Terrorism Legislation Would Make It Even Worse," *Jacobin*, January 12, 2021.

139. Trevor Aaronson, "Terrorism's Double Standard," The Intercept, March 23, 2019.

140. "New Revelations about FBI Spying Renew Concern with Assessments," Defending Rights & Dissent, November 4, 2019.

141. For one such example, see the analysis of the FBI's surveillance of so-called "Black Identity Extremists," in Chapter 2 of this volume.

142. Sou Mi, "Patriot Act 2.0: Biden's Domestic Terrorism Laws are a Danger to the Working Class," Left Voice, January 15, 2021.

143. See, for example, Rachael Levy, "A Domestic Terrorism Law is Debated Anew after Capitol Riot," *Wall Street Journal*, February 13, 2021; and David Weigel, "The Trailer: How Democrats Plan to Fight Domestic Terror," *Washington Post*, January 14, 2021.

144. See, for example, an opinion article by two representatives of the American Civil Liberties Union: Hina Shamsi and Manar Waheed, "After Capitol Riot, Biden Backs Domestic Terror Law. It's a Predictably Misguided Response," NBC News, January 15, 2021.

145. Claire Provost and Nandini Archer, "Revealed: $280m 'Dark Money' Spent by US Christian Right Groups Globally," openDemocracy, October 27, 2020.

146. Rachel Savage, "U.S. Christian Groups Spent $280m Fighting LGBT+ Rights, Abortion Overseas," Reuters, October 27, 2020.

147. Julie Moreau, "Anti-LGBTQ Hate Groups on the Rise in U.S., Report Warns," NBC News, March 30, 2020, which covered the study by the Southern Poverty Law Center's Intelligence Project and Booth Gunter, "The Year in Hate and Extremism 2019," Southern Poverty Law Center, 2020.

148. Suyin Haynes, "U.S. Christian Right Groups are Pouring Millions into Conservative and Anti-LGBTQ Causes in Europe, New Report Says," *Time*, October 27, 2020.

149. "First Alert," Dataminr, undated [accessed June 30, 2021].

150. Sam Biddle, "Police Surveilled George Floyd Protests with Help from Twitter-Affiliated Startup Dataminr," *The Intercept*, July 9, 2020; and "More about Restricted Uses of the Twitter APIs," Developer Platform, Twitter, undated [accessed June 30, 2021].

151. Quoted in Biddle, "Police Surveilled George Floyd Protests."

152. Deirdre Bosa and Jon Fortt, interview with Ted Bailey, "Dataminr CEO Ted Bailey on Eyeing an IPO in 2023," *Squawk Alley*, CNBC, March 23, 2021.

153. Jeff Horwitz and Parmy Olson, "Twitter Partner's Alerts Highlight Divide over Surveillance," *Wall Street Journal*, September 29, 2020.

154. Jack Morse, "Dataminr Helped Cops Surveil Black Lives Matter Protesters, Report Finds," Mashable, July 9, 2020; and Biddle, "Police Surveilled George Floyd Protests."

155. Sam Biddle, "Twitter Surveillance Startup Targets Communities of Color for Cops," Black Agenda Report, October 28, 2020.

156. Doug Johnson and Hakai Magazine, "Coastal Darkening is a Hidden Environmental Nuisance," *The Atlantic*, February 14, 2021.

157. Tiffany Duong, "What You Need to Know About Coastal Darkening," EcoWatch, February 25, 2021; and Arshad M. Khan and Meena Miriam Yust, "When Sea Levels Rise and Coastal Waters Darken . . .," Modern Diplomacy, February 24, 2021.

158. "The State of America's Children 2020," Children's Defense Fund, 2020, 28.

159. Ibid.

160. See, for example, Alexandra Kukulka, "Juvenile Justice Bill Signed into Law: Northwest Indiana Officials Reflect on Its Impact and the Work That Still Needs to be Done," *Chicago Tribune*, May 10, 2021; James Queally and Leila Miller, "Cut Off from Their Kids, Parents of Juvenile

Detainees Wait and Worry as Coronavirus Spreads," *Los Angeles Times*, April 6, 2020; and Samantha J. Gross, "Florida's Public Defenders Plea for COVID Testing in Juvenile Lockups," *Tampa Bay Times*, July 2, 2020, updated July 3, 2020.

161. "Forms of Emotional Battering," American Judges Association, undated [accessed June 7, 2021].

162. Richard Wolf, "International Child Custody Battle between Ohio and Italy Will Get Supreme Court Hearing," *USA Today*, June 10, 2019.

163. Associated Press, "Supreme Court Rules Against Ohio Mom in International Custody Case," Cleveland.com, February 25, 2020.

164. David Yaffe-Bellany, "The Three Abductions of N.: How Corporate Kidnapping Works," *New York Times*, August 13, 2020, updated August 20, 2020.

CHAPTER 2

Déjà Vu News

What Happened to Previous *Censored* Stories

SHEALEIGH VOITL, GRIFFIN CURRAN, RACHAEL
SCHWANEBECK, and STEVE MACEK

*Journalism is in fact history on the run. It is history written
in time to be acted upon: thereby not only recording events
but at times influencing them . . . Journalism is also the
recording of history while the facts are not all in.*

—THOMAS GRIFFITH, senior editor, *Time* magazine (1959)[1]

Each year, Project Censored draws attention to news
that has been overlooked, minimized, and, in some cases,
deliberately buried by the big corporate media. The Project's annual Top 25 list of underreported stories reveals
systematic gaps and omissions in the way such outlets
cover vital subjects, including racial oppression, economic
inequality, environmental degradation, the military–
industrial complex, and the criminal justice system. The
aim of this chapter is to investigate the fate of a handful
of the important stories included in previous years' Top 25
lists.

As news cycles accelerate, breaking stories and an end-
less flow of social media commentary make ever more
insistent claims on our attention and past stories quickly

fade from view. Resisting the pull of the 24/7 news cycle, the Déjà Vu News chapter begins from the premise that previous stories' enduring significance cannot be measured by narrow conceptions of "timeliness." Instead, we insist that past stories such as those reviewed here remain instructive in making sense of current issues and deserve to be part of the public discourse.

This year's Déjà Vu chapter looks back on five Top 25 stories from the past decade, tracks significant developments in their underlying facts, and investigates whether or not they have received any subsequent coverage by either corporate or independent news organizations. From *Censored 2012*, we update story #5, about private prison companies lobbying for draconian anti-immigration legislation. From *Censored 2018*, we review story #13, about right-wing funders promoting bogus "campus free-speech" legislation, and story #24, about eight "use of force" policies that, when adopted together, allegedly reduce police killings of civilians by 72 percent. From *Censored 2019*, we update story #10 about the FBI's use of the "Black Identity Extremists" label to classify racial justice activists as terrorists. Finally, we revisit story #3 from *Censored 2020*, about a proposal by Indigenous groups in the Amazon to create the world's largest protected area.

As with previous Déjà Vu chapters, we discovered that some of the stories we investigated—in particular, the story about the campus free-speech legislation—have indeed received considerably more corporate news coverage than when they first appeared on one of Project Censored's Top 25 lists. We also found that some of the stories—the story about private prison companies' lobbying efforts, the story about the eight "use of force" policies, and the story about the FBI's "Black Identity Extremists" label—have seen significant developments. Often these developments have been reported more thoroughly, with more analytical precision and with fewer factual omissions, by independent media than by the establishment press.

Overall, our review of these five stories underscores both the continuing importance of the stories themselves and the crucial role that independent media play in bringing such stories to the public's attention.

Censored 2012 #5

Private Prison Companies Fund Anti-Immigrant Legislation

Peter Cervantes-Gautschi, "Wall Street and the Criminalization of Immigrants," *Counter-Punch*, October 15, 2010.

Student Researcher: Caitlin Morgan (Sonoma State University)

Faculty Evaluator: Peter Phillips (Sonoma State University)

Between 2007 and 2010, approximately one million immigrants were held in detention facilities operated by our country's taxpayer-financed private prison system. The conditions in these facilities were hazardous, predatory, and deeply disturbing. Women and young children were regularly assaulted and abused, and men sometimes died due to a lack of appropriate medical attention.

At the helm of this diabolical operation were two of the largest private prison companies in the country: Core-Civic (formerly Corrections Corporation of America, or CCA) and GEO Group, based out of Nashville, Tennessee and Boca Raton, Florida, respectively. Each company had made sizable campaign donations to former Arizona governor Jan Brewer, who held office between 2009 and 2015. In fact, CoreCivic's top management in Nashville provided Governor Brewer her largest share of out-of-state campaign contributions. Brewer herself even appointed two former CoreCivic lobbyists as aides, both of whom helped shepherd Arizona's SB 1070 into law in 2010. SB 1070, known as the Support Our Law Enforcement and Safe Neighborhoods Act, is widely regarded as one of the most blatant and rigid anti-immigrant measures enacted in the United States.[2] Among other things, the Act requires police officers in Arizona to ascertain the immigration status of people they stop for routine traffic violations.

CoreCivic and GEO Group rely almost entirely on revenue from state and federal tax dollars and benefit greatly from the incarceration of immigrants seized by US Immigration and Customs Enforcement (ICE). Prior to SB 1070, Arizona already had several CoreCivic-run detention facilities. This number was expected to grow exponentially following the passage of SB 1070, further lining the pockets of CoreCivic executives and shareholders.

Update

In 2005 the Department of Homeland Security (DHS) and the Department of Justice launched Operation Streamline in Texas, which threatened federal prosecution for any person caught illegally crossing the border into the United States.[3] Many Border Patrol sectors in the Southwest established initiatives similar to Operation Streamline in the years that followed.[4] Private prison companies like CoreCivic and GEO Group, that imprison migrants in their detention facilities, championed these efforts.[5] By 2013, detention of migrants, often for longer than ten months at a time, earned these corporations approximately $1 billion each year in federal funds.[6]

Two different immigration reform plans put forth by the Obama administration and by a bipartisan group of US senators in 2013 focused heavily on comprehensive Border Patrol programs.[7] Using data from the Center for Responsive Politics, HuffPost reporter Laura Carlsen compiled a list of private prison lobbyists who pushed these plans. In 2012, Akin Gump Strauss Hauer & Feld, Mehlman Vogel Castagnetti Inc., and McBee Strategic Consulting respectively earned $220,000, $280,000, and $320,000 lobbying for CoreCivic. The company spent a total of $970,000 that year on lobbying that targeted the Department of Justice, Department of State, and US Marshals Service, according to OpenSecrets.org.[8] Similarly, Navigators Global and Lionel "Leo" Aguirre each received $120,000 for their services to GEO Group.[9]

Many of the senators who drafted the proposed bipartisan immigration reform legislation—Chuck Schumer (D-NY), Marco Rubio (R-FL), Bob Menendez (D-NJ), Michael Bennet (D-CO), Dick Durbin (D-IL), and Jeff Flake (R-AZ)—accepted significant contributions from private prison corporations in 2012. Schumer collected at least $64,000 from Akin Gump, the CoreCivic lobbyist, and nearly $35,000 from FMR (Fidelity), a part-owner of CoreCivic and GEO. Lindsay Graham (R-SC) and John McCain (R-AZ) also received contributions from GEO Group during their re-election campaigns; Graham accepted $1,000 in 2014, while McCain collected $1,500 in 2016, as reported by *Roll Call*.[10]

In August 2016 the *Washington Post* reported that the Justice Department intended to phase out the use of private prisons.[11] The memo issued by Deputy Attorney General Sally Yates instructed officials to reject offers to renew contracts or "substantially reduce" the contracts' scope.[12] Yates confirmed in the memo that private prisons "compare poorly" with government-operated correctional facilities in cost-effectiveness, rehabilitation services, and safety.[13] However, the Justice Department's directive did not include ICE's detention facilities, as they fall outside the scope of the Federal Bureau of Prisons's authority. Instead, it focused on the 13 privately-run prisons holding roughly 22,000 federal prisoners, representing about 12 percent of the total inmate population within the Bureau of Prisons system.[14]

The year prior to this announcement, both GEO and CoreCivic earned about half of their revenues from federal government contracts, but even after the policy change, each maintained their agreements with ICE and the US Marshals Service.[15] In fact, Jonathan Burns, a representative for CoreCivic, said that the memo only seriously impacted the Bureau of Prisons's correctional facilities, which accounted at the time for only approximately 7 percent of the company's business.[16]

By 2017 the corporate news media was covering America's 45th president, Donald Trump, every single excruciating second. *The New York Times* reported in March that, as the president and his administration openly disparaged and vilified immigrants, stock prices for CoreCivic and GEO rose drastically.[17] Additionally,

Yates's promise to end the use of private prisons was officially reversed by Jeff Sessions, Trump's attorney general, in February 2017.[18] By June 2018, according to OpenSecrets.org, the administration had spent $4 billion on contracts and grants dedicated to cracking down on illegal immigration, ensuring the growth and prosperity of companies like GEO and CoreCivic, which invested millions of dollars in lobbying efforts and had donated lavishly to Trump's 2016 campaign.[19]

OpenSecrets.org reported that in 2018 ICE signed contracts worth more than $450 million with GEO and more than $280 million with CoreCivic.[20] While their business model depends upon having the maximum number of people locked up in their detention facilities at any given time, the companies maintain that their extensive lobbying efforts have never attempted to influence the "basis for or duration of an individual's detention." Just incidentally, before resigning as Trump's DHS secretary in April 2019, Kirstjen Nielsen penned an "urgent request" to Congress on March 28—not to immediately reunite the thousands of immigrant children the administration separated from their families under her watch, but rather to address a shortage of detention beds and processing facilities at the border.

At the beginning of the Biden administration, the tangled traces of the previous administration's immigration policies remained in place. During his first days in office, Biden did roll back Trump's ruthless 2017 travel ban, which had prevented people from countries with largely Muslim populations from securing any kind of visa, and he launched a task force to reunite families separated at the border.[21] He also signed orders officially stalling the construction of Trump's infamous border wall and promised to strengthen the Deferred Action for Childhood Arrivals program, which protects undocumented youths known as Dreamers.[22] Still, immigration activists have called for Biden to examine all the manifold immigration policy modifications made by Trump during his four years as president.[23] Lucas Guttentag, a law professor at Stanford and Yale, developed the Immigration Policy Tracking Project, which uncovered 1,064 immigration-related policy changes made by Trump during his time in office.[24]

In January 2021, Biden reinstated Yates's promise to terminate contracts between the Justice Department and federal private prisons.[25] Yet the plan does not include any steps to do the same for deals made with for-profit immigration centers, which account for the bulk of the ICE detention system's facilities and make up one-third of GEO's and CoreCivic's total revenues.[26]

Censored 2018 #13

Right-Wing Money Promotes Model Legislation to Restrict Free Speech on Campuses

Alex Kotch, "Right-Wing Billionaires are Funding a Cynical Plot to Destroy Dissent and Protest in Colleges Across the U.S.," AlterNet, March 18, 2017.

Student Researchers: Dawn M. Lucier (College of Marin) and Emily von Weise (University of Vermont)

Faculty Evaluators: Susan Rahman (College of Marin) and Rob Williams (University of Vermont)

The #13 story on Project Censored's 2018 Top 25 list highlighted conservative billionaires' assault on campus free speech. In 2016 and 2017, raucous protests rocked college campuses over controversial right-wing speakers like Milo Yiannopoulos, Ann Coulter, and Ben Shapiro. Early in 2017 the Goldwater Institute, a libertarian think tank that receives funding from wealthy conservatives such as the Koch and Mercer families, began promoting model legislation ostensibly designed to protect free speech on campus. However, as UnKoch My Campus—a group that monitors the influence of conservative funders such as the Kochs on colleges and universities— pointed out, the Goldwater proposal would actually create stiff penalties for certain sorts of speech, specifically student protests against controversial speakers like Yiannopoulos. Under the model legislation, any student found guilty more than once of infringing on the expressive rights of others would be suspended from school for a minimum of one year.

Despite the bill's blatant flaws, Republican representatives introduced versions of it in several state legislatures, including Illinois, North Dakota, Virginia, Tennessee, Colorado, and Utah.

The original model for the Goldwater legislation was written by Stanley Kurtz, James Manley, and Jonathan Butcher. Kurtz is a fellow at the Ethics and Public Policy Center, a right-wing think tank that applies "the Judeo-Christian moral tradition to critical issues of public policy." This think tank has received millions of dollars in donations from conservative family foundations along with hundreds of thousands from two vehicles for Koch donations, Donors Trust and Donors Capital Fund. Manley, the Goldwater Institute's senior attorney, previously worked for the Mountain States Legal Foundation which has received donations from the same groups.

Butcher had worked at the conservative Heritage Foundation which received funding from the Koch family.

Update

More than a year after the publication of Kotch's AlterNet article, the story of the Right's dark money campaign for Orwellian "free-speech" legislation finally began to receive some corporate media attention. Although much of the coverage still framed legislation based on the Goldwater bill as a legitimate response to the "crisis" of free speech on campus, there were important exceptions. In a May 30, 2018 article published in the *Los Angeles Times*, author Michael Hiltzik sought to set the record straight. Hiltzik compared the "Campus Free Speech Act" to right-to-try legislation which provides terminal patients with last-chance experimental treatments: Though on the surface that legislation appears to benefit the public, in reality it undermines the Food and Drug Administration's ability to regulate potentially dangerous treatments. Hiltzik argued that both types of legislation purport to advance popular principles while covertly pushing a conservative agenda.[27]

According to the academic freedom watchdog group Foundation for Individual Rights in Education (FIRE), as of December 2019, 18 states have passed campus free-speech laws, including 14 states that did so after the publication of the Goldwater Institute's model legislation.[28] Although it is unclear what, if any, influence the Goldwater model legislation has had on the climate for free expression at colleges and universities in these states, the sudden spike in the number of states with such laws is noteworthy. Not long after these laws were passed, controversy over offensive speech on campus broke out at the University of Texas at San Antonio after students protesting against homophobic evangelical preachers were subjected to violence.[29] Although in this instance no legal action was taken against the students who were shoved and allegedly punched, the Goldwater model legislation would have required the protesting students to be disciplined.[30]

In April 2018, as several states were adopting "campus free-speech" legislation, the American Association of University Professors (AAUP), the largest general association of university faculty in the country, released a ten-page analysis of the Goldwater legislation and other similar bills. The AAUP came to the same conclusion as other critics of the legislation: the free-speech laws promoted by the Right are false friends of students and would do more to endanger students' rights than to protect them. Furthermore, the legislation uses the idea of free speech to mask a political agenda. The AAUP concluded that the Goldwater legislation is specifically designed to respond to incidents that have affected celebrity conservative speakers on campus.[31] Shortly after the publication of this report, conservative commentators lambasted the AAUP, claiming that it was attacking free speech and disputing the Association's contention that schools should be the ones deciding campus policy, not state legislators.

Perhaps the biggest development in this story since the publication of *Censored 2018* came in March 2019, when President Donald Trump signed an executive order requiring any institution receiving government funding for research to take adequate steps to promote free speech.

As Adam Harris of *The Atlantic* noted, the problem with Trump's executive order is that it mandates schools to do what they are already required to do by law: obey the First Amendment.[32] *The Washington Post* described the order's supporters as those who felt that colleges have been "fostering an unbalanced, liberal indoctrination of students."[33] Senator Lamar Alexander, a Republican from Tennessee, said he supported most of Trump's order. However, as a former college president, he said he did not like seeing Congress, the president, or anyone else creating speech codes to define what can be said on campus.[34]

Beyond the *Washington Post*, Trump's order received extensive coverage from other major news outlets, including a report by CNN, which commented that the executive order, while promising a lot, remained vague on details and that it was "unclear how the measure will affect college campuses in practice."[35] *USA Today* published an article which mirrored *The Atlantic* by quoting Senator Alexander's doubts about the necessity of the order.[36]

Censored 2018 #24

Eight Use of Force Policies to Prevent Killings by Police

Kate Stringer, "We Already Know How to Reduce Police Racism and Violence," *YES! Magazine*, July 8, 2016.

Alice Speri, "Here are Eight Policies That Can Prevent Police Killings," The Intercept, September 21, 2016.

Jamilah King, "Study: More Restrictive 'Use of Force' Policies Could Curb the Epidemic of Police Violence," Mic, September 21, 2016.

Student Researcher: Malcolm Pinson (San Francisco State University)

Faculty Evaluator: Kenn Burrows (San Francisco State University)

In September 2016, Campaign Zero published a study that highlighted eight use of force policies that police departments throughout the United States could implement to reduce the number of killings by police. Formed shortly after the fatal police shooting of Michael Brown and the protests that ensued in Ferguson, Missouri, Campaign Zero advocates against police violence, which disproportionately affects Black people in the United States, and works to reform the police system as a whole.

The report concluded that by adopting all eight of the specified policies, police departments could reduce civilian deaths by 72 percent. The eight policies Campaign Zero recommended were:

- Require officers to de-escalate situations before resorting to force

- Limit the kinds of force that can be used to respond to specific forms of resistance

- Restrict chokeholds

- Require officers to give a verbal warning before using force

- Prohibit officers from shooting at moving vehicles

- Require officers to exhaust all alternatives to deadly force

- Require officers to stop colleagues from exercising excessive force

- Require comprehensive reporting on use of force

Researchers studied data from police departments in 91 of the country's largest cities and reviewed reports, collected by the *Guardian* and the *Washington Post*, of police-involved killings going back to 2015. As reported in Mic, Campaign Zero's study found that US police departments in cities such as Washington, DC and Miami, which already enforced four or more of the eight guidelines, saw lower rates of police killings than departments in places like Orlando or Oklahoma City, which employed fewer than four of the policies.

Samuel Sinyangwe, one of the study's authors, told Alice Speri in an interview for the Intercept that departments were reluctant to adopt these policies because many believed they put officers at greater risk. However, the study found that departments with a high number of use of force policies in effect saw fewer instances of violence against officers. In Mic's 2016 story by Jamilah King, Sinyangwe acknowledged that publishing this study would not have been possible even two years earlier. Being able to document which departments were doing the most harm and how allowed researchers to develop concrete policies they believed would prevent police killings. As of June 2017 there had been no corporate media coverage of Campaign Zero's extensive study.

Update

On June 3, 2020, a little over a week after the killing of George Floyd in Minneapolis, Campaign Zero officially rolled out its "#8CantWait" platform, which highlighted the eight police guidelines featured in their 2016 study that were projected to reduce police killings by 72 percent.[37] In an interview with *GQ*, co-founder DeRay Mckesson said he wanted to "demystify these policies" and police reform in general.[38] Mckesson shared that all eight of the guidelines are "simple and clear enough for anyone to be an expert on."

A year earlier, the nonprofit had released its "Police Scorecard," which studied 100 of California's largest municipal police departments.[39] Campaign Zero then calculated and assigned grades to those departments based on several factors, including "use of less-lethal and deadly force" and "police actions that left a person seriously hurt or killed." The report concluded that nearly half of the people who had been critically wounded or killed by officers in these areas were unarmed during their encounters with police. The "Scorecard" received coverage in the *Los Angeles Times*, *OC Weekly*, and the Davis Vanguard, which reported that 39 of California's sheriff's departments scored an F on Campaign Zero's data map in "violence alternatives, accountability, and approaching policing."[40] However, in an article for *The Atlantic*, Conor Friedersdorf advised readers to approach the data "with caution."[41] The study neglected major agencies in the state, including the Los Angeles County Sheriff's Department, which employs about 9,400 deputies.[42]

By the summer of 2020, when Campaign Zero had fully unveiled "#8CantWait," substantial concerns over inaccuracy in the group's research surfaced. As detailed in a comprehensive June 18, 2020 article by Shani Saxon published in ColorLines, once "#8CantWait" publicized the claim that eight restrictive use of force policies could reduce violence by police by 72 percent, it received almost immediate pushback from community organizers protesting on the frontlines.[43] In a letter posted to Medium two days after the "#8CantWait" initiative was announced, activists Cherrell Brown and Philip V. McHarris said the "data and study design do not support that staggering statistic put forth in the least bit."[44] Brown and McHarris wrote that releasing such extreme and unsubstantiated figures when dealing with matters of life and death was "irresponsible" and "may serve as an out for leaders and politicians looking for alternatives to more transformative demands."

The Campaign Zero study focused on 91 police departments throughout the country over the span of 18 months.[45] Brown and McHarris wrote that, because the use of force policies hadn't been widely implemented, the study was "extrapolating beyond the actual data in creating stylized estimates." Additionally, Campaign Zero's "#8CantWait" only included seven control variables and used a 95 percent confidence interval. Brown and McHarris maintained in their letter that "99% is the confidence interval often used in medical sciences, and at that level of confidence, the policies studied by #8cantwait would fail to be statistically significant at reducing police killings."

Critics on Twitter quickly echoed Brown's and McHarris's sentiment. Many people expressed reservations about the campaign's messaging, and many worried that the "#8CantWait" campaign would distract from widespread demands for defunding the police as a means to abolish the system entirely.[46] Detractors pointed out major flaws in the campaign's contention that enacting policies would be enough to actually curtail violence. For example, the campaign's first policy called for a total ban on chokeholds and strangleholds; yet in 2014, when police violently forced Eric Garner to the ground and strangled him outside of a beauty supply store on Staten Island for selling loose cigarettes, chokeholds by police had already been banned in New York City for more than two decades.[47]

Moreover, San José's police department boasted on social media on June 11 about having already adopted all eight recommended reforms. They posted this public pat on the back less than two weeks after their officers shot rubber bullets at protestors, including their own bias trainer, causing serious injury.[48]

In response to the "#8CantWait" campaign, community organizers developed "#8toAbolition," a comprehensive plan (which mirrored the design and aesthetic of "#8CantWait") to defund, demilitarize, and abolish police and the prison–industrial complex.[49] Authored by a group of ten organizers, and championed by Critical Resistance and other Black abolitionist organizations, "#8toAbolition" sought to shift the conversation away from Campaign Zero's core aim of "fewer police killings" to a goal of "a world where there are zero police murders because there are zero police."[50]

On June 9, 2020, Brittany Packnett Cunningham announced her departure from Campaign Zero, the organization she co-founded.[51] Days after the release of "#8CantWait," Packnett Cunningham shared her sincerest regret over promoting Campaign Zero's latest initiative. She wrote that the concerns over the inconsistent data were new to her: "[G]iven what I have now become aware of, I chose to resign and to focus on other important work, for and with our most marginalized communities."[52]

The same day, Samuel Sinyangwe, Campaign Zero's leading data scientist, also issued a formal apology via social media.[53] He acknowledged that the initiative itself had been "rushed," and although both he and Packnett Cunningham requested that the release be postponed, "#8CantWait" launched anyway.

On June 10, 2020, following the organization's shake-up and sweeping criticism, *Fast Company* reported that Campaign Zero added three additional icons to their website: "immediate harm reduction, comprehensive community safety, and abolition."[54] In a message posted to their website the same day, the organization apologized for having "detracted from efforts of fellow organizers invested in paradigmatic shifts that are newly possible in this moment."[55] Even after receiving President Obama's endorsement, the "#8CantWait" campaign was only briefly profiled by *Rolling Stone* and Business Insider, while the subsequent controversy was covered by *Politico*.[56]

Censored 2019 #10

FBI Racially Profiling "Black Identity Extremists"

Jana Winter and Sharon Weinberger, "The FBI's New U.S. Terrorist Threat: 'Black Identity Extremists,'" *Foreign Policy*, October 6, 2017.

Hatewatch Staff, "FBI 'Black Identity Extremists' Report Stirs Controversy," Southern Poverty Law Center (SPLC), October 25, 2017.

Amy Goodman, interview with Christian Picciolini, "Life After Hate: Trump Admin Stops Funding Former Neo-Nazis Who Now Fight White Supremacy," *Democracy Now!*, August 17, 2017.

Brandon E. Patterson, "Police Spied on New York Black Lives Matter Group, Internal Police Documents Show," *Mother Jones*, October 19, 2017.

Student Researcher: Hailey Schector (Syracuse University)

Faculty Evaluator: Jeff Simmons (Syracuse University)

In August 2017 the Federal Bureau of Investigation (FBI) issued a warning to other law enforcement agencies about the dangers of "Black Identity Extremists." As Jana Winter and Sharon Weinberger reported for *Foreign Policy*, the FBI seemed to be more concerned about these hypothesized extremists than the active threat to public safety posed by violent white supremacists. The intelligence assessment used the term "Black Identity Extremists" (BIE) to describe any person of color responding to "perceived racism and injustice in American society," "wholly or in part, through unlawful acts of force or violence"—a definition vague enough to apply to practically any Black participant in unsanctioned gatherings about social injustice, Black nationalism, or police abuses of power.[57] Historians, scholars, and former government officials alike criticized the Bureau for its warning and its use of the designation.

The Southern Poverty Law Center suggested the FBI's coining of the term "Black Identity Extremists" might be a diversion from "the more serious threat of white supremacists and other far-right extremists." Indeed, in the same month that the FBI prepared their report, independent news outlet *Democracy Now!* observed that the Trump administration was defunding programs to counter violent white supremacist groups.

The initial corporate media coverage of this story was often uncritical. While some corporate news outlets challenged the use of the "BIE" label, others reported without questioning the FBI's assessment of Black protest groups as a violent domestic threat. A November NBC News report correctly pointed out that the FBI has a long history of targeting Black activist organizations like the

Black Panthers. However, that same report misleadingly implied that "lawmakers," not activists, were leading the fight against the FBI's racial profiling.[58]

Update

Since Project Censored first spotlighted this story, there has been a dramatic increase in coverage by both the corporate and independent media.

A widely reported April 2019 House Judiciary Committee hearing underscored the problems with the FBI's "BIE" classification. Kristen Clarke, president and chief executive of the Lawyers' Committee for Civil Rights Under Law, told the House Judiciary Committee, "This is [a] mere distraction from the very real threat of white supremacy that we face today."[59] Clarke also argued that "Black Identity Extremists" do not really exist: "It harks back to the dark days of our federal government abusing its power to go after civil rights activists during the heyday of the civil rights movement. There is no such thing as black identity extremism."[60]

As Alice Speri reported in October 2019 for the Intercept, documents obtained by the American Civil Liberties Union (ACLU) and the racial justice group MediaJustice show that "between 2015 and 2018, the FBI dedicated considerable time and resources to opening a series of 'assessments' into the activities of individuals and groups it mostly labeled 'black separatist extremists.'" Unlike full-blown investigations, "assessments" do not need to be based on evidence of criminality or a threat to national security and can be launched for such purposes as recruiting new informants.[61]

This secret intelligence program appears to have followed in the footsteps of earlier efforts by the FBI to spy on and delegitimize the Civil Rights movement from the mid-1950s to the early 1970s.[62] The FBI similarly monitors immigrants and people from Middle Eastern or South Asian communities, rationalizing that they might be, or become, potential recruits for terrorist organizations.[63] As a 2019 report by the civil liberties group Defending Rights & Dissent noted, when choosing targets for an assessment, agents are allowed to use ethnicity, religion, or speech protected by the First Amendment as a factor, "as long as it is not the only one."[64]

Despite widespread criticisms of the FBI's decision to classify Black activists as a terrorist threat, the Bureau nevertheless listed that bogus threat as one of their top counterterrorism priorities for 2018, according to leaked internal strategy documents published by The Young Turks in August 2019.[65] Yet, in the leaked internal documents, the FBI failed to cite a single attack or incident attributed to "BIE." The documents show that the FBI introduced a new program, "IRON FIST," to mitigate the imagined threat of "Black Identity Extremists" and to gather new information about the "movement." As part of this program, the Bureau planned to expend more resources on surveilling and investigating Black activists, including through undercover agents. Although the Bureau has released hundreds of pages of documents, it continues to shield the majority of its records from public scrutiny, so the full extent of the FBI's anti-"BIE" efforts remains unknown.

The FBI's director, Christopher Wray, testified at a July 23, 2019 Senate Judiciary Committee hearing that in early 2018 the Bureau dropped the use of the term "BIE," as well as the term "white supremacy," in favor of a new terrorist threat classification, "Racially Motivated Violent Extremism." Wray said that the new classification gave a broad indication of how the Bureau has now come to understand all racially motivated crime.[66] Many lawmakers claimed that the FBI's new designation, like the original "BIE" label, obfuscates the true threat of militant white supremacist groups and grants the FBI cover to continue monitoring Black activists who pose no threat to national security at all.[67] FBI Director Wray attempted to justify the new designation by arguing that the Bureau "only investigate[s] violence. We don't investigate extremism. We don't investigate ideology."[68] But the ACLU has criticized the FBI's new designation as little more than a disguised version of the earlier classification, charging that "the FBI simply renamed the label."[69]

Since the publication of the 2019 *Censored* yearbook, the *Washington Post* and other establishment papers have reported on the controversy surrounding the "Black Identity Extremist" designation. However, only independent media have given extensive coverage to the leaked documents about the IRON FIST program and to evidence of ongoing FBI spying on Black social justice activists.

Censored 2020 #3

Indigenous Groups from Amazon Propose Creation of Largest Protected Area on Earth

Jessica Corbett, "Calling for 'Corridor of Life and Culture,' Indigenous Groups from Amazon Propose Creation of Largest Protected Area on Earth," Common Dreams, November 21, 2018.

Jonathan Watts, "Amazon Indigenous Groups Propose Mexico-Sized 'Corridor of Life,'" *The Guardian*, November 21, 2018.

Student Researcher: Robert Andreacchi (Sonoma State University)

Faculty Evaluator: Peter Phillips (Sonoma State University)

The Amazon rainforest has long been threatened by sweeping, unregulated development. At the 14th United Nations Biodiversity Conference in November 2018, an alliance of some five hundred Indigenous groups from nine countries, known as COICA—the Coordinator of the Indigenous Organizations of the Amazon River Basin—proposed preserving a "sacred corridor of life and culture" covering more than 700,000 square miles, an area about the size of Mexico, to safeguard what they called "the world's last great sanctuary for biodiversity."

As reported by Common Dreams, the alliance's proposal would protect biodiversity in the "triple-A" corridor that spans the Andes mountains, the Amazon, and the Atlantic Ocean. This region faces challenges from agribusiness, mining, and the global climate crisis. But members of the alliance also aim to address territorial rights, as the Indigenous inhabitants of the proposed preserve "don't recognize modern national borders created by colonial settlers."

Right-wing governments in Brazil and Colombia oppose COICA's plans. In October 2018, far-right politician Jair Bolsonaro, who is now Brazil's president, indicated that he would stay in the Paris climate agreement only if Brazil was guaranteed sovereignty over Indigenous land and the "triple-A" region. Juan Carlos Jintiach of COICA told Common Dreams that Bolsonaro's comments about environmental and Indigenous issues were concerning because three-fourths of the environmental defenders assassinated in 2017 were Indigenous leaders, and opposition to agroindustry is "the main cause for assassination of our leaders." Observing that Indigenous peoples and communities "face costly and difficult processes to legalize their lands," while corporations "obtain licenses with ease," Jintiach called for Bolsonaro to ensure the rights and safety of the people of Brazil.

Although the corporate and independent press covered Bolsonaro's intent to undermine Indigenous rights in order to open Amazonian land for development, the coverage almost entirely ignored COICA's proposal to create the world's largest protected area. For example, in January 2019 the *New York Times* reported Bolsonaro's order giving the business-friendly Ministry of Agriculture authority over the certification of Indigenous territories but made no mention of COICA's proposal.[70] In March 2019 the *Times* ran an opinion piece on efforts by Indigenous groups to resist Bolsonaro's policies.[71] The penultimate paragraph of that article included one sentence on the coalition of Indigenous groups proposing an Amazon sanctuary, noting simply that Bolsonaro's election would pose problems for their proposal, and linking to the *Guardian*'s November 2018 report.

Update

The onset of the global pandemic in 2020, the ensuing economic crisis, and the contested US presidential election preempted all but a passing mention of COICA's proposed "corridor of life" in both the corporate and independent press. While Indigenous groups and their

Amazonian homelands continue to face destruction, they now must also contend with the deadly COVID-19 virus. In the Amazon, dozens of Indigenous groups lack access to basic healthcare and, because of their isolation from urban populations, their immune systems are less resilient against many of the viruses carried by outside contacts. Experts are concerned that the COVID-19 pandemic puts Indigenous peoples at increased risk of potential extinction.[72]

The rampant development that led Indigenous groups to propose the biodiversity sanctuary—in particular, illegal mining and logging operations—has brought with it the deadly virus.[73] National and local governments in the region remain reluctant to take steps to protect the Amazon or its Indigenous residents, as is clear from how they have responded to wildfires that ravaged the area. As Manuela Picq explained in a September 24, 2019 article on the Indigenous news site Intercontinental Cry, Bolivian president Evo Morales let his country burn during the fall of 2019 in the hope of opening new land to expanded agribusiness. The lack of government interest in controlling these fires constituted an act of ecocide, but the horrific impact on the Indigenous population eventually turned it into a genocide as well.[74]

While the governments of the region have made it clear that they have no interest in helping the Indigenous inhabitants of the Amazon, these remote communities have found new allies in an unusual place. In October 2019 Pope Francis hosted the fourth synod of his papacy in Rome, where he welcomed 185 bishops and cardinals as well as a collection of emissaries from the Amazon. The synod's goal was not to convert the tribes of the Amazon, but instead to show support for the preservation of their homelands and culture. This synod was not without its opponents: Some conservative Catholics objected to the display of "pagan" Amazonian symbols in the Vatican as sacrilegious (even going so far as to steal traditional Indigenous statues from a chapel where they were on display and throw them into Rome's Tiber River). Nonetheless, COICA received newfound acknowledgement of their plight from the Church and its supporters with open arms, as COICA's leadership believe that the Church's involvement could help reinvigorate discussions of the moral and spiritual aspects of Indigenous rights, social justice, and ecology—issues that more recently have been framed in exclusively political terms.[75]

In the wake of this meeting, COICA partnered with several Amazon aid foundations to organize a livestream of a May 28, 2020 global benefit concert involving a variety of artists including Barbra Streisand, Morgan Freeman, Jane Fonda, Sting, and Dave Matthews. The event aimed to fund rapid-response grants for Indigenous groups throughout the Amazon and to raise awareness of the severe impacts that both climate change and COVID-19 are having on the Amazon's Indigenous people.[76]

As of early 2021, corporate media continue to ignore the plight of the Indigenous peoples of the Amazon and to tune out COICA's call for preserving a "sacred corridor of life and culture" in the region. Although the establishment media have overlooked this issue, COICA continues to take action and forge alliances with everyone from the Pope to pop stars in an attempt to preserve the delicate balance of life in the Amazon and the people who call it home.

Conclusion

The developments charted by the brief updates included in this chapter demonstrate that corporate media continue to neglect stories with potentially enormous social or political impact even after those stories have been identified as unjustly overlooked by media watchdogs like Project Censored. The dogged persistence of gaps in corporate news coverage of certain taboo topics (such as police malfeasance, government corruption, and environmental destruction) coupled with the fact that all journalism, whether independent or corporate, is a "recording of history while the facts are not all in," underscores why a look back at previously overlooked news stories remains so necessary.[77]

SHEALEIGH VOITL is a 2021 graduate of North Central College, where she earned her degree in journalism and media communication. Beyond graduation, she hopes to explore pop culture reporting, as TV and music remain her truest loves, as well as social justice journalism, including stories examining healthcare disparities, the police and prison–industrial complex abolition movement, and immigrant rights.

GRIFFIN CURRAN is a recent graduate of North Central College with a degree in social sciences and secondary education. He intends to build a career working in high-need schools, combining both his passion for education and social justice in a way that will prepare his students to face any challenges that may come their way.

RACHAEL SCHWANEBECK is a student at North Central College studying history and library sciences. She is currently a junior and is set to graduate in spring 2022, after which she aspires to work in an archive.

STEVE MACEK is professor of communication and chair of the Department of Communication and Media Studies at North Central College. He is the author of *Urban Nightmares: The Media, the Right, and the Moral Panic over the City* (University of Minnesota Press, 2006) and writes frequently about media, politics, censorship, and academic freedom for newspapers, magazines, and online publications.

Notes

1. Thomas Griffith, "The Pursuit of Journalism," *Nieman Reports*, January 1959 (reprinted December 15, 1999).
2. Eileen Diaz McConnell, "Latinos in Arizona: Demographic Context in the SB 1070 Era," in *Latino Politics and Arizona's Immigration Law SB 1070*, eds. Lisa Magaña and Erik Lee (New York: Springer Science+Business Media, 2013), 1–18, 2.
3. Michael Corradini et al., "Operation Streamline: No Evidence that Criminal Prosecution Deters Migration," Vera Institute of Justice, June 2018, 1.
4. Ibid.
5. Laura Carlsen, "With Immigration Reform Looming, Private Prisons Lobby to Keep Migrants Behind Bars," HuffPost, March 5, 2013, updated May 5, 2013.
6. Ibid.
7. Ibid.
8. "Client Profile: Corrections Corp of America," OpenSecrets.org (Center for Responsive Politics), 2012.
9. Carlsen, "With Immigration Reform Looming."
10. Eric Garcia, "Private Prison Companies Continue Giving to Senate Candidates," *Roll Call*, October 20, 2016.
11. Matt Zapotosky and Chico Harlan, "Justice Department Says It Will End Use of Private Prisons," *Washington Post*, August 18, 2016.
12. Ibid.
13. Joseph Margulies, "This is the Real Reason Private Prisons Should be Outlawed," *Time*, August 24, 2016.
14. Zapotosky and Harlan, "Justice Department."
15. Ibid.
16. Ibid.
17. Jeff Sommer, "Trump Immigration Crackdown is Great for Private Prison Stocks," *New York Times*, March 10, 2017.
18. Ibid.

19. Geoff West and Alex Baumgart, "'Zero-Tolerance' Immigration Policy is Big Money for Contractors, Nonprofits," OpenSecrets.org (Center for Responsive Politics), June 21, 2018.

20. Camille Erickson, "Detention Center Contractors Will Keep Reaping Profit Even after DHS Upheaval," OpenSecrets.org (Center for Responsive Politics), April 15, 2019.

21. "Biden Reverses Controversial US Travel Bans," BBC News, January 21, 2021.

22. Michael D. Shear and Miriam Jordan, "Undoing Trump's Anti-Immigrant Policies Will Mean Looking at the Fine Print," *New York Times*, February 10, 2021, updated July 16, 2021.

23. Ibid.

24. Ibid.

25. Madison Pauly, "Biden Will End the Justice Department's Use of Private Prisons," *Mother Jones*, January 26, 2021.

26. Ibid.

27. Michael Hiltzik, "How a Right-Wing Group's Proposed 'Free Speech' Law Aims to Undermine Free Speech on Campus," *Los Angeles Times*, May 30, 2018.

28. The 14 states are Alabama, Arkansas, Colorado, Florida, Georgia, Iowa, Kentucky, Louisiana, North Carolina, Oklahoma, South Dakota, Tennessee, Texas, and Utah. "Campus Free Speech Statutes" archives, Foundation for Individual Rights in Education (FIRE), December 18, 2019. In updates to this webpage, FIRE has also documented that, as of May 2021, four more states have followed suit in enacting campus free-speech laws: Ohio, Montana, North Dakota, and West Virginia.

29. Dominic Anthony Walsh, "Campus Free Speech Law Leads to Protests, Violence at UTSA," KERA News (Texas Public Radio), March 1, 2020.

30. Stanley Kurtz, James Manley, and Jonathan Butcher, "Campus Free Speech: A Legislative Proposal," Goldwater Institute, January 30, 2017, 6.

31. "Campus Free-Speech Legislation: History, Progress, and Problems," American Association of University Professors (AAUP), April 2018.

32. Adam Harris, "Trump's Redundant Executive Order on Campus Speech," *The Atlantic*, March 21, 2019.

33. Susan Svrluga, "Trump Signs Executive Order on Free Speech on College Campuses," *Washington Post*, March 21, 2019.

34. Harris, "Trump's Redundant Executive Order." Note that one section of the President's order garnered widespread support: the requirement that colleges publish data on the average earnings of their graduates, average student-loan debt, and other financial information.

35. Maegan Vazquez and Betsy Klein, "Trump Signs Executive Order on Campus Free Speech," CNN, March 21, 2019.

36. Chris Quintana, "'I am with You': President Trump Signs Executive Order on Free Speech at College Campuses," *USA Today*, March 21, 2019.

37. Shani Saxon, "What Went Wrong with the #8CantWait Police Reform Initiative?" ColorLines, June 18, 2020.

38. Alex Shultz, "DeRay Mckesson on the 8 Reforms That Could Dramatically Reduce Police Violence," *GQ*, June 3, 2020, updated June 10, 2020.

39. "Police Scorecard," PoliceScorecard.org (Campaign Zero), undated [accessed October 13, 2020].

40. James Queally, "'Police Scorecard' Raises Questions about Use of Force and Accountability in California," *Los Angeles Times*, May 29, 2019; Anthony Pignataro, "Campaign Zero Grades 12 OC Police Departments," *OC Weekly*, June 3, 2019; and David Greenwald, "39 California Sheriff's Departments Score an F on Violence Alternatives, Accountability, and Approaching Policing," Davis Vanguard, December 10, 2019.

41. Conor Friedersdorf, "A Scorecard for Police Departments," *The Atlantic*, May 30, 2019.

42. Ibid.

43. Saxon, "What Went Wrong."

44. Cherrell Brown and Philip V. McHarris, "#8cantwait is Based on Faulty Data Science," Medium, June 5, 2020.

45. Ibid.

46. Saxon, "What Went Wrong."

47. Jordan Freiman, "New York Lawmakers Pass Anti-Chokehold Bill Named for Eric Garner," CBS News, June 8, 2020.

48. San José Police Department (@SanJosePD), Twitter post, June 11, 2020, 2:58 p.m.; and Travis Gettys, "San Jose Cops Rupture Testicle of Their Own Bias Trainer in Violent Response to Protests," Raw Story, June 11, 2020.

49. "#8toAbolition," 8 to Abolition, undated [accessed October 13, 2020]. See also Marcia Brown, "How Police Abolitionists are Seizing the Moment," *American Prospect*, June 19, 2020.

50. DeRay Mckesson, Samuel Sinyangwe, Johnetta Elzie, and Brittany Packnett, "Police Use of Force Policy Analysis," Campaign Zero, September 20, 2016; and "#8toAbolition."

51. Brittany Packnett, "A Choice to Transition," Medium, June 9, 2020.

52. Ibid.

53. Samuel Sinyangwe (@samswey), Twitter post, June 9, 2020, 10:10 p.m.

54. Lilly Smith, "In the Fight for Police Reform and Abolition, Design Plays a Key Role," *Fast Company*, June 10, 2020.

55. "#8CantWait," 8CantWait.org (Campaign Zero), undated [accessed October 19, 2020]; quoted in Shultz, "DeRay Mckesson on the 8 Reforms."

56. Daniel Kreps, "Campaign Zero's '8 Can't Wait' Project Aims to Curtail Police Violence," *Rolling Stone*, June 4, 2020; Meg Teckman-Fullard, Elizabeth McCauley, and Liz Kraker, "Explained: The Eight Policies That Could Decrease Police Violence in the 8 Can't Wait Campaign, Backed by Obama," Business Insider, June 12, 2020; and Laura Barrón-López, "Why the Black Lives Matter Movement Doesn't Want a Singular Leader," *Politico*, July 22, 2020.

57. "Black Identity Extremists Likely Motivated to Target Law Enforcement Officers," Federal Bureau of Investigation Counterterrorism Division, August 3, 2017.

58. Chandelis R. Duster and Donna M. Owens, "'I Know They're Watching Us': Black Lawmakers, Activists Alarmed Over FBI Report," NBC News, November 9, 2017.

59. Michael Brice-Saddler, "Democrats to DOJ: Investigate White Nationalists with Same Intensity as Global Terrorism after 9/11," *Washington Post*, August 8, 2019.

60. Ibid. See also Eugene Scott, "At a Hearing, an Expert Said the FBI Should Focus on the Rise of White Nationalism, Not 'Black Identity Extremists,'" *Washington Post*, April 10, 2019.

61. Alice Speri, "The FBI Spends a Lot of Time Spying on Black Americans," The Intercept, October 29, 2019.

62. Scott, "At a Hearing." Between 1956 and 1971, the FBI's notorious COINTELPRO (Counter Intelligence Program) monitored and actively attempted to sabotage the Southern Christian Leadership Conference, the Congress of Racial Equality, the Black Panther Party, the Nation of Islam, the Young Lords, the American Indian Movement, and other civil rights and racial justice organizations. The existence of this program and the shocking facts about its operations were ultimately brought to light by activists from the Citizens' Commission to Investigate the FBI and by a 1975 Senate investigation into intelligence abuses, the so-called Church Committee investigations. For more information on COINTELPRO, see Ward Churchill and Jim Vander Wall, *Agents of Repression: The FBI's Secret Wars Against the Black Panther Party and the American Indian Movement* (Boston: South End Press, 1990).

63. Nusrat Choudhury and Malkia Cyril, "The FBI Won't Hand Over Its Surveillance Records on 'Black Identity Extremists,' so We're Suing," American Civil Liberties Union (ACLU), March 21, 2019.

64. Chip Gibbons, "Still Spying on Dissent: The Enduring Problem of FBI First Amendment Abuse," Defending Rights & Dissent, 2019, 23.

65. Ken Klippenstein, "Leaked FBI Documents Reveal Bureau's Priorities Under Trump," The Young Turks, August 8, 2019; and "Leaked FBI Documents Raise Concerns about Targeting Black People Under 'Black Identity Extremist' and Newer Labels," American Civil Liberties Union (ACLU), August 9, 2019.

66. Byron Tau, "FBI Abandons Use of Term 'Black Identity Extremism'; Bureau Has Reorganized Domestic Terrorism Categorization in Favor of 'Racially Motivated Violent Extremism' Category," *Wall Street Journal*, July 23, 2019.

67. Brice-Saddler, "Democrats to DOJ"; and Felicia Sonmez, "Democrats Accuse Trump Administration of Trying to 'Obfuscate the White Supremacist Threat' with New Categories for Domestic Terrorism," *Washington Post*, May 2, 2019.

68. Tau, "FBI Abandons Use of Term 'Black Identity Extremism.'"

69. American Civil Liberties Union, "Leaked FBI Documents Raise Concerns."

70. Ernesto Londoño, "Jair Bolsonaro, on Day 1, Undermines Indigenous Brazilians' Rights," *New York Times*, January 2, 2019.

71. Carol Giacomo, "Brazil's New President Threatens 'the Lungs of the Planet,'" *New York Times*, March 19, 2019.

72. François-Michel Le Tourneau and William Milliken, "COVID-19, Isolated Indigenous Peoples and the History of the Amazon," The Conversation, April 21, 2020.

73. Luciana Magalhaes and Juan Forero, "Coronavirus Spreads Deep Into the Amazon, Imperiling an Ancient Tribe," *Wall Street Journal*, September 27, 2020.

74. Manuela Picq, "Evo Morales' Ecocide is a Genocide," Intercontinental Cry, September 24, 2019.

75. Alexander Zaitchik, "Can the Catholic Church Save the Amazon?" *New Republic*, November 14, 2019.

76. Amazon Watch, "Amazon Watch, Amazon Aid Foundation, Rainforest Foundation US, COICA, and EMA Team up for 'Artists United for Amazonia' Livestream Global Event," Cision Canada, May 28, 2020.

77. Griffith, "The Pursuit of Journalism."

CHAPTER 3

TikToking Our Return to a New Normalcy

Shrinking Attention Spans, Pervasive Inanities, and the Persistence of Humilitainment—Junk Food News (2020–2021 Pandemic Edition)

JEN LYONS, SIERRA KAUL, MARCELLE LEVINE
SWINBURNE, VIKKI VASQUEZ, GAVIN KELLEY,
and MICKEY HUFF

*America's present need is not heroics, but healing;
not nostrums, but normalcy.*
—WARREN G. HARDING, Boston, May 1920[1]

I'm sure y'all got a story to tell.
—JOHN REINKE, from the Netflix series *Tiger King*[2]

From social distancing to Zoom fatigue, Americans dove headfirst into the "new normal" of 2020–2021. Confined to their homes due to COVID-19, the seemingly unending global pandemic, many Americans struggled to make ends meet and stay healthy, but also searched for new ways to entertain and distract themselves, turning to a plethora of media outlets. Once reliant on newspapers, magazines, books, and corporate television news networks, Americans instead turned to apps and other online streaming services on their phones and tablets to access the outside world, and especially to binge-watch epic distractions both low brow and high: from the murder, mayhem, and madness of *Tiger King* to the banal, bourgeois, bedroom battles of *Bridgerton*. Of course, many also flocked in droves to social media for daily contact and communication, and for news about the pandemic, but it wasn't just the posts on Facebook or even the 280-character-limited tweets on Twitter that kept Americans up-to-date—it was also the ever-expanding rabbit hole of TikTok. Indeed, as John Reinke noted on the smash reality TV series *Tiger King*, everyone's "got a story to tell," and they were certainly telling on apps like TikTok, where Andy Warhol's old adage that one day everyone will be famous for 15 minutes was edited down to about 15 seconds, or a generous minute.

TikTok is basically Twitter on street-grade crack. According to a *Forbes* interview with University of Southern California Professor Julie Albright, TikTok has "adopted the same principles that have made gambling addictive."[3] A digital drug for anyone with a phone, and especially young people, the TikTok app uses random reinforcement—similar to a slot machine on the Las Vegas strip—to keep users scrolling. It has changed the way Americans tell and view stories, interact with others, and even receive news and information. Its influence borders on the obscene. TikTok has become part of the new normal of the past year, but instead of helping us heal, it has functioned as a nostrum to the new normal—a rather ineffective remedy from an unqualified source during the pandemic.

TikTok feeds Americans nonstop Junk Food News

and infotainment, à la reality TV. "Junk Food News" is a term, originally coined by Project Censored's founder Carl Jensen, to identify a category of frivolous or inconsequential news stories that receive substantial coverage by corporate news outlets, thus distracting news audiences from other, more significant stories. Content appearing on TikTok definitely fits Jensen's Junk Food News descriptor, as the app has become so popular that many of its brief videos regularly appear on corporate news media outlets, distracting Americans from crucial independent investigative reporting.

This chapter aims to shed light on the mass media malaise this past year that distracted Americans from far more significant news stories. While a young woman inadvisably sprayed her hair with industrial glue instead of hairspray on TikTok, Americans were glued to their own hyper-partisan and biased news sources, deprived of any reporting on urgent humanitarian crises and food shortages in places like Ethiopia, Yemen, and beyond. As Fox News devoted hours to displaying its disgust of Cardi B and her wildly popular song "WAP," statistics regarding female unemployment and a decrease in living standards for American women were thrown out the window. As Americans were swept up in the vicarious power of cancel culture, celebrating "canceled" celebrity YouTube stars, reality TV hosts, and the British royal family, bills erecting new barriers to voting that would disproportionately impact voters from historically marginalized groups—in effect, canceling their votes—went mostly unseen on corporate news media outlets. Finally, the love Americans feel for professional sports seems to have been eclipsed over the past few years by their love for reality TV glimpses of athletes' behind-the-scenes shenanigans; by the profusion of corporate news fluff, one might imagine that audiences today enjoy watching athletes fail off the court with crazy antics and bad behavior more than their triumphs during the games. Yet even in the midst of this tomfoolery tsunami, the real sporting scandal of the past year was the underreporting of the obscene profits franchise owners made while many of their supportive employees suffered during the pandemic.

All of these Junk Food News stories, and others like them, can be found on cable news and in the corporate press, now supersized via social media sites such as Twitter and Big Tech apps like TikTok. It's more than most can possibly keep up with—especially after doggedly "Keeping Up with the Kardashians" after 20 years ... and now Kimye's divorce!

After more than a year of social isolation due to the pandemic, Americans are now eager—just like their historical counterparts of one hundred years ago—to return to "normalcy," as a then soon-to-be president Warren G. Harding put it. But, like the Americans of the 1920s who were emerging from a World War and global pandemic, we're likely to find such a return to normalcy nearly impossible to achieve given how much has changed. This year's top Junk Food News selections not only reflect this "new normal," but also survey the best of the worst, the stories you didn't necessarily want or need to know about but couldn't unsee, served fresh, and endlessly refreshed, off corporate news media's marvelous menu of mundane mediocrity.

TIKTOK TIME BOMB—ALGORITHMS
OF HUMILITAINMENT

We've all seen them: the teenagers and young adults doing synchronized dancing in a grocery store, park, mall, or coffee shop. You may have heard them duetting sea-shanties, or maybe you were told about the crowdsourced musical based off of the 2007 Pixar movie *Ratatouille*. All of these terribly essential activities have one thing, or specifically one app, in common: TikTok, where apparently *anyone* can cook!

Haven't heard of it? Many people's first exposure to the app may have been through Nathan Apodaca and his Ocean Spray TikTok post, vibin' to Fleetwood Mac's "Dreams," riding NFTs (nonfungible tokens) to block-chain authenticity (if anyone understands what that means). Apodaca's clip drew the attention of a TV show host excited to "sit down and tap into the mind of Nathan Apodaca, also known as 'Dogg Face.'"[4] It also brought him a hefty wad of cash.[5]

Those who *still* weren't privy to TikTok, even in the advent of these cultural milestones, most certainly became aware of its existence due to the glorious mishaps of Tessica Brown, also fondly known as "Gorilla Glue Girl." Her story took the internet, tabloids, and news cycles by storm after she repeatedly posted to TikTok in the early months of 2021 that it had been a "bad, bad, bad idea" for her to use Gorilla Glue to set her hairstyle when she had run out of her regular hairspray.[6] Her entranced audience collectively wondered, how could anyone ever make that mistake in the first place? The meme became a well-recognized source of humor, demonstrated by a *Saturday Night*

Live skit titled "Gorilla Glue."[7] For many, it appeared as another instance of finding amusement in someone else's humiliation. The internet is filled with videos in the so-called "fail" genre, including the slew of epic fails featured at FailArmy, Newsflare, and Funny Vines, sites and YouTube channels that all showcase their own Fails of the Week. Even ESPN's *SportsCenter* boasts a "Not Top 10" segment, which pokes fun at athletes' mishaps caught on camera. There is no shortage of "entertainment" that comes at the expense of others' misfortunes.

The specific term for this phenomenon is "humilitainment," a word coined by media scholars Brad Waite and Sara Booker in 2005 to refer to entertainment that capitalizes on someone else's humiliation.[8] This term is often used in conjunction with "schadenfreude," a German compound word that translates to "harm-joy" and describes finding joy in others' pain. Humilitainment often features as Junk Food News. It has become a common theme in "reality" television programming over the years, on shows like *Survivor*, *Big Brother*, *16 and Pregnant*, *90 Day Fiancé*, and *Jersey Shore*, just to name a few. Even decades-old TV series, dating back to *Candid Camera* and *America's Funniest Home Videos*, have presented "fails" that resulted in viewers literally laughing at a complete stranger's pain or misfortune.

From one screen to another, it's not just television that gives us humilitainment, but our phones and tablets as well. The viral videos of people failing at trends, poorly cutting their hair at home, or having fashion faux pas in public have been on the internet and our phones almost as soon as videos could be uploaded and watched. This trend certainly hasn't stopped, and it continues to weasel its way into our media feeds. TikTok is just the latest vehicle for consumers to binge on Junk Food News, infotainment, and humilitainment. But perhaps one of the most interesting aspects of TikTok is its algorithm: the more time a user spends on the app, the more data the algorithm collects. For the first few uses of the app, the algorithm will present the most popular videos and trends to the user, but eventually, after tracking the user's viewing habits, it will funnel the newcomer deeper into the app toward what the program *assumes* the consumer enjoys. Eventually, the user will only be recommended to very specific creators or videos that fit into the individual's established interests.[9]

In this way, TikTok closely resembles the corporate press. TikTok's algorithm divides viewers into specific groups, much as corporate media news outlets like Fox News and CNN divide and conquer audiences. According to a recent study by the Pew Research Center, there are consistent ideological divides between groups of Americans based on where they go to get their news about what is going on in the world.[10] In other words, the Gorilla Glue story wasn't the only one people were getting stuck to: many Americans also like to get stuck to particular news outlets, where they can tune in to their favorite sources to feed their political confirmation biases.

This market-driven division impacts the information that spreads among various demographics in society, which in turn is reflected across social media—creating an echo chamber of poorly informed people and often resulting in the mass circulation of half-truths and misinformation. In many cases, one person's (or niche group's) truth is another's fiction, yet another way in which TikTok's algorithm produces results similar to the corporate press.[11] As with the subjects of talk shows, reality TV, or sensationalist news stories, most TikTokers who produce content are average individuals who gain notoriety for dubious reasons, which can then be further exploited by the commercial press for ratings. And much like Fox News, MSNBC, or CNN, TikTok specially tailors its information to fit the narrative of a specific audience, and the corporate media outlets seem to have developed a symbiotic relationship with the app. Thus, not only do TikTok videos now count as news, but both corporate news stories and TikTok videos, whether accurate or not, have adapted to stick with audiences eager to have their beliefs reinforced. In this regard, TikTok and the corporate media are a match made in Junk Food News heaven. What could *possibly* go wrong?

While Americans were stuck on Gorilla Glue Girl online, corporate news outlets stove-piped the same stories, reinforcing information silos and creating filter bubbles as monetized coping mechanisms for chaotic and uncertain times. These Junk Food News stories distracted Americans while millions of people literally starved across the globe. *Democracy Now!*, quoting the World Food Programme's David Beasley, reported that Yemen, Ethiopia, and other impoverished and war-torn nations are "heading toward 'the biggest famine in modern history,' and many parts of [these countries] feel like 'hell on Earth' after years of food shortages and destruction brought on by the U.S.-backed, Saudi-led war."[12]

Why did that story not appear at the forefront of the corporate press, nor on the videos of TikTok? It is likely because Americans would rather bask in the glory of someone's humilitainment than recognize worldwide humanitarian issues. While millions of TikTok users post elements of their daily lives on an app for entertainment, the everyday reality of food shortages and starvation goes unreported. But then again, why would people want their news coverage to be civically driven when it could be viral and funny, especially when it comes at someone else's expense?

TUCKER CARLSON HATES WET A** PU*SIES: CARDI B'S "WAP"

By practicing the fine art of raining on conservatives' parade, Cardi B's hit song "WAP," featuring Megan Thee Stallion, created its own news cycle for more than nine months following its August 2020 release. Cardi B released the song "WAP," an acronym for "Wet A** Pu*sy," on August 7, 2020 alongside the song's official music video, gaining the full attention of NBC, CNN, the *Washington Post*, BBC, *Forbes*, and the *New York Times* in their culture, entertainment, music, and opinion sections. From pu*sy medium-rare to pu*sy rarely dropped from the establishment news cycle, what was once considered the purview of gossip rags like TMZ or Perez Hilton's blog is now unfulfilling fodder for even the most "serious" of publications.

Much of the positive press distributed immediately after the song's release praised the song and video for their empowering contributions to sex-positive feminism, citing historical precedents for this hyper-sexual, feminine artistic expression in music from the 1990s.[13] A few sources went considerably further back in American social history, comparing Cardi B and Megan Thee Stallion to Black female artists from one hundred years ago like Ma

Rainey, Lucille Bogan, and Bessie Smith, all criticized in their time professionally for expressions of female sexuality and pleasure.[14] The "WAP" song and video welcomed in important conversations across major news outlets on topics like sexuality, body positivity, feminism, intersectionality, and misogyny and misogynoir.[15]

Possibly the most representative and accepted of our society's white, male misogynists, Fox News host Tucker Carlson first became fixated on Cardi B's "Wet A*s Pu*sy" just after its release; Carlson carved time from his August 18, 2020 show to skewer Cardi B and her song.[16] In his three-minute pearl-clutching rant on *Tucker Carlson Tonight*, Carlson took aim at Cardi B's lyrics, musical talent, moral values, and political engagement. He lambasted an interview Cardi B conducted for her social media followers with then–presidential hopeful Joe Biden. Carlson explained his intense (almost irrational) anger over the lyrics of "WAP." He even excoriated Cardi B on a personal level, taking aim at the artist over a video clip in which she spoke candidly, humorously, and explicitly about vaginal health.

Not to say that this was out of character for Carlson; when audio recordings published on October 7, 2016 showed man's-man Donald Trump unapologetically using the word "pu*sy" to describe where, as a star, he could grab a woman, Carlson did concede that Trump's "words are indefensible"—though in that case, Carlson quickly followed up by claiming the outrage over the recordings was "manufactured," as "the press has no moral standing to judge anyone who talks like this."[17] For Cardi B, though, Carlson somehow seemed not quite so magnanimous, pulling instead from his fear-mongering playbook to decry the song as dangerous and Cardi B as the single biggest threat to American family values today.

Between August 2020 and April 2021, entertainment, business, and culture sections of news outlets sought to analyze, perhaps thanks to conservative men like Tucker Carlson, the deeper social and psychological issues at work behind this strong aversion to WAP and other expressions of female sexual pleasure. Like Carlson, Republican politician James P. Bradley condemned Cardi B and Megan Thee Stallion as "what happens when children are raised without God."[18] Because children raised *with* God are all loving, caring creatures who do no harm to anyone, right? (Perhaps Bradley should run that by Robert Aaron Long, the 21-year-old shooter in the Atlanta spa shooting spree that left eight people dead, most of them Asian women, who claimed he "loved God and guns").[19] Month after month, there was never a shortage of headlines, opinion pieces, and social media memes about "sexually repressed" Republican men becoming "hot and bothered" by "WAP" and its accompanying video.[20]

Months later, in March 2021, "Wet A*s Pu*sy" was once again at the forefront of Carlson's mind after Cardi B and Megan Thee Stallion's performance of the song at the Grammy Awards show. Carlson was joined on *Tucker Carlson Tonight* by conservative personality Candace Owens, and together they grumbled about the unfairness of life in a society that "canceled" Dr. Seuss and Mr. Potato Head but allows Cardi B to continue to make music and speak in public.[21] After taking swipes at Cardi B, once again, as a mother, artist, and popular figure, Carlson and Owens ended with a condemnation of Cardi B and "WAP" for causing harm to children and families.

One further hopes those children and families were not watching Carlson's show, lest they be even more scarred from such self-serving, degrading propaganda.

As an honorary voice of the nation's incels, Carlson was not alone in keeping "WAP" and its Grammy performance in the news cycle. A United States congressman from Wisconsin, Glenn Grothman, drew media attention after taking to the House floor on April 22, more than a month after Cardi B and Megan Thee Stallion's Grammy performance, to criticize the Federal Communications Commission's minimalist response to their infamous awards show appearance.[22] Cardi B made the Politics section of the *Milwaukee Journal Sentinel* when she struck back at Representative Grothman over his preoccupation with her performance only two days after the conviction of Minneapolis police officer Derek Chauvin for the murder of George Floyd.[23] Unlike Representative Grothman, Cardi B knows the difference between Junk Food distraction and substantive, relevant news.

Overwhelmingly, those who criticized "WAP" did so from within the righteous realms of family values and child welfare. A few criticized the song as being harmful to women, feminism, and even women's rights, implicitly. While it could take decades to study the 'traumatizing' impact of "WAP" on children or the detrimental effects on women's equality, there were news stories of urgent relevance to the lives of women and children that were completely ignored by corporate, establishment news outlets, including by every woman and child's savior, the chivalrous Tucker Carlson.

The same media voices and publications that exploited any living, breathing news about Cardi B and Megan Thee

Stallion as the harbingers of our decline conveniently forgot to cover the nationwide shutdown of childcare centers, which heavily contributed to a vast increase in unemployment among women. Some economists have used the term "shecession" for the tendency brought to a head by the pandemic, noting that the 2020 recession saw women's unemployment rates rise far more dramatically than men's.[24]

Less than two weeks before Tucker Carlson's original diatribe against Cardi B and "WAP," on August 6, 2020, the Hechinger Report published a piece about the accelerated threat of mass evictions caused by the COVID-19 crisis in cities such as Kansas City, Missouri. Central to coverage by the Hechinger Report, an independent news source with a focus on topics in education, was the distressing, negative impact that evictions would have on Kansas City Public Schools. A researcher with Princeton University's Eviction Lab warned that, without protections or relief, the imminent wave of evictions would mean a disruption in even remote learning for many students, a concern shared by Melissa Douglas, a liaison for homeless students in Kansas City Public Schools.[25]

Why did this report on the actual welfare, health, and education of children get buried in the news cycle under the numerous other stories about Pied Piper Cardi B and the imagined moral threat she poses against children? Why did condemnations of Cardi B's motherhood, femininity, and feminism dominate the news cycle over stories about skyrocketing women's unemployment, the looming risk of eviction, and more deeply rooted issues like women's access to employment and childcare? Because Junk Food News rules the news cycle.

So it is that "WAP" continues to get media coverage whenever celebrities like Gwyneth Paltrow, BLACK-PINK's Rosé, Kim Kardashian, and Addison Rae show their support for the song in the form of TikTok dance "challenges." "WAP" returns to the news cycle whenever politicians choose to step up to Cardi B on Twitter. And "WAP" lives rent-free even in the minds of those raring to evict some 19 to 23 million Americans, including millions of schoolchildren, in the wake of the pandemic. It's almost enough to make you wonder whether politicians and pundits denouncing the purported threat posed by a pop song might not be simply distracting us from actual crises they don't want to address.

"I CAN'T GIVE YOU THIS ROSE": CANCEL CULTURE MEETS *THE BACHELOR* FRANCHISE

Once beloved 20th-century children's author Dr. Seuss supposedly penned the phrase, "Be who you are and say what you feel, because those who mind don't matter and those who matter don't mind." Today, however, in 21st-century America, you must never fail to mind what you say, do, or think, especially if it has a chance of ending up on the internet. Now, it seems, there is no escaping the modern threat of being "canceled"—a dreaded fate that some conservative pundits have argued Dr. Seuss himself has suffered after his own estate said it was pulling several Seuss titles from future circulation due to evolving attitudes.[26] "Cancel culture," as it has become known, is the phenomenon of promoting the censorship of people, brands, and even shows and movies due to what some consider to be offensive or problematic remarks, actions, or ideologies.[27] Anyone can be "canceled," but it has become a particularly prominent practice among celebrities, authors, and politicians. In 2021 it has become the new normal to be canceled—from TikTok's biggest stars to the face of long-running television franchises like ABC's *The Bachelor*.

The internet has played a big part in enabling cancel culture: while the internet has revolutionized how we access information, it has also become an immortal safe, storing information and past ideas that many would rather forget. In addition, while the internet makes readily available information from the past, it does so often without context, leaving many to view the remnants of yesteryear through the lens of today's mores. This has resulted in classic animated Disney and Warner Brothers children's characters, including Dumbo, Peter Pan, the Aristocats, and Pepé Le Pew, being called out on the internet, especially on social media platforms like Twitter, TikTok, and Facebook.

In the midst of this cancel culture phenomenon, Disney Parks even announced that its classic Disneyland ride "Splash Mountain" would be "re-themed" to reflect the more recently released movie *The Princess and the Frog*. The reasoning? According to NPR, there was an influx of complaints on the internet regarding the ride's association with the 1946 film *Song of the South*, which is considered racist by today's standards (and should have been at the time, but that's another matter).[28] Former Disney CEO Bob Iger has conceded that *Song of the South*, whose characters are depicted in the animatronic portion of the ride, is "not appropriate in today's world."[29] Yes, the world is much different than it was in 1946. Disney's *Song of the*

South absolutely does not fit in with today's more equitable principles—though one would hope those principles include acknowledging errors of the past, rather than attempting to ignore or erase them from memory, because, whether positively or negatively, the world we live in today was ineffably shaped by that context; and, as philosopher George Santayana is reputed to have claimed, "Those who cannot remember the past are condemned to repeat it."

Yet in the realm where pulling repeats from circulation is the go-to solution to all potential offenses of the past, cancel culture has thrived, from nixing sitcoms featuring now-controversial figures like Bill Cosby or Louis CK to firing the eminently cancelable stars of reality TV. From the days when many tuned in to hear Donald Trump on *The Apprentice* yelling "you're fired" at poor contestants to a time when social media users obsess over whether or not Carole Baskin, featured in the Netflix reality series *Tiger King*, killed her husband and fed him to tigers—a stunning example of the ultimate cancelation—Americans seem to love a good canceling. When we aren't *Keeping Up with the Kardashians* or watching the train wreck of Big Ed on *90 Day Fiancé*, many among us bite our nails over who will accept the final rose on this week's rundown of *The Bachelor* (and, in turn, who will be rejected).

One of the most widely recognized and well-known reality franchises of all time, ABC's *The Bachelor* has had so much success across more than two decades that it has resulted in countless spin-offs, podcasts, televised weddings, hushed divorces, and thousands of advertisements. While cast members come and go, the face of *The Bachelor*, host Chris Harrison, has remained a constant part of the franchise. That is, until he was canceled himself in 2021 by offended viewers. In the most recent season of *The Bachelor*, frontrunner contestant Rachael Kirkconnell was "canceled" after photos surfaced of her taking part in an "Old South" plantation-themed party in 2018. Kirkconnell was further criticized for "liking" Instagram posts with MAGA hats and the Confederate flag and for having a politically conservative father. When the franchise's host Chris Harrison was asked for his opinion on the matter by former *Bachelorette* Rachel Lindsay, Harrison noted that our perspective now is different from our perspective in 2018 (the year Kirkconnell attended the "Old South" party).[30]

A lot of "Bachelor Nation" was outraged by Harrison's response, to the extent that he not only had to issue an apology, but also needed to announce that he would be "stepping aside for a period of time" from his hosting duties. To this point, Harrison had appeared on nearly every single episode of *The Bachelor*, including all its spin-offs. But, after nearly twenty years, Harrison was canceled. The story was everywhere: Twitter exploded, TMZ went ballistic, even Fox News host Dave Rubin called Harrison "deeply pathetic" for apologizing for his comments about cancel culture.[31] Dozens of articles were published on *The Bachelor* franchise, and Harrison was mentioned in talk shows, news reels, TikToks, and everything pop and cultural in between.

But amidst all this noise, what genuinely newsworthy story did this Junk Food News distract us from? Corporate media's indignant vidiots overshadowed a host of proposed laws intended to limit—some might even say "cancel"—certain Americans' voting rights. In the first 36 days of 2021, Republican leaders proposed more than one hundred voter suppression bills.[32] Similar to the

19th-century laws that once limited voters based upon literacy tests, property ownership, and skin color, these bills may make voting much more difficult in 2021. The suppressive tactics proposed in these bills include limiting mail-in voting access, imposing stricter ID requirements, rethinking successful pro-voter registration policies, restricting voting on Sundays, and enabling more aggressive voter roll purges—particularly among communities of color and other Democratic-leaning constituencies.[33] While corporate media "cancels" characters, movies, and reality television personalities for racial insensitivity, many of our own state governments are actively proposing bills canceling the voting rights of specific historically-marginalized groups of Americans, preventing them from freely participating in modern democratic elections. Where are the headlines and outrage over that, Fox News?

MEGXIT FROM BUCKINGHAM PALACE: OPRAH INTERVIEWS THE ROYAL DOWN AND OUT

On March 7, 2021 the American public waited with bated breath to see what "bombshell" revelations Oprah Winfrey would pull out of Meghan Markle and Prince Harry about their troubles with the British royal family. Viewers watched Oprah visit the couple's Montecito mansion chicken coop in a "stars are like us" moment, attempting to make the couple appear relatable and humble.[34] Banking on the American public's appetite for reality TV and drama surrounding British royalty, every major media outlet covered the interview. We may have become independent from the Brits all those years ago, but we still touch our collective knee to the ground in deference to their amazing *royal* drama (with apologies to Colin Kaepernick). As the couple sat down with Oprah, they dove into topics ranging from catfights to mental health, centered throughout on Meghan's terrible mistreatment. The royal family's tea was served piping hot.

The real shocker came when Markle, a woman of mixed race, disclosed that the royal family was worried about the darkness of her unborn child's skin.[35] Who would have thought that the British monarchy, with its rich colonial past and deep roots in the slave trade, would be uneasy about welcoming a child with African DNA into its family? Well, Markle was as blindsided by this news as anyone! She made a point to tell Oprah that she was "naive" and believed the royal family would "protect" her.[36] But the fact remained, Markle contended, that even though she is light-skinned, she is still Black in the eyes of several members of the royal family.

The role that colorism played in this drama should not be overlooked. Though some light-skinned individuals can "pass" as white and gain some privileges in the world, their dark-skinned counterparts cannot. On January 20, 2021, the United States welcomed not only its first female vice president (VP), but the first of African American and South Asian descent. People raved about the fact that the VP "looked like them" and how important it is to have a woman of color in this seat of power. While this accomplishment is undeniable and this moment in history is incredibly important, the fact nevertheless remains that, although VP Kamala Harris is part Black, she has a very light complexion. Lighter complexioned people of color hold privileges and are often afforded opportunities that remain unavailable to those with a darker complexion. This pigment privilege started during slavery, when dark-skinned slaves were assigned to work in the fields while those with a fairer complexion were allowed to work in the slaveholder's home.[37] The pain that Markle felt should not be overlooked, but the reality is that she was considered light enough to marry into the royal family even as she was still dark enough to be regarded as a threat to their genealogy (which should've been threatened by all the royal marriages between cousins, but that's a different matter). Her treatment speaks to the racism that continues to pervade even the wealthiest tier of society, yet her naivety also shows her privilege as a light-skinned woman of color. She identifies as mixed race, yet she did not claim her Blackness until it became a topic worthy of media attention.

Another revelation that came from Oprah's primetime interview was Markle's battle with her mental health and suicidal thoughts because of her vile treatment by the royals and the UK press. She disclosed that she attempted to get help but was denied it. Her decision with Prince Harry to "step back" from their senior roles in the family was her best course of action to regain mental stability, she explained to Oprah.[38] Markle's struggles with mental health were often pushed to the forefront of the news cycle by a wide array of outlets, including CNN, Fox News, and the *New York Times*, among others. CBS, the network that aired the interview in discussion, flaunted Markle's personal struggles with the hope of capitalizing on sky-high ratings—and to CBS's delight, a whopping 61 million viewers worldwide tuned in to the broadcast.[39] Countless articles ran about Markle's mental health, with many voices weighing in, from healthcare professionals to tennis star Serena Williams.[40] That corporate media and celebrities are attempting to "normalize" mental health matters is a good thing—but realistically, while Silicon Valley ventures like BetterUp (where Prince Harry is now a "chief impact officer") talk about the mental health of individuals, they do nothing to address the structural issues that impact mental health, including one big one, racism.[41]

Something that cannot be ignored in the "Megxit" interview is the obvious topic of social class. Harry and Meghan, while forced out of the royal family and cut off financially, will still end up on top. People all over the world are forced out of their families for a myriad of reasons, from sexual identity, to issues with addiction or mental health. The majority of people that this happens to do not have a safety net made up of millions of dollars from inheritance. There was even one fan of the royal couple who felt so bad for them losing all their unearned wealth that she set up a GoFundMe page to help with their expenses, and it did manage to raise a cool $110 before being shut down.[42]

In the interview with Oprah, Harry mentioned that all he had financially was the money his mother had left him. *Forbes* estimates that, after a $5 million down payment on their home and a $3 million repayment for their earlier home remodeling, their net worth at the time of the interview was likely a measly $10 million.[43] Yes, there is trauma for Harry from being denied by his family, but he and his family will certainly not suffer financially and apparently won't starve for attention, either. Not to mention the fact that Meghan has her own money from her previous acting career in the United States.[44] The royal couple did mention in the interview the deals they were making with Netflix and Apple TV+, yet they failed to mention the worth of such deals (which is estimated to be above $100 million).[45] So basically, they will be just fine, and able to afford the mortgage on their Montecito mansion in Santa Barbara County after all. Whew!

Another topic that was repeatedly mentioned in the "Megxit" interview was that the royal family will no longer provide Prince Harry, his wife, or child with security.[46] This news left the couple shocked—how dare they be denied protection? Having personal security can be necessary for the safety of people with high social or political standing, but this seems absurd. The entitlement of these two, to assume that the British taxpayers would continue to pay for their security after they moved overseas and left their royal titles behind, cannot be overstated. They are worth millions still, and will only continue to acquire more money. They can definitely afford to pay for their own private security.

Security in general is a privilege that many people do not know. While Harry and Meghan's interview was airing, the world continued to face the challenges associated with a global pandemic, so security was a very common and pressing issue for many. From feeling safe in society to job security, the COVID-19 pandemic affected not only peoples' mental states, but their livelihoods as well. And just as Markle felt the impact of racism from the royals, Black-owned businesses in America have been feeling the impact of a global pandemic in a racist country rooted in white supremacy.

Most Black-owned businesses are located in neighborhoods with a high minority population, often depending upon foot traffic. They are also mostly retail and restaurant businesses, which were some of the first workplaces to really feel the impact of the shelter-in-place and social distancing orders associated with COVID-19.[47] Though the government ultimately doled out more than $500 million for small business loans in two installments to cover payroll, the majority of at least the first installment—not surprisingly—went to businesses where the population had a low percentage of Black and Brown people, thus leaving that community financially out of luck at a crucial time.[48] In places like Lexington, Kentucky, the local government wanted to give 10 percent of its contracting dollars to businesses in need. This included female-owned and veteran-run businesses as well as minority-run businesses. The vast majority of those funds in 2020 went to non-Black female- and veteran-run businesses, leaving less than 1 percent for businesses that were Black-owned.

The media likes to focus on how corporations like Coca-Cola have "pledged to increase [...] purchases from Black-owned suppliers by $500 million over the next five years," but what happens after those five years? A pledge is not a contract.[49] These earmarking preferences and pledges from government and large corporations are band-aid solutions to larger problems for the Black community and are obviously not a sustainable answer, nor have they ever been. Like Markle, we really shouldn't be surprised by the mistreatment of Black people in our society. Unlike her, however, most people in the Black community don't have a $10 million safety net to fall back on or lucrative deals with Netflix when being Black works against them.

TOTALED CARS, INFIDELITY, DRUGS, AND STRIP CLUBS: JUST ANOTHER NIGHT . . . FOR A PROFESSIONAL ATHLETE

One of the greatest sources of Junk Food News has always been professional sports. You know: young, "good-looking" athletes with huge mansions and fancy cars, lavishly spending money and exemplifying lifestyles of the rich and famous. What could go wrong with that combination? Sports stories have long been used as analogies dating back to the days of traveling oral storytellers, when lessons were pulled from the trials and tribulations of losses and victories of our mighty sports figures. In the past, reporters might chronicle the struggles of an athlete hampered by an addiction or affliction to show his or her imminent rise from their darkest hour to triumph once again. But in a world where if-it-shames-it-leads reigns supreme, stories are not just related to the games on the field, but rather to the trials and tribulations off and well-off, as "fans" celebrate their heroes' accomplishments while razzing the failings of erstwhile icons, all through online hashtags, ratings, clicks, and likes. When corporate media is already an industry that feeds off of distraction, what news story could better steal the limelight from scoreboards or professional accomplishments than the humiliation of athletes-turned-celebrity-multimillion-aires? Scores of professional athletes provide a buffet to those who feed at the trough of Junk Food News. Totaled cars, infidelity, drugs, and strip clubs—misbehavior among the fallen warriors of today makes for salacious headlines direct from the wide, wearisome world of sports.

Many of these sports-star-gone-wild stories are forms

of humilitainment, where details are often left unexplored unless they might lead to sensationalism. There's a headline, a photo, and a two-sentence caption cracking its way across the airwaves of corporate news. For instance, we all know Tiger Woods: one of the world's most famous golfers. He was a Junk Food News goldmine in 2009 when, after crashing his car just outside his home in suspicious circumstances, he was revealed to have been cheating repeatedly on his wife Elin Nordegren for years, a story just strange and salacious enough to be thoroughly highlighted by the corporate press.[50] Years later, Woods returned to his place as America's sweetheart when he was filmed winning the prestigious Masters golf tournament and embracing with his son in 2019. All was forgiven and forgotten—well, until recently, when Woods found himself in the news yet again in February 2021, this time for crashing his luxury SUV at around 85 miles per hour in Southern California. Many fans were concerned about the professional golfer—not so much for his health and well-being, but instead for whether he would be able to compete in the 2021 Masters tournament.[51]

Americans love to stay up-to-date on the personal lives of professional athletes. Why do the Kardashians stay so relevant? Because they've apparently dated half the NBA! Whenever their names start to fizzle out, there seems to be another story on how Boston Celtic Tristan Thompson cheated on his baby mama Khloé Kardashian yet again.[52] Ever heard of Jennifer Lopez? When her ratings were down, she just dumped her partner, former Yankee baseball All-Star Alexander Rodriguez, to jump back into the limelight. For his part, "A-Rod" coped with his public breakup by introducing his own line of makeup for men.[53]

Then there's National Basketball Association (NBA) superstar James Harden. Considered one of the greatest guards of his time, the 2018 MVP and nine-time NBA All-Star explored a potential trade to the Miami Heat from the Houston Rockets. As one of the hosts of *The Complex Sports Podcast* noted on January 19, 2021, Harden "is a fit for the [Miami] nightlife and that culture, not necessarily the Heat culture."[54] In other words, Harden loves to party, and his reckless and sometimes questionable nightlife behavior has frequently been picked up by corporate media outlets. When the media are more concerned with the off-court fouls of athletes than their on-court moves, it creates a bad look for professional sports franchises and leagues. However, such misbehavior seems to constitute excellent entertainment for the rest of us and great ratings for news corporations. Harden's affinity for strip clubs was even picked up by the Australian news outlet news.com.au, which revealed that Harden reportedly spent $1.43 million at a strip club in Houston in just one night.[55] Accordingly, with a plethora of such distractions in Miami, the blockbuster trade was never finalized for Harden. He may have been denied the Heat, but by gossip reporters' estimation he still set ablaze in Houston! Miami Heat veteran Udonis Haslem noted, "I would've aged 15 years trying to be his OG down here."[56] Lucky for Haslem that Harden is now holding court in Brooklyn with the Nets. Look out, New York!

While Tiger "King" Woods is totaling expensive SUVs and James Harden is allegedly blowing millions of dollars at strip clubs, corporate news outlets failed to acknowledge a multitude of stories that actually need to be reported to the American public. In February 2021 the National Football League (NFL) produced a very COVID Super Bowl, proving global pandemic guidelines do not apply to multi-billion-dollar sports leagues. Despite the fact that millions of NFL fans have fallen ill, lost jobs, lost homes, lost family members, and lost lives due to the global pandemic, NFL owners only added to their net worth over the past year. Since March 2020 the 64 billionaire NFL franchise owners enjoyed a $98.5 billion rise in their net worth, collectively.[57] That insane spike in revenue could be used as a stimulus check of $1,400 for more than 70 million Americans, many of whom are avid NFL supporters.[58] The private gain of these sporting capitalists in the midst of so much public pain is particularly upsetting due to the fact that many of the franchises have been the beneficiaries of recent tax-payer handouts, with 28 professional sports teams receiving $9 billion in taxpayer subsidies over the past few decades.[59] Nevertheless, thousands of low-wage stadium workers' jobs were eliminated by the pandemic, while greedy owners continued to stuff their pockets. Of course, the obscene influx in net worth among professional sports team owners remained almost entirely unreported by corporate outlets, which instead freed up airtime for reports on James Harden's spending habits—but hey, at least he is helping to support the economy.

CONCLUSION: JUNK FOOD NEWS—OF NOSTRUMS AND A NEW NORMALCY

The "new normal" associated with the COVID-19 lock-downs has caused Americans to turn to social media more than ever before to get their fix of infotainment. Trapped in their homes, expected to social distance, and addicted to their devices, Americans have found more pleasure than ever in others' humilitainment. And with less human contact than many have experienced in much of the modern era, for better or worse, Junk Food News has become even more of a societal norm that holds us together (almost as well as, say, Gorilla Glue). From Tucker Carlson's absolute outrage over a song, to an NBA All-Star allegedly spending an exorbitant amount of money at a local strip club, the everyday lives of celebrities are dissected under a corporate media microscope. The use of personal digital devices has become so ubiquitous that apps like Facebook, Instagram, Twitter, and now TikTok, have shrunk the global village, and with it the realm of privacy, further than we've ever imagined. It is as if every millisecond of the day can be regularly caught on camera or documented in some way and shared with the world, regardless of its insignificance.

As John Reinke of the *Tiger King* remarked, "I'm sure y'all got a story to tell." Do we ever. From the "stories" on Facebook, Snapchat "snaps," and Instagram "reels," to YouTube "shorts," an armada of Twitter "fleets," and ticktocking the time away on TikTok, we've all had stories to tell and way too much time on our hands. Regardless, these outlets have become the nostrums that make up the "new normal," foreshadowing a post-pandemic normalcy we should all collectively "eek!"

While some may bemoan this barrage of the banal, there's nothing new about indulging in celebrity gossip and tripe. For decades, Americans have read magazines, watched television programs, and followed the personal lives of celebrities and others to distract from the drudgery of daily life. A hundred years ago, journalists like

H.L. Mencken mocked the fickleness and anti-intellectual character of the country's masses, referring to them as the "booboisie."[60] This past year, during the pandemic, bingeing on mundane, meaningless material online was amplified by access to technology and time alone. But the "new normal" has taken this enduring obsession one step further.

Americans are now demanding far too much from their celebrity counterparts, finding new ways to "cancel" their actions when they don't live up to their expectations, and even, in some cases, hindering or destroying their careers. Too often, online policing such as this is a poor substitute for actual engagement in the wider community and politics. The reliance upon the lives of strangers through the mediated screen has developed into an addiction at worst and a cause for civic concern at best. These Junk Food News stories, sprinkled across social media and corporate news platforms alike, distract Americans from far more significant stories that could actually impact their personal lives and the lives of their fellow citizens. Indeed, though some TikTok teenagers fully believe their dance challenges will one day be in history textbooks, some of the truly significant stories of our time are passing unnoticed. As numerous states propose voting laws that could restrict certain groups of Americans from exercising their most basic democratic rights, we focus on what the host of a reality dating show said in a tabloid interview. And while Prince Harry and Meghan Markle cry poor from their sprawling mansion in affluent Montecito, Black-owned businesses continue to actually suffer deprivations in the unending shadow of the pandemic.

The corporate media, similar to the soul-stealing

TikTok algorithm, carefully choose the stories we see, and thus the ones many do not. In a digital world where people are reliant on communication devices, Americans should strive to recognize the stories that might actually impact their personal lives and better their communities rather than channel their energy toward their distaste for Cardi B's latest performance or sink into the humilitainment of the next fallen Tiger King. The future of our democracy may just depend on how carefully we fashion our "return" to a new normalcy, one guided by civic engagement and equitable principles and not algorithmically manipulated by society's baser elements.

JEN LYONS is an instructor of history at Diablo Valley College in the San Francisco Bay Area. Lyons earned her MA in history from the University of Nevada, Reno in May 2020. Her research primarily focuses on the United States in the 20th and 21st centuries, including how various modes of communication have impacted American social, economic, and political habits.

SIERRA KAUL is an honors history student, formerly at Diablo Valley College, now at UC Davis, who has interned with Project Censored for three years. When she isn't writing essays or being sarcastic about existing, she enjoys air conditioning and long naps in the dark. If you need her, you can find her in the trenches of Twitter complaining about something mundane.

MARCELLE LEVINE SWINBURNE teaches women's history, US history, and California history at Diablo Valley College and Solano Community College. Her passions include gender politics, K–12 special education, travel, comedy, and "other hot-girl stuff."

VIKKI VASQUEZ is a history student at Diablo Valley College and will be attending California State University, East Bay in Fall 2021. Her plan is to become a history teacher for high school students, and she hopes to teach them critical media literacy when exploring the past and present.

GAVIN KELLEY is a graduate of Cal State Long Beach with a degree in creative writing. He wields his pen as an arts organization administrator and is currently manager of operations for the Colburn School's dance program. A kung fu practitioner and martial arts movie podcaster and fan, Gavin developed a keen eye for Junk Food News after years of studying straight-to-video B-movies. He co-hosts the *Martial Arts Mania Podcast*.

MICKEY HUFF is director of Project Censored and president of the Media Freedom Foundation. He is also a professor of social science, history, and journalism at Diablo Valley College, where he chairs the Journalism Department. He has co-edited and contributed to Project Censored's annual volumes since 2009, and Junk Food News analysis has long been one of his guilty pleasures.

Notes

1. William Deverell, "Warren Harding Tried to Return America to 'Normalcy' After WWI and the 1918 Pandemic. It Failed," *Smithsonian Magazine*, May 19, 2020.
2. Thomas West, "Tiger King: 15 of the Best Quotes from the Documentary Series," Screen Rant, June 27, 2020.
3. John Koetsier, "Digital Crack Cocaine: The Science behind TikTok's Success," *Forbes*, January 18, 2020.
4. Angie Goff, interview with Nathan Apodaca, "Viral Tik Tok Star Nathan Apodaca, Known for Ocean Spray and 'Dreams' Video, Sits Down with FOX 5 DC," *Oh My Goff*, FOX 5 Washington DC, posted to YouTube by FOX 5 Washington DC on December 15, 2020.
5. Sandra Song, "Nathan Apodaca is Selling His Viral 'Dreams' TikTok as an NFT," *Paper*, March 18, 2021.
6. Marie Fazio, "Gorilla Glue as Hair Spray? 'Bad, Bad, Bad Idea,'" *New York Times*, February 8, 2021, updated February 12, 2021.

7. "Gorilla Glue," *Saturday Night Live*, NBC, broadcast on February 13, 2021 and posted by Saturday Night Live to YouTube that same night.
8. Sarah Booker and Brad Waite, "Humilitainment? Lessons from 'The Apprentice': A Reality Television Content Analysis," Presented at the 17th Annual Convention of the American Psychological Society, Los Angeles, May 2005; and Richard H. Smith, "Joy in Another's Shame: Humilitainment Anyone?" *Psychology Today*, March 16, 2014.
9. Sara Fischer, "Inside TikTok's Killer Algorithm," Axios, September 10, 2020.
10. Amy Mitchell, Mark Jurkowitz, J. Baxter Oliphant, and Elisa Shearer, "How Americans Navigated the News in 2020: A Tumultuous Year in Review," Pew Research Center, February 22, 2021.
11. Ibid.
12. Amy Goodman, "World Food Programme Warns 34 Million Face Famine in Yemen, Ethiopia and Beyond," *Democracy Now!*, March 12, 2021.
13. Dream McClinton, "Cardi B and Megan Thee Stallion's WAP Should be Celebrated, Not Scolded," *The Guardian*, August 12, 2020.
14. Kate Lister, "Cardi B's WAP Follows a Long History of Black American Women Singing about Sexual Pleasure," inews.co.uk, August 20, 2020.
15. See Moya Bailey, *Misogynoir Transformed: Black Women's Digital Resistance* (New York: New York University Press, 2021). "Misogynoir" is defined as the specific hatred, dislike, distrust, and prejudice directed toward Black women. Scholar Moya Bailey coined the term to describe sexist, racist sentiments toward Black women specifically.
16. Tucker Carlson, *Tucker Carlson Tonight*, Fox News, August 18, 2020; the clip on "WAP" is viewable, with a transcription of the rant, via Media Matters Staff, "Tucker Carlson Launches Unhinged Attack on Cardi B for Promoting Proper Hygiene," Media Matters for America, August 18, 2020.
17. Howard Kurtz, interview with Tucker Carlson, *MediaBuzz*, Fox News, October 9, 2016; that clip is viewable, with a transcription of the interview, via Media Matters Staff, "Fox's Media Criticism Show Claims Other Reporters are 'Overplaying' Trump Tapes with 'Manufactured Outrage,'" Media Matters for America, October 9, 2016.
18. August Brown, "California Congressional Candidate Slams Cardi B and Megan Thee Stallion's 'WAP,'" *Los Angeles Times*, August 7, 2020.
19. "Atlanta Shootings: Suspect Charged with Murder as Victims Identified," BBC News, March 18, 2021.
20. Lake Schatz, "Sexually Repressed Fox Anchor Tucker Carlson Freaks Out over 'WAP' Video: Watch," Consequence of Sound, August 19, 2020; and Wren Graves, "A Republican Congressional Candidate is All Hot and Bothered about Cardi B and Megan's 'WAP Video,'" Consequence, August 7, 2020.
21. Tucker Carlson, interview with Candace Owens, *Tucker Carlson Tonight*, Fox News, broadcast March 15, 2021 and posted by "TuckerOnly" to YouTube that same night.
22. Glenn Grothman, "Keeping Obscene and Indecent Content Off Our Airwaves," *Congressional Record*, Vol. 167 No. 70, April 22, 2021, H2060.

23. Molly Beck, "Cardi B, Glenn Grothman Clash over 'WAP' Performance," *Milwaukee Journal Sentinel*, April 22, 2021.

24. Kimberly Cataudella, "The Pandemic is Worsening a Long-Running Crisis: Child Care," The Center for Public Integrity, March 26, 2021.

25. Barbara Shelly, "Children Will Bear the Brunt of a Looming Eviction Crisis," Hechinger Report, August 6, 2020.

26. Jeremy Engle, "Lesson of the Day: 'Dr. Seuss Books are Pulled, and a "Cancel Culture" Controversy Erupts,'" *New York Times*, March 5, 2021.

27. Brooke Kato, "What is Cancel Culture? Everything to Know about the Toxic Online Trend," *New York Post*, March 10, 2021, updated June 25, 2021.

28. Austin Horn, "Disney Announces Redesign of Splash Mountain after Some Call Ride Themes Racist," NPR, June 25, 2020.

29. Ibid.

30. Rachel Lindsay, interview with Chris Harrison, *Extra*, Fox, broadcast February 9, 2021 and posted by "extratv" to YouTube that same night.

31. Stephanie Giang-Paunon, "'Bachelor' Host Chris Harrison 'Deeply Pathetic' for Apology to 'Woke Mob': Dave Rubin," Fox News, March 4, 2021.

32. Kenny Stancil, "'Downright Scary': In 2021 Alone, GOP Introduces 100+ Voter Suppression Bills in 28 States," Common Dreams, February 5, 2021.

33. Ibid.

34. Oprah Winfrey, interview with Harry Mountbatten-Windsor and Meghan Markle, *Oprah with Meghan and Harry: A CBS Primetime Special*, CBS, March 7, 2021.

35. Ibid.

36. Ibid.

37. Margaret L. Hunter, "'If You're Light You're Alright': Light Skin Color as Social Capital for Women of Color," *Gender and Society*, Vol. 16 No. 2 (April 2002), 175–93, 176 [accessed June 3, 2021].

38. Winfrey, interview with Mountbatten-Windsor and Markle, *Oprah with Meghan and Harry*.

39. Dominic Patten, "'Oprah with Meghan and Harry' Viewership Tops 60M Worldwide; Royal Special Rebroadcast Tonight on CBS—Update," Deadline, March 12, 2021.

40. Alex Gurley, "Serena Williams Had the Nicest Things to Say about Meghan Markle, Proving We All Need a Friend Like Serena Williams," BuzzFeed, March 25, 2021.

41. Natalie Shure, "Prince Harry's New Fake Mental Health Care Job is a Farce," *New Republic*, March 29, 2021.

42. Jelisa Castrodale, "A Woman Set Up a GoFundMe to Help Harry and Meghan Pay for Their $14M House," Vice, March 19, 2021.

43. Dawn Chmielewski, "How Much are Prince Harry and Meghan Markle Worth? Surprisingly, Not That Much," *Forbes*, February 26, 2021.

44. Ibid.

45. Brandon Katz, "Harry & Meghan's Big Hollywood Deals Helped Them Weather the Family Chaos," *Observer*, March 8, 2021.

46. Winfrey, interview with Mountbatten-Windsor and Markle, *Oprah with Meghan and Harry*.

47. Carlos Avenancio-Leon and Isaac Hacamo, "How the Pandemic Recession Targets Black and Hispanic-Owned Small Businesses," *YES! Magazine*, March 4, 2021.

48. Lydia DePillis, "COVID Has Put a Whole Generation of Black-Owned Businesses at Risk," Truthout, March 7, 2021.

49. Ibid.

50. Tom Lutz, "Tiger Woods Driving at 87mph in 45mph Zone at Time of Car Crash, Police Say," *The Guardian*, April 7, 2021.

51. Ibid.

52. Johnni Macke, "All the NBA Players the Kardashian-Jenner Family Have Dated: Lamar Odom, Kris Humphries, Devin Booker and More," *US Magazine*, June 21, 2021.

53. Joanna Taylor, "Jennifer Lopez's Ex Alex Rodriguez Launches Concealer for Men," *Evening Standard*, May 26, 2021.

54. Quoted in Emily Bicks, "Miami Heat Veteran Admits He's Relieved James Harden Didn't Join Team," Heavy, January 22, 2021.

55. "Houston Rockets Star James Harden Reportedly Had a Big Night Out," news.com.au, June 7, 2020.

56. Bicks, "Miami Heat Veteran Admits He's Relieved."

57. Chuck Collins and Omar Ocampo, "Billionaires Win and We Lose at Pandemic Super Bowl 2021," Truthout, February 6, 2021.

58. Ibid.

59. Ibid.

60. H.L.M., E.A.B., and A.F.L. [H.L. Mencken, probably Ernest A. Boyd, and probably a misprint for Abraham L. Flexner], "The Boob Dictionary: Being a Contribution Toward the Enrichment of the American Language," (Baltimore) *Evening Sun*, February 15, 1922, 12; reprinted in the *Baltimore Sun*, February 20, 2016.

CHAPTER 4

False Balance in Media Coverage Undermines Democracy

News Abuse in 2020–2021

ROBIN ANDERSEN

When former Project Censored director Peter Phillips coined the term "News Abuse," he sought to identify the numerous ways that media language, logics, framing, and sourcing serve to distort and obscure the accurate reporting of news that is necessary in a democratic society. False and misleading interpretations of current affairs, people, and groups leaves a democratic public in the dark. As citizens, we not only have a right to know, but an obligation to be informed. As the political Right promotes fiction over fact, it has become increasingly clear that accurate information is at the heart of a democratic society, and that lies and distortions are antithetical to the democratic process. This chapter seeks to shed light on the accuracy and validity of news and information in an age of "fake news" and a "post-truth" media environment.

News Abuse has become a key concept over the years because it encourages us to cast a critical eye toward what is presented as news, and to understand how news practices and conventions frequently blunt the forces of democracy and obstruct the fight for racial, gender, and economic justice and struggles against oppression, inequality, and environmental collapse.

THE YEAR IN NEWS

Capping one of the most momentous years in recent American politics, the 2020 presidential election brought an end to the devastating four-year reign of Donald J. Trump, and it was followed by an angry backlash by right-wing rioters who stormed the US Capitol building on January 6, 2021. As news outlets broadcast images of pitched battles between Capitol police and rioters—benignly characterized as "Trump supporters"—forcing their way up the Capitol steps and into the congressional chambers, media commentators seemed to be as surprised as viewers by the TV footage. The country and the world watched for hours as the violence raged, and media tried to catch up with the story that was unfolding before their eyes. What became evident almost immediately was that rioters were stoked by a conspiracy-fueled rage of stolen-election rhetoric and racism, incited by Trump and other Republicans as they attempted to overturn the outcome of the 2020 presidential election.

Another crisis, generations in the making, brought on by the structural racism that permeates the United States—especially within the ranks of law enforcement—had already hit the country on May 25, 2020, when Minneapolis police officer Derek Chauvin, with the complicity of three other cops, brutally murdered George Floyd while bystanders bore witness and documented the crime. The world was watching then too, as state-sanctioned killers took the life of yet another Black person in

America. Initial news reports across the media spectrum from ABC to PBS would rely on the vague, mystifying lexicon that has served to shield police from justice for decades, claiming Floyd "died in police custody."[1]

Black Lives Matter (BLM) protests erupted immediately as American citizens took to the streets in outrage, and further actions spread throughout the world. Comparing the law enforcement response to BLM protests with that of the white insurrectionists who rioted on January 6th, President-Elect Joe Biden gave voice to what had become obvious to many when he said, "No one can tell me that if it had been a group of Black Lives Matter protesting yesterday, they wouldn't have been treated very, very differently from the mob of thugs that stormed the Capitol."[2] Biden added, "Don't dare call them protesters." Media coverage would also reveal a striking double standard in reporting on the two utterly disparate groups.

The 46th president of the United States, Joe Biden, was inaugurated in the middle of an economic, environmental, political, and public health crisis of unthinkable dimensions in a ceremony that took place primarily over media channels and platforms. In stark contrast to Trump's fearful rhetoric of "American carnage" four years earlier, Biden's message was generous and unifying, and his inauguration featured uplifting performances, including a young Black female poet named Amanda Gorman, who became the youngest inaugural poet in US history and a notable celebrity.[3] Present at the inauguration, and photographed sitting alone with his arms crossed over his chest and wearing a simple cloth mask and colorful handmade mittens, Bernie Sanders quickly became a social media meme. Sanders's perhaps skeptical or impatient look sparked a nerve and seemed to remind the country that his presidential campaigns had given voice to a renewed political vision, one that looked back to the New Deal and policies that embraced a more just economy where inequality, oppression, and corporate domination would no longer define what America had become after decades of neoliberal policies. The new administration was put on notice that the power and strength of progressive forces within the Democratic Party could not be ignored, would not stand for continued social and economic injustice, and would demand action to prevent environmental collapse.

President Biden's first one hundred days were a whirlwind of policy initiatives, diverse cabinet appointments, and executive orders, many of which overturned the anti-environmental, anti-labor, and anti-immigrant actions of the Trump era. Biden commemorated those who died from COVID-19, offered solace to a country reeling from the loss of half a million people in a pandemic made worse by Trump's public information disaster, and changed the tenor of discourse from toxic to humane. In a somewhat surprising break from a good number of past policies of corporate Democrats, the new president's more progressive agenda seemed to take establishment media by surprise.

Coverage of President Biden was mixed, but the primary focus used to cover the new administration was an inside-the-Beltway lexicon, a tired, constructed frame that calls for "bipartisanship," which, as detailed below, undermines democracy and disavows the will of the American people. Even though such false balance, sometimes referred to as "both-sidesing," wobbled under the weight of Republican obstructionism, media continued to frame debates about policies as legitimate differences between two equally democratic political parties.[4] As the GOP blocked every Democratic initiative, Republicans claimed they were being unfairly censored by "cancel culture," a claim that was definitively belied in May 2021, when the party censured and purged its own conservative politicians, including Senator Liz Cheney of Wyoming and Representative Anthony Gonzalez of Ohio, for insufficient loyalty to Trump, as they had refused to go along with his Big Lie of election theft.[5]

As the year wore on, media reporting would represent the fragmented world of politics with coverage that failed to make the connections necessary to understand the full extent and true dangers of the country's political crises. Even more than usual, media relied on superficial reporting, often dominated by shocking visuals devoid of meaning and substance that presented the mere simulacrum of life on the ground.

Reviewing the book *A Brief History of Fascist Lies* by Federico Finchelstein, chair of the History Department at the New School for Social Research, Eric Black described being "troubled by certain similarities between Trump's methods (including lying frequently while always claiming to be telling the truth) and those of Hitler and Mussolini."[6] Black also pointed out how relevant the book is "to the world we're living in today." Though Trump is no longer in office and has been "deplatformed" (removed from social media platforms), his lies continue to be upheld by the GOP. Indeed, a majority of Republicans still believe Trump's 2020 election loss "resulted from illegal voting or election rigging."[7] News media, in not confronting those lies head-on and instead insisting upon "both sides" narratives even in the midst of anti-democratic maneuvering, have played an outsized role in the growth and perpetuation of a truly dangerous politics.

MEDIA CAUGHT BY SURPRISE ON JANUARY 6TH

From the first images of rioters festooned in Trump gear, wielding Confederate flags, throwing aside metal barriers, clinging to the steep outer walls of the Capitol building, and storming up its steps to wreak havoc once inside, media were caught off guard as commentators scrambled for words to describe the perpetrators and the nature of the mayhem taking place. Throughout the long afternoon the language would evolve, but the innocuous-sounding terms "Trump supporters," "demonstrators," and "protesters" were being used for the rioters on many news programs even after the breach of the Capitol.[8] This Trump creation was a beast that stubbornly remained out of focus, indefinable, and seemingly inexplicable.

From magazines to comedy shows, practically all media seemed to have a team on the ground or a compilation video. Indeed, the *Daily Show*'s Jordan Klepper walked with the mob to the Capitol building and was the first to call their actions "sedition."[9] *The Nation*'s Elie Mystal said the first word that sprang to mind while watching the insurrection was "Whiteness."[10]

Video footage revealed heated confrontations between Capitol police and rioters, as well as some officers standing aside, warmly greeting the trespassers, or even taking selfies with the crowd of mostly white men who seemed awestruck and confused about what they might do next once they entered the majestic Capitol rotunda. Rioters wore various costumes; some donned MAGA hats or were draped in Trump flags, and others mingled with the notorious QAnon "shaman" who entered the media spotlight in face paint, with horns on his head, tattoos on his stomach, and fur on his legs. Men in paramilitary garb carried weapons, and some sprayed police with chemical irritants, beating and pushing officers down the steps.

Watching the documentation emerge was equivalent to experiencing media whiplash. Footage of rioters smashing through windows and doors was seen over and over, and cameras followed their frenzied hunt for congressional prey as they chanted "Where is Pence?" and "Hang Mike Pence." Journalists were also under attack. Rioters made their intentions clear when they painted "Murder the media" on one of the building's doors. Belligerent shouting rioters surrounded and threatened reporters and destroyed their equipment with glee.[11] Photographs revealed a noose hanging ominously from the inaugural scaffolding, a reference to the violent racist history that forged so much of the background of the day.

From one hour to the next on January 6th, and for days to come, dozens of descriptors were used, tested, tried, and rejected. Were the people who stormed the Capitol insurrectionists, violent rioters, traitors, patriots, or just a mob? Did they commit sedition, an attempted coup, or a "political protest that got out of hand"?[12] In a flourish of descriptive prose in the *New York Review of Books*, Mark Danner would narrate his impressions as he strode alongside rioters to the Capitol steps. Understanding that "Trumpism is driven by cruelty and domination even as its rhetoric claims grievance and victimization," Danner rightly deemed the event a "stupid coup."[13]

Trump's words before the riot calling for Mike Pence to overturn the election results and for the mob to stop "the steal" (that is, Congress's confirmation of the verified results of a legitimate election) were later shown to have also been promoted by a number of other Republican leaders, from Ted Cruz to Jim Jordan, who had enthusiastically egged on extremists' conspiracy theories for weeks. This mob had been incited by Trump as they pursued lawmakers, many of whom were forced to flee their chambers in terror. As police held back the rioters, congresspeople cowered under furniture and desperately called for help and their families. Capitol police were ultimately the last line of defense for the US Congress and Constitution against a raging horde of Trump fanatics.

By the time members of Congress came out of hiding to certify Joe Biden as the 46th president of the United States, Senator Chuck Schumer (D-NY) identified the people who stormed the Capitol as "domestic terrorists," words that the corporate media would quickly forget.[14]

Media Miss the Story of the Decade

When *Washington Post* editors Leonard Downie Jr. and Robert G. Kaiser wrote about American journalism in peril in 2002, they admitted that the press completely missed the Iran–Contra scandal, saying, "We didn't get one of the biggest stories of the Reagan years until it was handed to us on a platter."[15] Certainly the same can be said for corporate media and the Capitol Insurrection of January 6th.

When investigations by government and the press into the forces that created the mob began, they quickly revealed the near-total lack of preparedness and security at the Capitol (at times deliberate), and the failure of information leading up to the attack, even though the planning and threats of violence were readily available to government and journalists months earlier. As *Wired* magazine observed, researchers who study far-right movements had been "expecting—and warning—of the likelihood of violence around either the Electoral College vote or the upcoming inauguration since Biden's victory, especially since Trump and right-wing media outlets have been stoking baseless conspiracy theories about election fraud for weeks."[16] Luke Mogelson's long article in the *New Yorker* about the insurrection was subtitled "a chronicle of an attack foretold."[17] In it, Mogelson detailed the many warnings of what would unfold on January 6th, from Trump's own words in statements and speeches in the weeks leading up to Biden's confirmation, to a protest at the Pennsylvania state capitol in Harrisburg on Election Day where hundreds of heavily armed militia members vowed to revolt. Mogelson also noted that militant pro-Trump gangs like the Proud Boys—a national organization dedicated to "reinstating a spirit of Western chauvinism" in America—had been "openly gearing up for major violence." In early January, on Parler, a social media website frequented by the Far Right, one of the leaders of the Proud Boys had warned that lawmakers "should be dragged out of office and hung."

Before the election, Trump himself repeatedly announced that if he didn't win, the election must be deemed fraudulent.[18] In a gamble that the outcome might mirror the 2000 election results that brought George W. Bush to the White House, Trump made it clear to media that he would do everything in his power to attempt to halt counting of mail-in ballots beyond Election Day.[19] Right up to the moment before the Capitol was stormed, Trump was urging his supporters to "fight like hell, [or] you're not going to have a country anymore."[20] In other words, there were many indications that Trump was rallying his forces to steal the election, and even inciting his mob to attempt a potentially violent coup d'état.

Corporate Media Fail the American Public before and after the 2020 Election

Though major news organizations reported on the dozens of lawsuits that Trump's clownish legal team were crisscrossing the country to file—before and after Biden was elected—stories failed to connect the dots and show the bigger picture of the reasons for the flurry of litigation. For example, Business Insider reported on an "all-out legal war to stop the expansion of vote-by-mail," detailing actions against New Jersey, Nevada, North Carolina, Iowa, Pennsylvania, and Montana, states that were allowing voters to cast their ballot by mail more easily because of the pandemic.[21] But after detailing the suits, the article simply ended, with no explanation for what it all meant, why such legal maneuvering was being done, and what the consequences might be for the election—and democracy. Connections between Trump's "legal war" and voter suppression strategies were not made.

In threats issued two days before the election, Trump told reporters in Charlotte, North Carolina, "We're going to go in the night of, as soon as that election is over, we're going in with our lawyers."[22] *The Washington Post* reported that the "president's comments are among his most unam-

biguous yet . . ." Here the paper could have followed with
". . . of Trump's ongoing efforts to steal the election."[23]
But instead, the sentence continued with passive legal-
istic wording, ". . . that he is embracing an aggressive legal
strategy in an election that has already been beset with a
multitude of lawsuits."[24]

Trump had been setting the stage to steal the election for
months, but as Fairness & Accuracy In Reporting (FAIR)
pointed out, "it appears to be taboo for journalists at the
biggest newsrooms in the country to straightforwardly
report the fact that Trump is trying to do so."[25] FAIR even
conducted a Nexis search for "Trump" + "election" + "steal"
of most of the biggest newspapers in the country from July
7 to September 7. Out of all election-themed coverage,
there wasn't a single article reporting that Trump was trying
to steal the 2020 election.[26]

Yet a robust discussion—and reporting critical of
media silence on the issue—was taking place on independent and alternative media outlets.[27] As early as June in
the *New Yorker*, Bill McKibben noted that Trump seemed
to be gearing up for "a coup," pointing out that his "constant shout-outs to 'the Second Amendment people'"
was nothing less than a "clarion call" for violent disruption.[28] *The Nation* presented Democrats with a three-point
strategy of what they must do should Trump try to stage
a coup.[29] And writing in the Intercept, Frances Fox Piven
and Deepak Bhargava offered grassroots activism as their
answer to the question posed in the headline, "What If
Trump Won't Leave?"[30]

OPENING THE FRAME

While corporate outlets caught up with a reality they had refused to acknowledge for months, some alternative and historical explanations began to enter public discourse, a phenomenon recognizable to media scholars. When predominant narratives fail to explain a sudden crisis or surprising event, the boundaries that contain standardized reporting break down and an opening for a broader range of information and perspectives can develop. Frequently such information has been pushed to the margins, but as it is made more central to public debate the dynamics of history become visible, if only briefly, as media scramble to impose another framework for coverage.

The Turner Diaries

The day after the storming of the Capitol, the *New York Times* published a piece by journalist Seyward Darby titled "The Far Right Told Us What It Planned. We Didn't Listen."[31] In the piece, Darby connected the language and iconography of the rioters to the long-standing narratives of white supremacists. She noted similarities between the Capitol riot and *The Turner Diaries*, a racist dystopian novel written by a white supremacist in 1978. A noose, like the one seen hanging over the inaugural scaffolding on January 6th, unmistakably recalls the history of white vigilantes lynching Black people. As Darby explained, the gallows erected in front of the Capitol also alluded to an event in *The Turner Diaries* known as the "'day of the rope,' when the terrorists lynch their enemies: 'the lawyers, the businessmen, the TV newscasters, the newspaper reporters and editors, the judges, the teachers, the school officials, the "civic leaders," the bureaucrats, the preachers.' And, yes, 'the politicians.'"[32] Hannah Gais, a senior researcher for the Southern Poverty Law Center, agreed with Darby's assessment, adding on Twitter that some among the more than 5,000 viewers on a livestream of the siege proclaimed "hang all the congressmen" and "give them the rope."[33]

Darby also asserted that the press was complicit in hiding the depth of the white supremacist violence that had become increasingly common in Trump's America by perpetuating the narrative of the "lone wolf," the myth that growing right-wing violence is a matter of "isolated incidents" perpetrated by disturbed individuals, disconnected from any larger pattern of organized racist violence.

Other critical perspectives likewise found their way into the public sphere: for example, an essay by Eric Foner on the history of American racism appeared in *The Nation* two days after the riot, and racist violence was a central theme in some reporting.[34] Other reports helpfully referred to an *On the Media* podcast by WNYC Studios that explained the roots of the QAnon conspiracy and the iconography that appeared so frequently in images from January 6th.

QAnon Rooted in American Gnosticism and the Anti-Semitic Blood Libel

In an interview with *On the Media* host Bob Garfield, Jeff Sharlet, professor of English at Dartmouth College, said of QAnon, "You've heard this song before."[35] As Sharlet explained, the far-right conspiracy theory QAnon is rooted in American Gnosticism and the basic premise that experts and institutions always hide the truth. Followers of QAnon believe that what we see before us is not real, a logic that opens a deep rabbit hole of conspiracy theory that has been burrowing at the fringes of American culture for a long time. Present-day Trump conspiracy theorists frequently speak of people in the "dark shadows" in power, and they are certain that Trump will bring down forces shrouded in darkness and expose them to the light. In this narrative, only their leader knows the truth and independent facts disappear.

Conspiracy theories tend to have similar structures, and the brutal QAnon narrative that Democrats are kidnapping children and cannibalizing them is little more than a makeover of the old anti-Semitic conspiracy theory of the Blood Libel. The Gnostic mindset that divides the world into purely good and evil forces and that insists the truth can't be trusted has actually been "uniting very disparate followers in belief about something sinister."[36] The idea that the election was stolen and that believers must Stop the Steal of course had no basis in fact, but that didn't matter to Trump's base as they fought to bring the latest "hidden truth" into the light.

The QAnon conspiracy theory and its iconography underlie a variety of phrases used on January 6th as well as the slogan popular among the rioters, "Dark to Light!"[37] The conspiracists' twisted logic also explains their intransigence, preventing even visual evidence from challenging beliefs that they hold as uncontested truths. In early April 2021 a Reuters/Ipsos poll demonstrated the power and scope of these conspiracy theories, finding that about half of Republicans believe the siege was largely a nonviolent "protest," or was the handiwork of left-wing activists.[38]

So the various elements that came together as the January 6th mob amounted to a toxic mix of delusional extremists that Trump gave voice to and helped unify into a violent movement. The symbolism and iconography of the costumes, secret hand signals, QAnon references, and Confederate flags of white supremacist and anti-government militias united far-right fringe believers together with anti-vaxxers, anti-maskers, and racist members of law enforcement and the military. In the absence of a sufficiently critical media, Trumpists believing in a bizarre mélange of lies seized the moment to attempt to violently overthrow American democracy.

The best way to counter conspiracy is to expose the logic of its meanings and its purpose, and then proceed to counter the lies it tells. Yet corporate media have consistently failed to expose Trumpism for what it is, and thus have been complicit in its rise.

As Trump Sets News Agenda, Media Ignore QAnon Conspiracy Codes

Trump regularly used right-wing racist, ethno-nationalist, and anti-immigrant codes and narratives, a strategy that media failed to notice even though it accounted for much of his electoral success in 2016.[39] From the moment Trump began his bid for the presidency, the phrase "false claims" proved to be entirely inadequate for countering Trumpian disinformation. Throughout his 2020 presidential campaign, no less than in 2016, Trump regularly spoke in conspiracy codes, a language that should have been easy for journalists to identify and call out, yet corporate media rarely did.

For instance, in an interview on *Fox News* with Laura Ingraham, Trump alluded to QAnon logic by saying "people that are in the dark shadows" are "controlling the streets."[40] From what he had just been discussing, he was apparently referring to BLM protests. When host Laura Ingraham pointed out that it "sounds like conspiracy theory," Trump doubled down, launching into a tale of a mysterious plane that allegedly flew from an unnamed city to Washington loaded with "thugs wearing these dark uniforms, black uniforms, with gear." Trump was likely referring to the "anarchists, paid by outsiders" in Portland, Oregon, from a point he made earlier in the interview. To QAnon followers, his vague words represented coded, secret messages about the hidden liberal forces that Trumpists must prevent from manipulating reality and causing violence. In reporting on the interview, the *Washington Post* said only that Trump's comments were met with "bafflement" or "head-scratching" from critics.[41]

Beyond failing to call out Trump's conspiracy coding, the press allowed him to establish its framing of left-wing protesters, and specifically the Black Lives Matter movement, as violent lawbreakers. That assertion was headlined in corporate media and became the dominant theme for reporting on what was, in fact, the largest people's movement in the history of the country.[42]

CORPORATE MEDIA PORTRAY BLM PROTESTORS AS VIOLENT LAWBREAKERS

Throughout the summer of 2020, media asserted in lock-step that BLM protesters were violent looters causing chaos across America's cities, a message the GOP—the "party of law and order"—also promoted. Writing for FAIR, Joshua Cho wrote that "throughout the ongoing protests this year, corporate media seemed to take every opportunity to vilify the Black Lives Matter (BLM) movement by spinning the protesters—rather than the racist and authoritarian US regime they are protesting against—as the primary instigators of violence."[43] Headline after headline in corporate media demonstrated bias against the protesters.

On June 1, 2020, an NBC News headline read "Some George Floyd Protests Turn Violent in Several West Coast Cities." The story claimed, "From Colorado to California, nearly every protest started peacefully before some people provoked confrontation."[44] The next day the *Wall Street Journal* published an article titled "Protests Sparked by George Floyd Death Descend into Violence Despite Curfews."[45] ABC News cited law enforcement reports, saying, "Police Declare Riots as Protests Turn Violent in Cities Nationwide; 1 Demonstrator Dead in Austin."[46]

Many headlines characterized protesting as an excuse for stealing and looting. One *Washington Post* headline used a euphemism for police violence while accusing protesters of criminal behavior: "Looters Smash Business Windows along Chicago's Magnificent Mile after Police-Involved Shooting."[47]

"Police are Rioting across the Nation"

Police violence was evident on the ground, and the reporting of BLM protests by media free from corporate control was strikingly different from corporate sources and far more accurate. Alternative news reported on the police riots, detailing how law enforcement routinely initiated violence. For example, as Common Dreams reported just beneath one article's headline, "Police are rioting across the nation."[48] On June 6, 2020, the Intercept offered ideological analysis and historical perspective on the protests, writing, "Police Attacks on Protesters are Rooted in a Violent Ideology of Reactionary Grievance."[49] As the Intercept noted, peaceful protesters stood bravely against "a lawless police culture" of state-sanctioned violence. Amnesty International identified human rights violations faced by protesters. The organization released a report on June 5, 2020, documenting many acts of brutality perpetrated by law enforcement against BLM protesters.[50] The study recorded 125 separate incidents of attacks against demonstrators, medics, journalists, and legal observers in forty states and Washington, DC, and told the stories of more than fifty people who were victims of the police's violence and use of excessive force.

"It's Difficult to Tell . . . Who Started What"

In many cases, US corporate media covered violent right-wing counter-demonstrations to BLM protests using the false-balance frame.[51] Coverage of a rally in Texas for Hank Gilbert, the Democratic challenger to Rep. Louie Gohmert, offers a good example. Armed counter-protesters carrying Confederate and Thin Blue Line flags—many toting military-style firearms—crashed the event, beating and robbing attendees and injuring several. Though video documentation clearly showed who instigated the attack, local news coverage portrayed it as a clash as opposed to the targeted political violence that it was.

The Tyler Morning Telegraph featured the far-right Republican Louie Gohmert claiming, "It is difficult to tell, from what I understand today, who started what."[52] Deploying a narrative of "both sides" to justify the political violence of one side ignores facts and uses neutered language to obscure the actual perpetrators of the violence. As FAIR pointed out, "Armed supporters of a far-right politician holding Confederate flags and attacking people in broad daylight in front of police, in a place like East Texas with a history of white supremacist violence, is an important event with national implications about the growing boldness and militancy of the far right."[53]

Deploying a narrative of "both sides" to justify the political violence of one side ignores facts and uses neutered language to obscure the actual perpetrators of the violence.

By August the *New York Times*, among other news outlets, employed a somewhat novel approach, worrying about the effect of BLM "violence" on swing-state voters.[54] This reporting accepted without qualms that violence was perpetrated by BLM protesters, effectively reversing reality. Preemptively blaming Trump's reelection on BLM also ignores how Trump's election-theft efforts included stoking violence by white supremacists on his behalf. As FAIR documented, corporate media ignored and minimized right-wing extremist violence, even though, as early as October 22, 2020, the *Guardian* reported that white supremacists were behind most US domestic terror attacks in 2020.[55]

Corporate media coverage left the misleading impression that the BLM uprisings spawned a massive wave of violence and property damage, yet a Princeton University/US Crisis Monitor study found that, as of September 3, 2020, 93 percent of all racial justice protests during the summer were peaceful and non-destructive.[56] More damning still were the conclusions drawn in a series of reports evaluating the police response to the summer protests. The reports, prepared by outside investigators, watchdogs, consultants, city-hired risk-management companies, and even several police departments, were compiled and reviewed by the *New York Times*, and, to the newspaper's credit (despite coming nearly nine months after the protests), it detailed the study's findings, noting the "widespread failure in policing" evident in the "startling display of violence and disarray" that law enforcement agencies were responsible for throughout the country.[57] Reviewers found that "officers behaved aggressively, wearing riot gear and spraying tear gas or 'less-lethal' projectiles in indiscriminate ways, appearing to target peaceful demonstrators and displaying little effort to de-escalate tensions," the *Times* reported. In many cities, the actions of officers made matters considerably worse.

Racist Violence on the Rise

With the exception of a long, well-researched piece in Vox, which detailed the ideology of American policing and how it justifies racist violence, corporate media failed throughout the summer of 2020 to paint a clear picture of the systematic, structural nature of police violence and killings, or its connections to white supremacy, the military, and capitalism.[58] These connections would only become apparent after investigations of the Capitol riots drew them out and establishment media then followed the story. In April 2021, Daily Kos, along with the *New York Times* and the *Washington Post*, reported on a study that traced the 377 violent rioters arrested at the Capitol and found that they were not motivated by election theft or the economy, but instead by "deep-seated resentments having nothing to do with democracy but rather with preserving and maintaining white power in this country."[59] When the study's author, Robert A. Pape, warned that political violence would not go away without "*additional information* and a strategic approach," he spoke directly to the need for vigorous and truthful reporting on white supremacist and police violence.[60]

Derek Chauvin Found Guilty on All Counts

The guilty verdict handed down to Derek Chauvin for the murder of George Floyd came about because Floyd was killed in front of dozens of witnesses who will have to live with the trauma of what they saw and filmed that day for the rest of their lives. Their documentation and testimony proved Chauvin's guilt beyond doubt. After the verdict was announced, CNN examined the language police initially used to describe Floyd's death in a story that decoded the official Minneapolis Police Department's press release, which stated "Man Dies after Medical Incident during Police Interaction."[61] Above a video clip from the trial, CNN compared witness testimony to the police language, with the heading "How Police Language Obscured the Truth." Still, no mention was made of language media used or the years of corporate reporting that parroted police reports. Instead, the many linguistic conventions that media employed for decades to obscure the truth of police killings remained unexamined.

Close to three months after Floyd was killed, *New York* magazine's website The Cut still used "died in police custody" as a descriptor of the event, but then proceeded to use more explicit language: "following a brutal police assault that was captured in a bystander video."[62] Here the magazine could have acknowledged what media studies scholars have long understood: namely, that citizens' use of cell-phone video to capture police brutality and the killing of Black people, alongside the unprecedented attention focused upon police violence by BLM organizing and protesting, created a historic anti-racist movement that ensured a murderous officer would finally be held accountable. Without such documentation and BLM protests, Derek Chauvin would most certainly have gotten away with murder—yet those same protests that have shaped contemporary American politics and shifted the way police killings can be reported were not only ignored by corporate media, they were also actively slandered, disparaged, and certainly "news abused."

GOP Election Denialism and Domestic Terrorism down the Memory Hole

As Republicans once again refused to impeach Donald Trump—this time by ignoring his incitement of the Capitol riot while holding tight to the "Big Lie" of a stolen election—media reporting of party politics remained virtually unchanged. During Biden's first one hundred days, what should have been reported as a struggle for democracy against authoritarianism, for economic justice against extreme inequality, and for diversity over white supremacy or even fascism, was couched instead as a period sorely in need of bipartisanship, with demands that Biden and Democrats negotiate with Republicans as the most important political mandate. This frame has consistently allowed Republicans to block policies popular with the American public.

Indeed, many Sunday morning shows continue to showcase Republicans who voted to overturn the election results. *Washington Post* columnist Margaret Sullivan argued that "Big Journalism" has shoved "the undemocratic efforts by some Republican elected officials to delegitimize or overturn the 2020 presidential election" down the memory hole.[63] Republican members of Congress such as Kevin McCarthy, Ted Cruz, and Ron Johnson appear without a word to viewers about how they "encouraged the Trumpian lies about election fraud that led to the violent assault on the U.S. Capitol"—and Sullivan's article was published less than four months after the coup attempt, since which time the corporate media's recuperation of these figures, as well as the memory hole necessary for their recuperation, have only grown. Princeton University history professor Kevin Kruse told Sullivan, "There's a kind of clubby atmosphere on these shows, part of the Beltway Bubble mentality, in which it's become almost impolite to raise the topic of the insurrection."

Sullivan applauded CNN's show *State of the Union*, which she cited as declining to provide a venue for the "Sedition Caucus," the 147 Republicans who, even after the

January 6th riots, voted to overturn the election results.[64] But she saved her highest praise for one all-news public radio station in Harrisburg, Pennsylvania, WITF, where journalists decided not to let Republicans forget their "damaging lies." In light of an "unprecedented assault on the fabric of American democracy," the newsroom regularly reminds listeners that some state legislators urged Congress to vote against certifying the Pennsylvania election results, and that members of Congress had voted against certifying the state's election results for President Biden. Tim Lambert, WITF's news director, told Sullivan that months before the election, "We could see the disinformation really taking hold, this idea that the only way President Trump could lose is if the election were rigged."[65]

Democracy deserves better journalism that is capable of making contextual connections between inequality and insecurity, local and global issues, health and the environment, and race and violence.

In a series of tweets dated May 16, 2021, Matt Negrin, a producer at the *Daily Show*, chided ABC's preference for Republican sources, saying, "ABC has been pushing the Big Lie for months, giving their platform to Steve Scalise, Rand Paul and other Republicans ... every week."[66] Negrin continued, "This is exactly what a coordinated misinformation campaign looks like and it's happening on a legitimate news outlet." In response to Negrin, Aaron Rupar also called out ABC for traveling "to Wyoming to interview random Trump supporters. One was given airtime to push a wild conspiracy theory about the 2020 election without any pushback." Negrin went on to argue that ABC "is not just being complicit. They are making conscious choices to air misinformation deliberately." By presenting election conspiracy theories with a veneer of legitimacy, ABC was "worse than Fox News," Negrin tweeted, because the platform provided for anti-democratic politicians by ABC "looks like a real news show."

BOTH-SIDES FRAMING OF VOTER SUPPRESSION AND THE VOTING RIGHTS BILL

Nowhere has the corporate media's both-sides framing distorted the struggle for democracy more than in coverage of new voter suppression laws and the federal voting rights bill known as the For the People Act of 2021. Investigative reporter Jane Mayer, who specializes in how "dark money" sabotages the political process, published an incisive piece in the *New Yorker* on the Republican panic over the proposed election reforms contained in the For the People Act.[67] The bill strengthens voting rights by creating automatic voter registration and expanding access to early and absentee voting. It would overhaul government ethics and campaign finance laws, and stem the flow of dark money from organizations that serve as vehicles for political donors such as the billionaire oil magnate Charles Koch.

On a conference call between dark-money groups and an aide to Mitch McConnell, Mayer reported, participants conceded that the bill was so popular, among liberal and conservative voters alike, that it wasn't worth trying to mount a public-advocacy campaign to shift opinion; indeed, polling data found overwhelming support for key provisions in the For the People Act. With the help of Data for Progress, Vox surveyed 1,138 likely voters nationally between April 16 and April 19, 2021, and found that more than "80 percent of respondents said they supported ... limiting the influence of money in politics, and modernizing election infrastructure to increase election security."[68] Those provisions would help block restrictive state bills—on redistricting, closure of polling places, voter ID requirements, and other measures that tend to decrease voter turnout and the power of the vote—that disproportionally affect Black and low-income voters. As Mayer reported, instead of trying to change such strongly positive public opinion, "a senior Koch operative said that opponents would be better off ignoring the will of American voters and trying to kill the bill in Congress."

That strategy was a perfect fit for the "both-sides" media frame employed ceaselessly on network television. Corporate media presented the story as a congressional battle, not as an example of anti-democratic Republican obstructionism against the will of the American public. One CBS headline read, "Senate Committee to Hold Markup on Controversial Voting Bill."[69] But why call a popular bill "controversial"? The popular voting bill is controversial only for dark-money donors who would prefer to restrict voting rights. CBS continued with a standardized back-and-forth, framing the controversy as a difference of opinion: "Democrats claim the bill is necessary to counter new voting restrictions being considered by multiple states, while Republicans decry it as federal overreach." Thus the struggle for democracy against the threats of authoritarianism and white supremacy are obscured and denied.

A look at the media coverage of one of the first voter suppression bills to grab national attention since the 2020 election also exemplifies this media framing. Julie Hollar's critique in *Extra!*, titled "Both-Sidesing Georgia GOP's Racist Suppression of Democracy," offers examples of "perfect false balance."[70] For example, ABC News reported,

> Democrats and voting rights advocates have blasted the bill as a voter-suppression tactic and legislative "power grab" in response to former President Donald Trump and GOP allies peddling false conspiracy theories. . . . But Republicans contend the bill increases accessibility and is meant to streamline elections, provide uniformity and address a lack of confidence in Georgia's elections "on all sides of the political spectrum," a notion Democrats dispute.

CBS followed suit, reporting, "Conservative groups hailed the legislation's passage, while liberals voiced their concern."

That style of reporting refuses to distinguish fact from fiction. There is simply no way that the Georgia voter suppression bill "increases accessibility." If journalism is to provide information to a democratic public, the claim that the bill addresses "a lack of confidence" in elections should also be exposed as a solution to a problem created by Republican conspiracy theories and lies that the election was stolen.

The false-balance frame used for Democrats and Republicans should no longer be considered actual journalism. It is simply a linguistic strategy that refuses to inform the public while blurring the line between information and wild, baseless assertion.

CONCLUSION: NEWS ABUSE ALIVE AND WELL (AND DANGEROUS AS EVER)

As we have seen, alternative media have remained far more likely to offer accurate reporting than their corporate peers; this fact makes the employment of draconian algorithms that have targeted alternative media, "de-ranking" them in search results or bouncing them from search engines entirely, ever more dangerous for American journalism and democracy.[71] At the same time, the dependency corporate press rooms formed for Trump's perpetual ratings-boosting, conspiracy-laced outrages, and the interest in all things Trump, made corporate media even less informative and more prone to "both-sidesing" than ever before.[72] As Nolan Higdon and Mickey Huff noted, corporate media that profited from Trump admitted to becoming dependent on lazy and reckless coverage of the 45th president, and it led to their failure to connect Trumpian rhetoric and his "cult of reality TV personality" to the bigger picture of "the decades-long, bipartisan embrace of neoliberalism," and it fostered their incompetence in reporting how conspiracy lies accelerated racist violence and ultimately led to domestic terrorism.[73] Because of this,

Big Journalism either missed the biggest stories of the decade or got them wrong in fundamental ways.

In the face of the ongoing rehabilitation of the Republican Party, establishment media often fail to reveal how American democracy remains at risk. Many states temporarily expanded mail and early voting in 2020 because of the COVID-19 pandemic, leading to the largest voter turnout in more than a century and a decisive win for Joe Biden. With less than 25 percent of voters now self-identifying as Republican, the GOP plan to maintain its grip on power is to push hundreds of voting restriction laws in 43 states in what critics say is the "most sweeping contraction of ballot access in the United States since the end of Reconstruction" and the beginning of Jim Crow.[74] As Robert Reich points out, "The greatest danger to American democracy right now is not coming from Russia, China, or North Korea. It is coming from the Republican Party."[75]

Today, with GOP-fueled right-wing domestic terrorism a major security threat, a militarized US foreign policy continues to drive a bloated Pentagon budget aimed at belligerencies outside of US borders, with barely a pittance aimed at cooperation with other nations to thwart a now near-certain climate catastrophe.[76] Such spending is pushed through with bipartisan agreement and little debate in US newsrooms, despite millions of Americans being out of work and in need, devastated by a pandemic that has exposed extreme racial and economic inequalities throughout the world.

Democracy deserves better journalism that is capable of making contextual connections between inequality and insecurity, local and global issues, health and the environment, and race and violence. Global and local publics need a press willing to distinguish truth from lies, not media reporting that hides behind a tired Beltway frame incapable of illuminating policies to address fairness, peace, sustainability, and global well-being.

ROBIN ANDERSEN is professor emerita at Fordham University and an award-winning author and media commentator. She is currently co-editor of the Routledge Focus Book Series on Media and Humanitarian Action. Her latest book, *Media, Central American Refugees, and the U.S. Border Crisis*, is available in paperback. She is a Project Censored judge.

Notes

1. See, e.g., Meredith Deliso, "Timeline: The Impact of George Floyd's Death in Minneapolis and Beyond," ABC News, April 21, 2021; and Yamiche Alcindor and Amna Nawaz, "What We Know about George Floyd's Death in Minneapolis Police Custody," *PBS NewsHour*, PBS, May 26, 2020, updated May 29, 2020.

2. Adam Edelman, "Biden Slams Capitol Rioters as 'Domestic Terrorists': 'Don't Dare Call Them Protesters,'" NBC News, January 7, 2021.

3. Amanda Gorman was 22 years old when she performed her poem titled "The Hill We Climb" at President Biden's inauguration. In 2017 she was also appointed the first-ever National Youth Poet Laureate. See Julia Barajas, "How a 22-Year-Old L.A. Native Became Biden's Inauguration Poet," *Los Angeles Times*, January 17, 2021, updated January 20, 2021. And Gorman appeared on the cover of *Vogue* magazine in May 2021. See Doreen St. Félix, "The Rise and Rise of Amanda Gorman," *Vogue*, April 7, 2021.

4. Media scholars have long criticized media's "both-sides" professional canon. The term "false balancing" was used by Michael Parenti in his introduction to *20 Years of Censored News*, eds. Carl Jensen and Project Censored (New York: Seven Stories Press, 1997), and in his article "Monopoly Media Manipulation," posted on the Michael Parenti Political Archive, May 2001. The terms "both-sidesing" and "false balancing" are used interchangeably here.

5. Zachary Petrizzo, "Republicans are Trying to Bully a GOP Lawmaker out of Congress for Insufficient Loyalty to Trump," Salon, May 10, 2021.

6. Eric Black, "On 'A Brief History of Fascist Lies' and Its Current Relevance," MinnPost, May 1, 2020.

7. "Majority of Republicans Still Believe the 2020 Election was Stolen from Donald Trump," Ipsos, April 2, 2021.

8. Marisa Peñaloza, "Trump Supporters Storm U.S. Capitol, Clash with Police," NPR, January 6, 2021, 9:33 a.m., updated 3:08 p.m.

9. Jordan Klepper, "Jordan Klepper Sees It All at the Capitol Insurrection | The Daily Social Distancing Show," *The Daily Show with Trevor Noah*, Comedy Central, posted to YouTube by The Daily Show with Trevor Noah on January 12, 2021.

10. "Nation Conversation | Insurrection 2021," a livestreamed panel featuring Melissa Harris-Perry, Elie Mystal, and Eric Foner, hosted by Katrina vanden Heuvel, and moderated by John Nichols, *The Nation*, January 13, 2021. Mystal's comment begins at 14 minutes 55 seconds.

11. See the U.S. Press Freedom Tracker, which aggregated all documented instances in which members of the press were assaulted, arrested, or had their equipment damaged while covering the riot. The phrase "Murder the media" was documented by the *New York Times*: Tiffany Hsu and Katie Robertson, "Covering Pro-Trump Mobs, the News Media Became a Target," January 6, 2021. See also Katherine Jacobsen and Lucy Westcott, "'Three People Threatened to Shoot Me.' Journalists Describe Covering Mob Violence at the US Capitol," Committee to Protect Journalists, January 7, 2021.

12. Amanda Taub, "It Wasn't Strictly a Coup Attempt. But It's Not Over, Either," *New York Times*, January 7, 2021, updated February 12, 2021; and Caleb Ecarma, "Tucker Carlson Bizarrely Blames the FBI for MAGA Riot," *Vanity Fair*, June 16, 2021.

13. Mark Danner, "'Be Ready to Fight,'" *New York Review of Books*, February 11, 2021.

14. "Chuck Schumer's Statement to the Senate on the Storming of the Capitol," *U.S. News & World Report*, January 6, 2021.

15. Leonard Downie Jr. and Robert G. Kaiser, *The News about the News: American Journalism in Peril* (New York: Alfred A. Knopf, 2002), 54.

16. Emma Grey Ellis, "The DC Mobs Could Become a Mythologized Recruitment Tool," *Wired*, January 8, 2021.

17. Luke Mogelson, "Among the Insurrectionists," *New Yorker*, January 15, 2021.

18. Morgan Chalfant, "Trump: 'The Only Way We're Going to Lose This Election is If the Election is Rigged,'" The Hill, August 17, 2020.

19. Barbara Sprunt, "Trump Falsely Claims That Votes Shouldn't be Counted after Election Day," NPR, November 1, 2020.

20. Brian Naylor, "Read Trump's Jan. 6 Speech, A Key Part of Impeachment Trial," NPR, February 10, 2021.

21. Connor Perrett, "The Trump Campaign is Waging an All-Out Legal War to Stop the Expansion of Vote-by-Mail in 7 Different States," Business Insider, September 27, 2020.

22. Tim Elfrink, "Trump Says That as Soon as Election Day Ends, 'We're Going in With Our Lawyers,'" *Washington Post*, November 2, 2020.

23. Robin Andersen, "Media Fail to Prepare Public for Potential Trump Coup," Fairness & Accuracy In Reporting (FAIR), November 4, 2020.

24. Elfrink, "Trump Says That as Soon as Election Day Ends."

25.   Joshua Cho, "Journalists Need to be Clear about a Clear Threat to Democracy," Fairness & Accuracy In Reporting (FAIR), September 15, 2020.

26.   The newspapers identified in FAIR's research were the *New York Times*, *Washington Post*, *Wall Street Journal*, *Houston Chronicle*, *Chicago Tribune*, *Star Tribune*, *Los Angeles Times*, and *USA Today*. They are among the largest newspapers in the country based on circulation.

27.   Andersen, "Media Fail to Prepare Public."

28.   Bill McKibben, "If Trump Goes Even Lower, We'd Better be Prepared," *New Yorker*, June 3, 2020.

29.   Zack Malitz, Brandon Evans, and Becky Bond, "To Stop Trump Stealing the Election, Democrats Must Do These 3 Things," *The Nation*, October 29, 2020.

30.   Frances Fox Piven and Deepak Bhargava, "What If Trump Won't Leave?" The Intercept, August 11, 2020.

31.   Seyward Darby, "The Far Right Told Us What It Planned. We Didn't Listen," *New York Times*, January 7, 2021.

32.   Ibid., quoting from "Andrew Macdonald" [pseud. William Luther Pierce], *The Turner Diaries* (Washington, DC: National Vanguard Books, 1978), Chapter XXIII.

33.   Hannah Gais (@hannahgais), Twitter post, January 6, 2021, 2:15 p.m.

34.   Eric Foner, "The Capitol Riot Reveals the Dangers from the Enemy Within," *The Nation*, January 8, 2021; and see, for example, Averi Harper, "Capitol Attack Conjures American Legacy of Racial Violence," ABC News, January 19, 2021.

35.   See "Extended Version: The Ancient Heresy That Helps Us Understand QAnon," *On the Media*, WNYC Studios, produced by Eloise Blondiau and hosted by Bob Garfield, November 23, 2020; Sharlet's quote begins at 8 minutes 45 seconds. Sharlet also reported for *Vanity Fair* on Trump's 2020 campaign.

36.   Ibid., spoken by Bob Garfield at 20 minutes 55 seconds.

37.   Kerry Howley, "QAnon and the Bright Rise of Belief," Intelligencer, January 29, 2021.

38.   James Oliphant and Chris Kahn, "Half of Republicans Believe False Accounts of Deadly U.S. Capitol Riot—Reuters/Ipsos Poll," Reuters, April 5, 2021.

39.   Robin Andersen, "Weaponizing Social Media: 'The Alt-Right,' the Election of Donald J. Trump, and the Rise of Ethno-Nationalism in the United States," in *The Routledge Companion to Media and Humanitarian Action*, eds. Robin Andersen and Purnaka L. de Silva (New York: Routledge, 2017), 487–500.

40.   Laura Ingraham, interview with Donald Trump, *The Ingraham Angle*, Fox News, August 31, 2020. Posted to YouTube by "Factbase Videos" on September 1, 2020; Trump's quote begins at 15 minutes 25 seconds.

41.   Katie Shepherd, "Trump Blames People in 'Dark Shadows' for Protest Violence, Cites Mysterious Plane Full of 'Thugs' in Black," *Washington Post*, September 1, 2020.

42.   Civis Analytics, a data science firm, along with three other data research organizations, found that 15 to 26 million people had participated in protests during the weeks that followed George Floyd's killing, a number

significantly larger than the three to five million people who participated in the Women's March of 2017. See Larry Buchanan, Quoctrung Bui, and Jugal K. Patel, "Black Lives Matter May be the Largest Movement in U.S. History," *New York Times*, July 3, 2020.

43. Joshua Cho, "Corporate Media Reverse Reality by Blaming BLM Protesters for Everything," Fairness & Accuracy In Reporting (FAIR), November 3, 2020.

44. "Some George Floyd Protests Turn Violent in Several West Coast Cities," NBC News, June 1, 2020.

45. Andrew Tangel, Erin Ailworth, Akane Otani, and Katie Honan, "Protests Sparked by George Floyd Death Descend into Violence Despite Curfews," *Wall Street Journal*, June 2, 2020.

46. Bill Hutchinson, "Police Declare Riots as Protests Turn Violent in Cities Nationwide; 1 Demonstrator Dead in Austin," ABC News, July 26, 2020.

47. Mark Guarino, Tim Elfrink, and Teo Armus, "Looters Smash Business Windows along Chicago's Magnificent Mile after Police-Involved Shooting," *Washington Post*, August 10, 2020.

48. Eoin Higgins, "Despite Claims from Officials, Demonstrators Say Police, Not Protesters, are Real 'Outside Agitators,'" Common Dreams, June 1, 2020. The article attributed the statement to Gregory McKelvey, a political organizer from Portland, Oregon.

49. Ryan Devereaux, "Police Attacks on Protesters are Rooted in a Violent Ideology of Reactionary Grievance," The Intercept, June 6, 2020.

50. "Black Lives Matter Protests: Mapping Police Violence across the USA," Amnesty International, June 5, 2020.

51. See "Portland Protest Turns Violent, Federal Police Clear Plaza," Associated Press, August 22, 2020.

52. See John Anderson, "Police and Gohmert React to Violent Protests in Tyler," *Tyler Morning Telegraph*, July 27, 2020, updated September 4, 2020; and John Anderson, "Tyler Protests: New Video of Assault," *Tyler Morning Telegraph*, July 30, 2020, updated June 17, 2021.

53. Henry Brannan, "On Right-Wing Violence in Texas, Media's Silence Sends Message," Fairness & Accuracy In Reporting (FAIR), August 11, 2020.

54. Sabrina Tavernise and Ellen Almer Durston, "How Chaos in Kenosha is Already Swaying Some Voters in Wisconsin," *New York Times*, August 26, 2020, updated October 16, 2020.

55. Brannan, "On Right-Wing Violence"; and Lois Beckett, "White Supremacists Behind Majority of US Domestic Terror Attacks in 2020," *The Guardian*, October 22, 2020.

56. Roudabeh Kishi and Sam Jones, "Demonstrations & Political Violence in America: New Data for Summer 2020," US Crisis Monitor (Armed Conflict Location & Event Data Project [ACLED]), September 2020.

57. Kim Barker, Mike Baker, and Ali Watkins, "In City After City, Police Mishandled Black Lives Matter Protests," *New York Times*, March 20, 2021, updated June 28, 2021.

58. Zack Beauchamp, "What the Police Really Believe," Vox, July 7, 2020.

59. "Dartagnan," "Study Indicates the Jan. 6 Riots were Motivated by Racism and White Resentment, Not 'Election Theft,'" Daily Kos, April 6, 2021. See also Alan Feuer, "Fears of White People Losing Out Permeate

Capitol Rioters' Towns, Study Finds," *New York Times*, April 6, 2021; and Robert A. Pape, "What an Analysis of 377 Americans Arrested or Charged in the Capitol Insurrection Tells Us," *Washington Post*, April 6, 2021.

60. Feuer, "Fears of White People." Emphasis added.

61. Eric Levenson, "How Minneapolis Police First Described the Murder of George Floyd, and What We Know Now," CNN, April 21, 2021.

62. Hannah Gold, "Everything We Know about the Killing of George Floyd," The Cut, August 10, 2020.

63. Margaret Sullivan, "The Politicians Who Tried to Overturn an Election—And the Local News Team That Won't Let Anyone Forget It," *Washington Post*, May 2, 2021.

64. Ibid. See also Karen Yourish, Larry Buchanan, and Denise Lu, "The 147 Republicans Who Voted to Overturn Election Results," *New York Times*, January 7, 2021.

65. Sullivan, "The Politicians Who Tried to Overturn an Election."

66. Matt Negrin (@MattNegrin), Twitter post, May 16, 2021, 10:26 a.m.

67. Jane Mayer, "Inside the Koch-Backed Effort to Block the Largest Election-Reform Bill in Half a Century," *New Yorker*, March 29, 2021.

68. Andrew Prokop, "Republicans Feared Democrats' Voting Protections Bill Polls Well. A New Poll Says They're Right," Vox, May 3, 2021. Furthermore, Vox reported, "More than 60 percent of respondents supported requiring nonpartisan redistricting commissions, a 15-day early voting period for all federal elections, same-day registration for all eligible voters, automatic voter registration for all eligible voters, and giving every voter the option to vote by mail."

69. Bob Brigham, "Top Dem Lawyer Blasts CBS News: 'Do You Really Need to Both-Sides Democracy?'" AlterNet, May 9, 2021. This article comments on and quotes from Grace Segers, "Senate Committee to Hold Markup on Controversial Voting Bill," CBS News, May 9, 2021.

70. Julie Hollar, "Both-Sidesing Georgia GOP's Racist Suppression of Democracy," *Extra!*, Vol. 34 No. 4 (May 2021), originally posted online as "Media Manage to Both-Sides Georgia GOP's Suppressing Democracy," Fairness & Accuracy In Reporting (FAIR), April 8, 2021. This article comments on and quotes from Quinn Scanlan, "Kemp Signs Sweeping Elections Bill Passed by Georgia Legislature. Here's What's in It," ABC News, March 25, 2021; and "Georgia Republicans Pass Sweeping Voting Restrictions," CBS News, March 26, 2021.

71. Robin Andersen, "Backlash Against Russian 'Fake News' is Shutting Down Debate for Real," Fairness & Accuracy In Reporting (FAIR), November 29, 2017.

72. Ken Doctor, "Trump Bump Grows into Subscription Surge—And Not Just for the New York Times," TheStreet, March 3, 2017.

73. Nolan Higdon and Mickey Huff, "Ripe for Fascism: A Post-Coup d'Trump Autopsy of American Democracy," *CounterPunch*, January 14, 2021.

74. "Party Affiliation," Gallup, undated [accessed July 2, 2021]; and Amy Gardner, Kate Rabinowitz, and Harry Stevens, "How GOP-Backed Voting Measures Could Create Hurdles for Tens of Millions of Voters," *Washington Post*, March 11, 2021. See also Jake Johnson, "In 'Perilous

Moment for Our Democracy,' 100+ Push Schumer, Dems to Nuke Filibuster," *Common Dreams*, June 3, 2021.

75. Robert Reich, "The Republican Party is an Existential Threat to American Democracy," *Common Dreams*, June 1, 2021.

76. "Domestic Violent Extremism Poses Heightened Threat in 2021," Office of the Director of National Intelligence, shared by the *New York Times*, March 1, 2021; and Medea Benjamin and Marcy Winograd, "Schumer's Anti-China Bill Sacrifices Climate for Empire," *CounterPunch*, June 4, 2021.

CHAPTER 5

Media Democracy in Action

Contributions by MICHELLE RODINO-COLOCINO and
BRIAN DOLBER (*The Gig Economy*), JOHN K. WILSON
(Academe Blog), MICHAEL GORDON (The Propwatch Project),
SONALI KOLHATKAR (*Rising Up with Sonali*), RACHAEL
JOLLEY (Centre for Freedom of the Media, University of Sheffield),
and ALISON TROPE and DJ JOHNSON (Critical Media Project)

Edited and introduced by ANDY LEE ROTH

"Under the impact of propaganda," Walter Lippmann wrote a century ago, in 1922, "the old constants of our thinking have become variables."[1] Writing in the aftermath of the First World War, the 1918 influenza pandemic, and the Palmer Raids, Lippmann asserted that it was no longer possible to believe in "the original dogma of democracy."[2] Despite his grave diagnosis, Lippmann, one of his era's leading journalists and political commentators, articulated a strenuous vision of a revitalized democracy and better future. His call a century ago—for institutions and education that could sharply distinguish "the realities of public life" from "self-centered opinion"—is newly relevant now.[3]

We, too, live in an era when the dogma of democracy is subjected to the sharpest criticism, and democracy is under threat from citizens who prize self-centered opinion above the common good. Many of our constants have also become variable. These changes can lead to anxiety and conflict—as Americans confront privilege and reckon with the nation's legacies of systemic racism and economic inequality, for instance; but questioning the "constants of our thinking" can also produce new ways to make sense of the world and our place in it.

This possibility informs each of the contributions to this year's Media Democracy in Action chapter. The chapter's authors provide insights into the kinds of institutions and education we need to make good on Lippmann's vision—one where the destruction of prejudice leads to a "radical enlargement of the range of attention," disintegrating our "hard, simple version of the world" and constructing a new understanding that is "vivid and full."[4]

To begin this chapter, Michelle Rodino-Colocino and Brian Dolber show how digital platforms have contributed to the development of a "gig economy" based on an increasingly large and precarious force of temporary and on-call workers, framed as "independent contractors." Where Rodino-Colocino and Dolber highlight the double-edged qualities of digital platforms in gig workers' efforts to establish and expand basic working rights, John K. Wilson's article on Big Tech's threats to higher education shows how companies such as Zoom jeopardize colleges and universities' moral and legal obligations to reject censorship.

Censorship and propaganda are two sides of the same coin: silence the undesirable voice, promote the "correct" one.[5] The Propwatch Project exposes how and why basic propaganda techniques work. As Michael Gordon describes here, the Propwatch Project website features a unique video repository of propaganda techniques, allowing visitors to view and identify often stealthy and otherwise unnoticed techniques at work in real-time. We believe Lippmann would have applauded this crucial work.

Sonali Kolhatkar reflects on lessons learned from pursuing independent investigative journalism as a vocation. Even as she confirms "the gargantuan task of pushing back against powerful media institutions," Kolhatkar's insights, based on creating and sustaining a progressive news program run by women, will no doubt inspire subsequent generations of muckrakers.

Kolhatkar draws parallels between her work as an independent journalist and her past experience as a scientist. In her teaching of journalism, Rachael Jolley invokes another comparable profession by drawing on classic and contemporary detectives from novels and TV as models of inquiry. Here Jolley highlights how she encourages budding journalists to hone their skills of detection as they investigate clues and construct cases.

Digging beneath the surface to discern hidden patterns is also an aim of the Critical Media Project (CMP). As Alison Trope and DJ Johnson explain, the Critical Media Project hosts an extensive collection of clips from movies, television, advertisements, news, documentaries, and online viral videos that are tagged and categorized to allow the website's visitors to explore media constructions of social identity. Promoting critical media literacy, the CMP not only shows how media systems uphold hierarchies of power, but also how those same systems can be used to upend them.

The individuals and projects spotlighted here exemplify what Project Censored means by 'media democracy in action.' Their work provides keen insights and proven resources to rescue democracy from dogma, by countering what Lippmann characterized as "self-centered opinion" with "the realities of public life." Read on to become informed and inspired.

Gig Work in the Age of Convergence

MICHELLE RODINO-COLOCINO AND BRIAN DOLBER

So-called "gig economy" companies have peddled myths of tech-enabled flexibility and entrepreneurship for more than a decade, masking their extension of familiar forms of exploitation. Wage theft, contingency, and risk of bodily harm have defined labor under capitalism from slavery to manufacturing and from service jobs to gig work. Since the start of the COVID-19 pandemic, these injustices have taken on new dimensions, as workers have been compelled to work harder for less while assuming greater risk. For Uber and Lyft drivers as well as for domestic workers, employment in the pandemic has required labor in close contact with people, without company-supplied personal protective equipment (PPE), without payment for risk to health or additional time worked (disinfecting vehicles and equipment, for example), and without paid sick or caregiving leave for those stricken by COVID. The usual indignities persist: working long hours often at sub-minimum wage, in unsafe conditions, without full payment for time worked, and, in the United States, without employer- or tax-funded healthcare benefits.

The Gig Economy: Workers and Media in the Age of Convergence, our new edited collection, examines the complex and historical relationships among gig labor, media, and workers that predate the pandemic with the aim of exposing and ending exploitation in the gig economy and beyond.[6] We define 'convergence' as the coming together of social, economic, political, cultural, historical, and technological forces. While many analyses uncritically cast the nebulous "platform" as an agent of change or focus ahistorically on present forms of gig labor, this volume takes a critical approach, grounded in political economy, to explore broader questions around convergence that connect history and relationships to wider systems of power,

---

"The COVID-19 pandemic converged with gig labor to create new class formations under the rubric of 'essential work' that put workers' lives and livelihoods at additional risk."

—Michelle Rodino-Colocino and Brian Dolber

---

including capitalism and struggles for social justice.[7] From taxi and Uber drivers, to hospitality workers and Airbnb hosts, from podcasters and radio presenters (working in fields historically dominated by white male hosts) to Latina audiobook narrators and women web cammers of color, the book's contributors explore how media and telecommunications systems integral to the extraction and circulation of value under capitalism can innovate in new contexts and expand opportunities for creating a fair economy. Each chapter examines experiences of and resistance to exploitative aspects of the gig economy, employing multiple theoretical perspectives (such as political economy and feminism) and methodologies (including ethnography, history, discourse analysis, and community-based participatory research) in a variety of national contexts. We consider the roles played by media, policy, culture, and history, alongside gender, immigrant status, ethnic background, and racial identity in forging working conditions in the "gig economy."

The Gig Economy draws on editors' and authors' engaged research into gig labor and organizing as well as their experiences as scholar-activists. Editors Brian Dolber, Chenjerai Kumanyika, Michelle Rodino-Colocino, and Todd Wolfson have worked as organizers and scholars of gig work (even back before it was called "gig work") in their local communities. Authors critically analyze efforts to collectively organize as gig workers, sometimes through the use of digital platforms. These struggles occur in par- adigmatic gig occupations, such as rideshare and delivery, and in academia. *The Gig Economy* argues that the con- tradictions and convergences of the gig economy produce new possibilities for collective organizing.

For Brian, who worked as a scholar-activist organizer with Rideshare Drivers United (RDU), the year leading up to the 2020 pandemic and elections underscored the importance of workers' organizing to shape public dis- course and change working conditions. In March 2019 the fledgling, independent California-based union orga- nized a one-day strike in Los Angeles and San Diego several days ahead of Lyft's Initial Public Offering (IPO). Countering major unions' neglect of on-the-ground orga- nizing of platform workers, RDU engaged in app-based organizing and social media advertising to initiate work-er-to-worker conversations that helped build a strong, militant community of drivers in California.[8] Press coverage connected RDU to emerging driver organizations throughout the United States and across the globe, leading to calls for a larger, international strike on May 8, 2019, the week of Uber's much-hyped IPO.

Although only a small fraction of workers participated, the March and May strikes of 2019 generated significant attention from corporate and progressive media outlets. Joining the wave of organizing that swept digital newsrooms, gig workers challenged Silicon Valley and Wall Street celebrations of tech entrepreneurship and flexibility with stories of declining wages, longer hours, poverty, and houselessness.[9] Drivers impacted investor confidence, translating into falling stock prices and an investor lawsuit, while also attracting the attention of a broad coalition of unions and lawmakers. With the media's legitimation, RDU helped to win recognition of gig workers' employee status and, by extension, collective bargaining rights through a state law known widely as AB5 (California Assembly Bill 5).

Yet if media power was instrumental in this victory, it was also central to workers' subsequent defeat. By unleashing 220 million dollars' worth of propaganda onto the California electorate—including ads on social media, TV, and billboards—Uber, Lyft, DoorDash, and Postmates (as it was being acquired by Uber) overturned the victory of AB5 with the passage of Proposition 22. Prop 22 is a reactionary law that exempts app-deployed drivers and delivery workers from AB5 and places them in a unique category of second-class workers who lack basic worker rights. For weeks leading up to the November 2020 election, Uber and Lyft funded "woke washed" ads boasting a multiracial cast of gig workers proclaiming desires for freedom and advocating for the substandard benefits that Prop 22 offered.[10] Rideshare Drivers United waged their own campaign, in solidarity with a broader coalition of unions and rideshare organizations, culminating in a statewide caravan that doubled as a media and organizing event. But the regressive measure ultimately passed with 58.6 percent of the vote, a case study in the power of political advertising and our system of journalism's inability to sufficiently challenge it.

As we write during our second pandemic spring, contradictory forces that alternately threaten and support gig workers continue to converge. With much of the United States preparing to "reopen," amid California's Right-led recall effort to unseat Democratic Governor Gavin Newsom, Uber and Lyft are offering attractive bonuses to entice drivers back onto the road, where they risk driving without paid sick leave, PPE, or fair pay. Meanwhile, the Biden administration supports the PRO Act (Protecting the Right to Organize Act) that would extend collective bargaining rights to misclassified workers (among other crucial reforms to the 1947 Taft–Hartley Act). Additionally, the Department of Labor has reversed a Trump administration memo that held app-based workers were independent contractors.

Our edited collection, coming in the wake of 2020's myriad challenges, underscores the importance of organizing even amidst crises and contradictions to advance workers' rights. As we conclude in *The Gig Economy*, the COVID-19 pandemic converged with gig labor to create new class formations under the rubric of "essential work" that put workers' lives and livelihoods at additional risk. Such developments highlight enduring exploitation as well as the potential for new class identities and democratic media to build solidarity and means for collective organizing. New paths for creating solidarity and systemic change are emerging. We call on readers of *State of the Free Press 2022* to join collective efforts for wider political economic reform that will embolden workers on the job, in the media, and in the streets.

MICHELLE RODINO-COLOCINO is associate professor of media studies in the Bellisario College of Communications at Penn State. The author of more than fifty publications in major journals of critical communication and feminist media studies, books, and outlets for public scholarship, she is currently writing a strategic history of labor management, media, and organizing. She has studied and engaged in labor organizing since the late 1990s with WashTech (Washington Alliance of Technology Workers/TNG-CWA Local 37083). Find her satirical performances @rocofem on Instagram.

BRIAN DOLBER is associate professor of communication at California State University San Marcos, and holds a PhD in communication from the University of Illinois, Urbana-Champaign. He is the author of *Media and Culture in the U.S. Jewish Labor Movement: Sweating for Democracy in the Interwar Era* (Palgrave, 2017), and his articles have appeared in venues including *Communication, Culture & Critique*; *Communication Theory*; and *tripleC: Communication, Capitalism & Critique*. Dolber is an organizer with Rideshare Drivers United and has twenty years of experience working in the labor movement.

Big Tech and the Threat to Academic Freedom

JOHN K. WILSON

As the COVID-19 pandemic swept the world, billions of people became more dependent on technology. Higher education in particular made tech companies essential partners to put classes and events online. But the power of technology to reach a global audience is also the power to censor, and colleges have seen new threats to academic freedom from Big Tech.

The most notable case of censorship began on September 23, 2020 at San Francisco State University (SFSU), when an open classroom webinar featuring Leila Khaled was banned by Zoom, Facebook, and YouTube.[11] Earlier, 86 organizations signed a letter to SFSU President Lynn Mahoney demanding the cancelation of the event and the permanent deplatforming of Khaled.[12] When that attempt at censorship failed, these anti-Palestinian groups turned to the corporations that provide access to technology. Tech companies, flooded with complaints, turned to a familiar excuse for censorship: Terrorism. Khaled is a member of the Popular Front for the Liberation of Palestine, a designated terror organization in the United States, and she hijacked two planes in 1969 and 1970.[13]

When groups accused Zoom, Facebook, and YouTube of providing "material support" to terrorists by allowing an academic discussion, the tech companies quickly gave in and canceled the platforms they provided for streaming the event, even though the law also applies to the universities organizing the panel and none have ever been prosecuted for providing material support to terrorists as a result of hosting an academic discussion. To protest the censorship, the American Association of University Professors (AAUP) chapter at New York University held an event on October 23, 2020 that included Khaled, and it was also censored by Zoom.[14]

The University of California faculty senate's Committee on Academic Freedom issued a statement condemning the power of Big Tech to censor campus events and classrooms: "Zoom has the ability to censor University content on the basis of criteria—such as indecency, falsity, goriness, or the promotion of hostility—that would be unconstitutional for the University to employ in some contexts, and a serious violation of academic freedom in many other contexts."[15]

"Colleges have a moral and legal obligation to reject censorship, and they cannot outsource repression to private corporations."

—John K. Wilson

In response to criticism, Zoom issued a new policy in April 2021, "On Academic Freedom for Our Higher Education Users," declaring that the company will not act on outside complaints based on Zoom's broad content-based rules when meetings are hosted by a college.[16] Zoom's move received very positive responses in the media, with headlines such as "Zoom Addresses Academic Freedom Concerns."[17] However, legal-based complaints were not covered by the new rule, and a few days later (with almost no media coverage), Zoom banned yet another anti-censorship event with Khaled. The University of California at Merced event "Whose Narratives? What Free Speech for Palestine?" was planned for April 23, 2021, but was banned by Zoom, Facebook, YouTube, and Eventbrite.[18]

Big Tech censorship of academia is spreading. In April 2021, Facebook deleted the entire page of the Arab and Muslim Ethnicities and Diasporas program at San Francisco State University, which co-sponsored the April 23rd event with Khaled.[19]

Online censorship goes far beyond the question of terrorism. In October 2020 the Critical Media Literacy Conference of the Americas (co-sponsored by Project Censored) took place online, but a few weeks later all recordings of the event mysteriously disappeared from YouTube. As Mickey Huff noted, "There is no violation, there was no reasoning, there was no warning, there was not an explanation, there was no nothing. The entire channel was just gone."[20]

Unlike academia, where detailed policies and due process procedures govern complaints, the tech world's approach to censorship has been full of mystery. Videos are disappeared and events are banished with a Kafkaesque uncertainty about what has happened or why, and no avenue can be found for an appeal. Colleges have a moral and legal obligation to reject censorship, and they cannot outsource repression to private corporations. Higher education needs to demand better policies from tech companies to ensure that free expression in academic work is protected, and must monitor the problem to help bring high standards of academic freedom to the tech world.

For those on the Left who demand that tech companies censor speech that they think wrong or offensive, this should serve as a chilling reminder that censorship remains a dangerous weapon often turned against progressives. It's also a reminder of the vulnerability of online learning under corporate control, as companies that always value profit over principle will gladly abandon academic freedom at any opportunity.

JOHN K. WILSON is a contributing editor at https://academeblog.org/ for the American Association for University Professors. He was a 2019–20 fellow at the University of California National Center for Free Speech and Civic Engagement, and he is the author of eight books, including *Patriotic Correctness: Academic Freedom and Its Enemies*, *The Most Dangerous Man in America: Rush Limbaugh's Assault on Reason*, and *Trump Unveiled: Exposing the Bigoted Billionaire*.

Combating Propaganda and Disinformation through the Messaging Strategy of Inoculation: The Propwatch Project

MICHAEL GORDON

On January 6, 2021, on a 52-acre park just south of the White House, President Donald Trump delivered a speech at the "Save America Rally" to a large crowd of supporters.[21] His speech, which lasted more than an hour, centered on claims of election fraud in the 2020 presidential election. He declared, "They rigged an election. They rigged it like they've never rigged an election before. [...] Today I will lay out just some of the evidence proving that we won this election and we won it by a landslide."[22] After the rally ended, the crowd of thousands walked up Pennsylvania Ave., forced their way through police lines, and stormed the US Capitol.[23]

The road to the siege of the Capitol that day didn't start with the rally at the Ellipse that morning; it didn't start on November 7th, the day the Associated Press called the race for Biden, or in mid-August, when Donald Trump started claiming that mail-in voting would guarantee a stolen election.[24] By that time, the American electorate had already been subjected to four years of a sustained propaganda and disinformation campaign—one which would leave the nation divided, mired in fear and conspiracy, confused, and mentally exhausted. The social unrest and mayhem of January 6th was not an aberration, but the predictable fruits of that campaign.

Many factors in the last decade have set the stage for propaganda's ominous resurgence, but perhaps none has been more pivotal than the rise of social media. What Sacha Baron Cohen called, in his 2019 Anti-Defamation League Award acceptance speech, "the greatest propaganda machine in history,"[25] social media has vastly increased the propagandists' reach and potential impact. These platforms make it both easy and cheap to microtarget political messaging to niche segments of society with certain pre-existing attitudes or values. Those same individuals can then amplify that messaging through interpersonal communications with family and friends, and that process can be repeated again and again.

Further exacerbating the situation are longstanding efforts to destroy the credibility of more traditional media, with average levels of trust in the media sinking to historic lows. Gallup polling from 2019 showed Americans' trust in newspapers and television and radio journalism has fallen four percentage points in just one year, with confidence in media veracity reported by 69 percent of Democrats, 36 percent of independents, and just 15 percent of Republicans.[26] All these factors—the rise of social media, the fall of trust in traditional news media, and the renewed pervasiveness of disinformation from the highest levels of government—together have culminated in a perfect storm, where propaganda has both the method and means to shape public opinion as at no other time in human history.

It is within this perfect storm that the Propwatch Project was conceived and launched. The unique platform catalogs and cross-references embedded video segments to deliver the world's first searchable video repository of propaganda techniques. Visitors to the propwatch.org website can not only view and identify propaganda techniques being executed in real time, but can learn how and why they work.

The project's methodology is based on the preemptive messaging strategy of inoculation, one of the few methods scientifically proven to protect an individual's attitudes and beliefs against devices of manipulation.[27] Similar to the medical inoculation process, by preemptively exposing the message receiver to prior instances of propaganda, a process of threat identification and defense response can be triggered, which can then lead to future resistance to propaganda in any subsequent encounters.

At the core of the project are minute-by-minute analyses of current national and statewide debates, interviews, and speeches for the presence of propaganda, from which hundreds of authentic examples are isolated. For inoculation to work effectively, the message receiver must first realize the threat. Using authentic examples of propaganda techniques in action rather than scripting presentations or hypothetical scenarios helps drive home what makes these techniques so threatening and immediately relevant. It is one thing to read the definition of a propaganda technique; it is another thing entirely to see the technique being performed in a national debate by elected officials or those running for office.

The project also showcases leading academics, researchers, and authors from around the world, who discuss the devices of propaganda and disinformation and explain how and why they work. A recent filmed interview with Tom Stafford, cognitive scientist at the University of Sheffield, UK, explores the illusory truth effect and how repetition can influence what is perceived as truth. In another video, Eric Oliver, from the University of Chicago, discusses the roles that intuition and feelings of uncertainty play in fueling conspiracy theories and political polarization and what can be done to bridge the divisions they create. These experts provide a peek behind the curtain and help explain not only how these devices of persuasion work, but also what can be done to overcome them.

And overcoming the grip of propaganda and disinformation is critical, as the events of January 6, 2021 demonstrate. It is within that chaotic scene of Americans forcing their way through Capitol police barricades that we begin to confront the destabilizing and radicalizing influence propaganda and disinformation can have on an anxious public—an influence that not only manifests itself in an attack on an American institution, but an attack on democracy itself.

THE PROPWATCH PROJECT is a 501(c)(3) educational nonprofit, whose mission is to raise public awareness about the prevalence of propaganda and disinformation. Find the Propwatch Project online at https://www.propwatch.org/.

MICHAEL GORDON is the founder and senior editor of the Propwatch Project and a professor with the College of Computer and Information Technology at St. Petersburg College, a National Center of Academic Excellence in Cyber Defense.

Rising Up with Sonali: A Women-Run Progressive News Broadcast

SONALI KOLHATKAR

As an independent journalist working to report and analyze the news, I face plenty of obstacles in bringing a well-researched story to public attention, yet one of the biggest challenges I face is how to beat corporate media at their own game with only a fraction of the resources to draw on. Armies of writers, reporters, and editors working in for-profit corporate newsrooms shape the dominant narratives on stories of importance to the public, leaving out crucial context, downplaying historical frameworks, bowing to right-wing cultural influences for fear of being seen as too leftist, and offering simplistic analyses aligned with the political, military, and economic objectives of the State Department and corporate PR efforts. Often, well-funded, for-profit media outlets take no notice of stories until they become too big to ignore. Independent journalists like me face the gargantuan task of pushing back against powerful media institutions while struggling to maintain the tenuous funding needed to remain afloat. Even as we worry about next month's bills, we probe stories far deeper than our corporate competitors.

Unlike most professional journalists, I came into this field without a degree in journalism. I studied science in college, obtaining a Master of Science degree in Astrophysics with the hopes of pursuing an academic career. But in 2002 I switched careers, leaving a Caltech job to realize my desire to do something more meaningful: I began hosting a daily radio news show at KPFK Pacifica Radio in Los

---

"Journalism is a combination of science and education—making sense of society using something very much like the "scientific method" and synthesizing that information into a format that serves the public and fosters democracy. To me, it seems natural that journalism is about holding powerful elites accountable, exposing abuse, and centering struggles for justice."

—Sonali Kolhatkar

Angeles. As a brown-skinned immigrant woman with a foreign-sounding name and a perceptible accent, I realized I was in many ways the antithesis of a traditional broadcast journalist. But in the world of independent media, I was welcomed and found my true calling.

I learned new skills on the job, finding that my background as a scientist was well-suited to journalism. After all, the goal of science is to make sense of the physical world. Journalism is a combination of science and education—making sense of society using something very much like the "scientific method" and synthesizing that information into a format that serves the public and fosters democracy. To me, it seems natural that journalism is about holding powerful elites accountable, exposing abuse, and centering struggles for justice. The technical skills were easy enough to grasp in principle, and pretty soon I had learned through practice how to book guests, research and write stories, interview experts on live radio, engineer interviews, and edit audio files.

In the precious time between pledge drives, I covered movements against police brutality years before "Black Lives Matter" (BLM) became a rallying cry. Fifteen years ago, when Black people said they were routinely racially profiled and brutalized, journalists like me did not need video evidence to believe them. Well before Patrisse Cullors, co-founder of the BLM movement, appeared on the covers of major magazines and wrote a bestselling book, she was a guest on my show, discussing what a society free of police might look like.

For decades, independent journalists and organizations worked diligently to report the facts even as corporate media outlets ignored or misrepresented them. Indeed, those outlets began to take racist police brutality seriously only after they were forced to by mass protests in the wake of George Floyd's murder on the streets of Minneapolis in 2020—and even then, most of their reporting failed to fully explore what BLM's demand to Defund the Police really meant. Rather than examining how police budgets eat up disproportionate city funds to the detriment of public services and making clear that the "Defund the Police" slogan is a call to reconfigure those funding priorities, commercial media played into fears about how reduced policing might result in a new surge in crime. Their sensationalist and fear-driven coverage had the predictable effect of reducing public support for BLM over the course of 2020.

The corporate media's blind spots are just as acute and perilous for foreign policy as for domestic policy. In April 2021, when President Joe Biden announced that he was ending the longest war in US history, I had the novel idea to interview two Afghans: a former refugee turned professor and a women's rights activist and aid worker. These experts shared a starkly different perspective than the ones ceaselessly presented by commercial media outlets. While the *New York Times* quoted former military generals who worried about the negative consequences of withdrawing troops, my guests pointed out that there was already evidence the war would continue via unmanned drones. They recited a litany of disastrous policies the US military and successive administrations had carried out in nearly two decades of occupying Afghanistan. They recounted the long history of US involvement in the country as crucial to any meaningful understanding of its present circumstances—a history stretching back forty years, not twenty, with the arming of Afghan fundamentalist warlords as proxy soldiers against the Soviets.

Imagine how different our public and political discourse would be on matters such as domestic state violence and international military hostilities if the corporate media covered stories the way independent journalists do. Instead, our major papers and news outlets only serve to preserve a status quo in which their power is maintained—perhaps because asking the hard questions might upend their own existence.

Until well-funded corporate outlets live up to their responsibility to provide rigorous investigations and analyses, with legitimate representation, holding power accountable in the public interest, independent journalists must remain engaged in a constant battle between producing critical work and worrying about whether the funding sources for such work will remain intact. This conundrum is felt across the landscape of progressive, independent, nonprofit journalism. The same structures and systems that we critique hold the purse-strings in an ever-unequal society. Corporate media outlets are part of the fabric of free-market predatory capitalism which produces the inequality that all of us—nonprofit media included—struggle to overcome.

Check out https://www.RisingUpWithSonali.com/ for more information on Sonali Kolhatkar's journalism.

SONALI KOLHATKAR is an award-winning journalist, and host and executive producer of *Rising Up with Sonali*, a nationally syndicated television and radio program airing on Free Speech TV, Pacifica Radio, and dozens of other independent media outlets. She is also a writing fellow for the Independent Media Institute's Economy for All project, writing weekly columns that are published in outlets such as Salon, *CounterPunch*, and AlterNet. She is the author, with James Ingalls, of *Bleeding Afghanistan: Washington, Warlords, and the Propaganda of Silence* (Seven Stories Press, 2006).

Looking for Clues?

RACHAEL JOLLEY

Shout out to all those crime fiction fans out there. I've always been a voracious reader of Agatha Christie and Dorothy L. Sayers, and I also dip into Sara Paretsky on occasion.

As a journalist for more than twenty years, I've always thought that reporting skills have more in common with the classic detective methods than most people think. Here's my short list of how that works: Tracking people down? Yup. Finding out background information? Yup. Watching what they do on Twitter/Instagram as part of your research? Yes again.

So when I did a series of six workshops for journalism students in their third year at Liverpool John Moores University (LJMU), I decided that one way of making the session spark ideas and resonate was to frame the subject within a detective theme. Everyone likes a detective TV show, right? The genre has a broad following across all age groups and backgrounds, and it felt like, especially during lockdown, students could do with something different coming across their Zoom screens.

In addition to thinking about various styles of journalism, and different types of publications to theme the session around, I prepared for this series of workshops by creating a detective-themed Spotify playlist, which I used to introduce the session and to play when students moved to the breakout rooms. At that time, LJMU provided a mixture of remote and in-person teaching, and instructors were beginning to experiment with new formats. In that spirit, I decided that having musical as well as visual stimulation would be really important to break up the session but also to make the workshops a little bit more fun and stimulating. I wanted the students to finish the session with a bit more energy than before, and I felt that using those different elements, both the music and some detective images, could help to do that.

My music choices might not be the same as the ones the students would have made, but at least they would help keep the conversations lively. My playlist included the *Maigret* theme, "Secret Agent Man" from the CBS show, and the *Mission: Impossible* theme tune. Now that I think about it, though, the next time I run the workshops I'd like to get the students to have a little breakout space to choose some detective-themed tunes of their own.

While I don't think that the journalism students had necessarily thought of themselves as having detective skills before, I hope they left thinking more about similarities between the two professions, and about how they could use a detective's set of skills in their journalism careers.

The overall session was called Watching the Detectives, which was a little hat tip to Elvis Costello for any fans out there, and the strands within it were called "looking for clues," "shadowing and surveillance," and "investigative research."

In looking for clues, we talked about how you could use various methods to find out more about a company that you might be writing about, such as digging about on their website for financial records, looking at the history of the firm, and scrutinizing the profiles of the directors. Another way to learn more about UK companies, too, is to look at their postings on the Companies House website, https://beta.companieshouse.gov.uk/search/, where details of directors and recent financial filings can be found. Companies House is an official register of companies, which are required to file specific details that remain publicly accessible. In other words, an ideal resource for journalists (or detectives) looking to uncover more details.

In shadowing and surveillance, we looked at how, if you were writing a profile of someone, or looking into a business leader, for instance, you could learn a lot from studying their social media profile, and following them on Twitter to see what their interests are and what they post about. We also talked about how this might be helpful if you were applying for a reporter job on a news website and you wanted to know more about the editor, news editor, or team before applying.

In investigative research, again we played with the detective theme; we discussed how, in following companies on social media, you could learn a lot about the tone of the place and how the staff operated from what they posted and what kind of stories they were putting out. Here I drew some parallels with the detective work students might do on potential employers to strengthen their job applications: they could look for clues into whichever subjects they were investigating and then put those details to good use.

Of course, as I hope became clear during the session, it was about putting together all the skills the students had been taught to develop throughout their degree course, and looking at them in a different way, to see when and where they could use them. While part of the idea behind the detective-themed approach was using Zoom in a creative way, to get away from what, after all, can be a boring way to workshop or lecture, the other aspect was to spark ideas in the students about how they can use the journalistic skills they've studied constructively and imaginatively. They were given a chance to see firsthand how research, investigation, and shadowing can not only help them build their knowledge of different subjects they might be researching as trainee journalists, but also assist in creating the perfect pitch for their first job on the journalistic ladder.

Steve Harrison, senior lecturer in journalism at Liverpool John Moores University, sat in on the detective workshops. He said, "One of the challenges of online teaching is engaging the students with imaginative, appropriate material, and the idea of using the thread of detective work to draw together various strands related to employability was a refreshing change."

Overall, the Watching the Detectives workshop series got enthusiastic responses from some students, and hopefully got them all thinking about some of their developing investigative skills practically and creatively. Whether I converted any to my passion for detective novels is a different question.

RACHAEL JOLLEY is a visiting fellow in journalism at the University of Sheffield as well as a research fellow at the university's Centre for Freedom of the Media. She also guest lectures at Liverpool John Moores University and the University of East Anglia.

Critical Media Project: Re(presenting) Identity, Media Making, and Power

ALISON TROPE AND DJ JOHNSON

Critical Media Project (CMP) was founded in 2013 to raise awareness among US educators and students about representation in media by fostering critical consumption, active participation, and cultural competencies. Through a media-rich website, curriculum, and other programs, CMP helps youth decode media representations, see across differences, and imagine a better future. CMP's multi-pronged mission speaks to the need to reimagine media literacy education in relation to social identities.

As an educational intervention, CMP concentrates on identity, because we live in a society that defines us by and through our varied and intersectional identities. We also live within systems of power where inequities and injustices situate us, defining who we are and what we can be. Media ecosystems can reinforce divisions and uphold systems of power, but they can also be used to upend them. Critical media literacy and production holds enormous liberatory potential to create a more just and equitable world.

CMP promotes *exploration* (observing and becoming cognizant of messages about identity that surface in everyday media and culture), *expansion* (understanding and gaining perspective on the historical, social, and political contexts of media representations of different identities), *excavation and explication* (critically deciphering and cultivating skills to analyze the meanings and ideologies behind various representations of identity across media genres and platforms), and *expression*

254 STATE OF THE FREE PRESS 2022

and engagement (developing and deploying strategies and techniques to create one's own representations, tell one's own stories, and craft counter-narratives).

CMP focuses specifically on seven broad categories of social identity: (1) race and ethnicity, (2) gender, (3) sexual orientation, (4) socioeconomic class, (5) religion, (6) ability, and (7) age. This list is not meant to be hierarchical or definitive; rather, within each category we identify subcategories as represented in specific media. For each of the broad identity categories, we offer a text-based socio-historical overview as well as a lesson plan and classroom worksheet to contextualize and complement the media. These materials provide an overview of key historical and theoretical concepts, underscoring the role media play in perpetuating stereotypes around particular identities while also considering the impact of media representation on social and emotional development.

CMP's extensive collection of media representations of social identities includes more than 600 examples from movies, television and streaming services, advertisements, news and documentaries, online viral videos, and user-generated content. We believe the best way to encourage media literacy is to provide actual media examples for critical analysis, and to use them as models to inspire, reorient, and challenge cultural and representational norms. Each piece of media is tagged and categorized by identity (e.g., race and ethnicity, gender, religion) and media type (e.g., advertising, news and documentaries, film, television and streaming services, online and social media, user-generated content). Reflecting the intersectional nature of identity, a single media artifact may be tagged with multiple identity categories. In addition, the site includes a page where visitors can filter all media content by different identity categories simultaneously to provide examples that exhibit intersectional representations.

While the site as a whole serves as a repository, we have found that the sheer amount of media, even with the tagging system, can be overwhelming to users. To address this and offer additional guidance, we have also developed a selection of curated "playlists" that hone in on particular social identities or issues of media representation. Each playlist provides a selection of annotated media examples and discussion questions, which guide students through key dimensions, trajectories, and controversies in media representation. The structure of these playlists is designed to allow for their use as either a standalone tool, offering a deep dive into a particular identity or issue, or as part of an integrated and expanded set of lessons. Crucially, these playlists are also structured to build from critical understanding and analysis toward empowered participation, culminating in a section titled "Your Turn!" that encourages students to produce their own media and directs them to media-making activities and resources on the site.

We've created additional playlists to respond to major social and political issues such as "Feminism," "Immigration and the American Dream," and "Black Protest and Social Movements"; playlists on gentrification, the environment, cancel culture, body diversity, and gendered violence, among other topics, are also under development in consultation with students and educators.

For educators seeking a more structured pedagogical framework to adopt in full or integrate selectively into existing classes, we have also developed an expanded curriculum that extends the core concepts and objectives of the Critical Media Project across ten lessons. The curriculum encourages students to decode media representations, think intersectionally about who they are and who they can be, tell their own stories, and create their own representations. Rather than telling students what to think or attempting to protect them from media, CMP prompts complex and sometimes difficult discussions, challenging youth to examine questions of privilege and bias by having them consider where and how they and their peers are represented.

"Critical Media Project helps youth decode media representations, see across differences, and imagine a better future."

—Alison Trope and DJ Johnson

In addition to our curricular interventions, we also have established public programs that amplify CMP's outreach and impact. Under the umbrella of CMP's "I Too Am" programs, youth voices and experiences are centered through critical creative activities tied to environmental education, public exhibitions, and cross-school collaborations. "I Too Am: Teens, Media Arts, and Belonging" brought the experiential and project-based learning of CMP to environmental education, taking youth from three South Los Angeles high schools to different locations and ecosystems around the city to reflect on the ways that place shapes our identities. This program culminated in the "I Too Am" Media Festival in February 2020 that broadened the scope of participation by offering platforms for youth from throughout Los Angeles County to showcase their media projects. In response to the COVID-19 pandemic, we developed the "I Too Am Critical Makers Lab," a six-part media-making workshop focusing on key themes of identity, place, belonging, visibility, stereotypes, and advocacy. As part of the expanding CMP universe, these programs, along with further developments of the website and curriculum, bolster our efforts to align with emerging formulations of 21st-century civic education and media literacy.

To access the Critical Media Project as well as information on its playlists, public projects, and suggested DIY activities, see https://criticalmediaproject.org/.

ALISON TROPE, PHD, is clinical professor and director of undergraduate studies in the School for Communication at the University of Southern California's Annenberg School for Communication and Journalism. She is the author of *Stardust Monuments: The Saving and Selling of Hollywood* (Dartmouth College Press, 2012) and is founder and director of the Critical Media Project.

DJ JOHNSON, MFA, is associate professor of practice in the Division of Media Arts + Practice at the University of Southern California's School of Cinematic Arts. He is a filmmaker and educator with more than twenty years of experience in media education, specializing in media strategies for social change and community organizing. He serves as the associate director of the Critical Media Project.

Notes

1. Walter Lippmann, *Public Opinion* (New Brunswick, New Jersey: Transaction Publishers, 1998 [1922]), 248.
2. Ibid., 248–49.
3. Ibid., 310; see also 364–65.
4. Ibid., 410.
5. See Timothy Garton Ash, *Free Speech: Ten Principles for a Connected World* (London: Atlantic Books, 2016), 76.
6. Brian Dolber, Michelle Rodino-Colocino, Chenjerai Kumanyika, and Todd Wolfson, eds., *The Gig Economy: Workers and Media in the Age of Convergence* (New York: Routledge, 2021).
7. Janet Wasko, Graham Murdock, and Helena Sousa, "Introduction: The Political Economy of Communications: Core Concerns and Issues," in *The Handbook of Political Economy of Communications*, eds. Janet Wasko, Graham Murdock, and Helena Sousa (London: Blackwell Publishing, 2011), 1–10.
8. Brian Dolber, "Most Expensive Ballot Initiative in California History Pits Uber and Lyft Against Drivers Who Built a Union from Scratch," *Labor Notes*, November 3, 2020.
9. Nicole S. Cohen and Greig de Peuter, *New Media Unions: Organizing Digital Journalists* (New York: Routledge, 2020).
10. "Woke washing" is Francesca Sobande's term for how brands portray themselves as concerned with inequality and social justice even if the brand's actions do not reflect a genuine commitment to addressing injustices. Francesca Sobande, "Woke-Washing: 'Intersectional' Femvertising and Branding 'Woke' Bravery," *European Journal of Marketing*, Vol. 54 No. 11 (December 2019), 2723–45.
11. Nora Barrows-Friedman, "Zoom Censors Events about Zoom Censorship," Electronic Intifada, November 13, 2020.
12. "Letter to SFSU President Lynn Mahoney Concerning Upcoming Leila Khaled Event and Academic Freedom Abuse," AMCHA Initiative, September 17, 2020.
13. Colleen Flaherty, "Zoom Draws a Line," Inside Higher Ed, September 25, 2020.
14. NYU-AAUP Executive Committee, "Statement from the NYU-AAUP on Zoom Censorship Today," Academe Blog, October 23, 2020.
15. University Committee on Academic Freedom (University of California Academic Senate), "Censorship by Zoom and Other Private Platforms," Academe Blog, February 5, 2021.
16. "On Academic Freedom for Our Higher Education Users," Zoom, April 13, 2021.
17. Lindsay McKenzie, "Zoom Addresses Academic Freedom Concerns," Inside Higher Ed, April 19, 2021.
18. Nora Barrows-Friedman, "Tech Companies Block Another Leila Khaled Event," Electronic Intifada, May 3, 2021.
19. Ibid.

20. Alan MacLeod, "'At First I Thought It was a Joke': Academic Media Censorship Conference Censored by YouTube," *MintPress News*, February 1, 2021.

21. Lauren Leatherby, Arielle Ray, Anjali Singhvi, Christiaan Triebert, Derek Watkins, and Haley Willis, "How a Presidential Rally Turned into a Capitol Rampage," *New York Times*, January 12, 2021.

22. Brian Naylor, "Read Trump's Jan. 6 Speech, A Key Part of Impeachment Trial," NPR, February 10, 2021.

23. Leatherby, Ray, Singhvi, Triebert, Watkins, and Willis, "How a Presidential Rally Turned into a Capitol Rampage."

24. Terrance Smith, "Trump Has Longstanding History of Calling Elections 'Rigged' If He Doesn't Like the Results," ABC News, November 11, 2020.

25. Elizabeth Chuck, "'Greatest Propaganda Machine in History': Sacha Baron Cohen Slams Facebook, Other Social Media Companies," NBC News, November 22, 2019.

26. Megan Brenan, "Americans' Trust in Mass Media Edges Down to 41%," Gallup, September 26, 2019.

27. Joshua A. Compton and Michael Pfau, "Inoculation Theory of Resistance to Influence at Maturity: Recent Progress in Theory Development and Application and Suggestions for Future Research," *Annals of the International Communication Association*, Vol. 29 No. 1 (2005), 97–146.

Acknowledgments

We are blessed to work with so many remarkable scholars, journalists, and organizations. Here we are pleased to acknowledge those who contributed to *State of the Free Press 2022*.

We are grateful to partner with Michael Tencer, our extraordinary editor, whose vast knowledge and attention to every detail greatly improve our books each year.

At Seven Stories Press, we thank Dan Simon, publisher and editorial director; Jon Gilbert, operations director; Ruth Weiner, publicity director and co-publisher of Triangle Square Books for Young Readers; Claire Kelley, library and academic marketing director; Lauren Hooker, senior editor; Allison Paller, web manager; Stewart Cauley, art director; Elisa Taber, assistant editor and academic manager; Eva Sotomayor, publicist; Silvia Stramenga, rights director and editor of foreign literature; and Catherine Taylor, publicity manager at Seven Stories Press UK—all of whom have our respect and gratitude for their steadfast commitment to publishing the Project's yearbook.

For the fourth consecutive year, Santa Fe–based artist Anson Stevens-Bollen has created a striking cover image that perfectly captures this book's message. We also thank him for the new Censored Press logo and the story icons that add visual pop to this year's Top 25 story list.

Books like ours need a team of keen-eyed proofreaders. This year they include Jason Bud, Dasha Bukovskaya, Ama Cortes, Mischa Geracoulis, Sierra Kaul, Gavin

Kelley, Marcelle Levine Swinburne, Jen Lyons, Juliana Moreno, Troy Patton, and Matthew Phillips.

Vital financial support from donors sustains the Project. This year we are especially thankful to Cooper Atkinson, Sharyl Attkisson, Margli and Phil Auclair, John Boyer, Allison Butler, Chuck Callahan, Sandra Cioppa, James Coleman, Dwain A. Deets, Jan De Deka, Dmitry Egorov, Larry Gassan, Michael Hansen, Elizabeth Hegeman, Nolan Higdon, Louise Johnston, Sheldon Levy, James March, Sandra Maurer, Harry Mersmann, Nate Mudd, David Nelson, Daniel O'Connell, Christopher Oscar, Peter Phillips, Allison Reilly, Lynn and Leonard Riepenhoff, Krista Rojas, John and Lyn Roth, Katherine Schock, T.M. Scruggs, Bill Simon, David Stanek, Roger Stoll, Lana Touchstone, Sal Velasco, Elaine Wellin, Derrick West and Laurie Dawson, Michelle Westover, and Montgomery Zukowski.

The Media Freedom Foundation board of directors, whose members are identified below, provide invaluable counsel and crucial organizational structure. Emeritus president and director Peter Phillips continues to be an inspiration and one of the Project's most stalwart supporters.

Our longtime webmaster Adam Armstrong manages our website, social media channels, and related audio and video content, including the Project's weekly radio program and podcast. His technological counsel in a digital era is invaluable to the Project's mission.

Anthony Fest provides critical assistance for the Project's weekly public affairs program, where he's been senior producer for more than a decade now. Bob Baldock and Ken Preston, as well as Ephraim Colbert, José Gonzalez, and Kevin Hunsanger, at KPFA Radio continue partnering with the Project for co-sponsored public events.

For amplifying the Project's voice and extending its reach, we graciously thank Nolan Higdon; John Bertucci; John Crowley and the Aqus community; Marco Palmieri and family at Risibisi; Chase Palmieri and all at Credder; Raymond Lawrason and Copperfield's Books; Kevin Herbert at Common Cents; James Preston Allen, Paul Rosenberg, Terelle Jerricks, and the team at *Random Lengths News*, as well as the Association of Alternative Newsmedia; the Mount Diablo Peace and Justice Center; the Peace and Justice Center of Sonoma County; Jason Houk at KSKQ, and the folks behind Independent Media Week; our allies in the Union for Democratic Communications and the Action Coalition for Media Education; Davey D and Hard Knock Radio; Abby Martin of *The Empire Files* and Media Roots; Mnar Muhawesh and all at MintPress News and *Behind the Headline*; Eleanor Goldfield of *Act Out!*; Maximillian Alvarez, Kayla Rivera, and the great staff at The Real News Network in Baltimore; Maya Schenwar and Alana Yu-lan Price at Truthout; Eric Draitser and *CounterPunch Radio* as well as Jeffrey St. Clair and the crew at *CounterPunch*; the team at Common Dreams; Norman Stockwell of *The Progressive*; Jordan Elgrably, Mischa Geracoulis, and The Markaz Review; Susan Zakin and Journal of the Plague Year; Emily Dorrel, Frank Dorrel, and Rachel Bruhnke, along with CodePink, for the Cold War Truth Commission; James McFadden and the Alameda Greens; Michael Welch of *The Global Research News Hour*; Alison Trope of USC's Critical Media Project; Jeff Share; everyone behind the Critical Media Literacy Conference of the Americas; Megan Castillo, Bruno L'Ecuyer, Candace Wilkinson-Davis,

Wier Harman, and all at Town Hall Seattle; Scott Catamas and Saturday Night Alive for the Global Peace Tribe; David Rovics; Kevin Gosztola at Shadowproof and the *Unauthorized Disclosure* podcast; Lee Camp and *Redacted Tonight*; Sharyl Attkisson of *Full Measure*; Arlene Engelhardt and Mary Glenney, hosts of *From a Woman's Point of View*; Dana Porteous of *The Creatives* podcast; James Tracy and everyone at the Howard Zinn Book Fair in San Francisco; Chris Carosi, Greg Ruggiero, Elaine Katzenberger, and City Lights Publishers; Peter Kuznick; David Talbot at *The David Talbot Show*; Theresa Mitchell of *Presswatch* on KBOO; Jon Gold; Max Tegmark at Improve the News; John Collins, Amna Al Obaidi, and the team at Weave News; Betsy Gomez and the Banned Books Week Coalition, including Christopher Finan and our allies at the National Coalition Against Censorship and the American Library Association's Office for Intellectual Freedom; Ralph Nader and the Center for Study of Responsive Law; and Peter Ludes, Hektor Haarkötter, Daniel Müller, and Marlene Nunnendorf at the German Initiative on News Enlightenment.

At Diablo Valley College, Mickey thanks history program co-chairs Matthew Powell and John Corbally, as well as the people who have supported the Journalism Department's revitalization efforts, including Adam Bessie, Mark Akiyama, Rayshell Clapper, Alan Haslam, Katy Agnost, Maria Dorado, Adam Perry, Michael Levitin, Nolan Higdon, Lisa Smiley-Ratchford, John Freytag, Ann Patton-Langelier, Jason Mayfield, Nicole White, Sahra Bhimji, Toni Fannin, Todd Farr, Beth Arman, Catherine Franco, Marisa Greenberg, Douglas Phenix, Rosa del Duca, Albert

Ponce, Sangha Niyogi, and everyone involved in the social justice studies program and the Faculty Senate; dean of social sciences Obed Vazquez and administrative assistant Lisa Martin; senior dean of curriculum and instruction Kim Schenk; vice president of instruction Mary Gutierrez; as well as college president Susan Lamb. Thanks also to current research assistants and Project interns including Dasha Bukovskaya, Sierra Kaul, and Veronica Vasquez. Mickey would also like to thank all of his students for the inspiration they provide, as they are a constant reminder of the possibilities of the future.

Mickey thanks his family, especially his wife, Meg, for her amazing work, counsel, and care, and their children, for patience, moral support, sense of humor, and their love of a good argument. Andy could not do what he does without the support and love of Elizabeth Boyd.

Finally, we thank you, our readers and supporters, who continue to cherish a truly free press and remain allies in our fight against censorship in its many guises. Together, we can and do make a difference.

Media Freedom Foundation/Project Censored Board of Directors

Adam Armstrong, Nicholas Baham III, Ben Boyington, Kenn Burrows, Allison Butler (vice president), Eleanor Goldfield, Doug Hecker, Mickey Huff (president), Veronica Liu, Christopher Oscar, Andy Lee Roth, T.M. Scruggs, and Elaine Wellin; with bookkeeper Michael Smith.

Project Censored 2020–21 Judges

ROBIN ANDERSEN. Professor Emerita of Communication and Media Studies, Fordham University. She has written dozens of scholarly articles and is author or co-author of four books, including *A Century of Media, A Century of War* (2006), winner of the Alpha Sigma Nu Book Award. She recently published *The Routledge Companion to Media and Humanitarian Action* (2017), and *HBO's* Treme *and the Stories of the Storm: From New Orleans as Disaster Myth to Groundbreaking Television* (2017). Writes media criticism and commentary for the media watch group Fairness & Accuracy In Reporting (FAIR), The Vision Machine, and the *Antenna* blog.

AVRAM ANDERSON. Electronic Resources Librarian at Macalester College. A member and advocate of the LGBTQI+ community researching LGBTQ censorship, in print and online. Co-editor, *A Call for Change: Minnesota Environmental Justice Heroes in Action* (2021). Recent publications include "Queer Erasure" in the Spring 2020 issue of *Index on Censorship*; "Stonewalled: Establishment Media's Silence on the Trump Administration's Crusade against LGBTQ People," featured in *Censored 2020*; "The Corporate Media Failed to Warn Us about the Trump Admin's Attack on LGBTQ Workers" (*In These Times*); and "Corporate Media Biases Threaten the Passage of Landmark LGBTQ Protections" (Truthout).

JULIE ANDRZEJEWSKI. Professor Emeritus, St. Cloud State University. Served as director of the Social Responsibility master's program, and president of the faculty union. Publications include *Social Justice, Peace, and Environmental Education* (co-edited, 2009) and, most recently, a book chapter, "The Roots of the Sixth Mass Extinction" (2017). She is currently co-chair of Indivisible Tacoma and organizer of the WA Indivisible Town Hall Series.

OLIVER BOYD-BARRETT. Professor Emeritus of Media and Communications, Bowling Green State University and California State Polytechnic University, Pomona. Most recent publications include *News Agencies in the Turbulent Era of the Internet* (2010), *Hollywood and the CIA: Cinema, Defense, and Subversion* (2011), *Western Mainstream Media and the Ukraine Crisis* (2017), *RussiaGate and Propaganda* (2020), and *Media Imperialism: Continuity and Change* (2020).

KENN BURROWS. Faculty member at the Institute for Holistic Health Studies, Department of Health Education, San Francisco State University. Founder and director of the Holistic Health Learning Center and producer of the biennial conference, Future of Health Care.

ELLIOT D. COHEN. Professor of Philosophy and chair of the Humanities Department, Indian River State College. Editor and founder of the *International Journal of Applied Philosophy*. Recent books include *Making Peace with Imperfection* (2019), *Counseling Ethics for the 21st Century* (2018), *Logic-Based Therapy and Everyday Emotions* (2016), and *Technology of Oppression: Preserving Freedom and Dignity in an Age of Mass, Warrantless Surveillance* (2014).

BRIAN COVERT. Independent journalist, author, and educator based in Japan. Worked for United Press International (UPI) news service in Japan, as staff reporter and editor for English-language daily newspapers in Japan, and as contributing writer to Japanese and overseas newspapers and magazines. Contributing author to past *Censored* editions. Teaches journalism/media studies at Doshisha University in Kyoto.

GEOFF DAVIDIAN. Investigative reporter, war correspondent, legal affairs analyst, editor, photojournalist, data analyst, and educator. Founding publisher and editor of the *Putnam Pit*, *Milwaukee Press*, and ShorewoodNewsroom.com. Contributor to Reuters, magazines, newspapers, and online publications.

ROBERT HACKETT. Professor Emeritus of Communication, Simon Fraser University, Vancouver. Co-founder of NewsWatch Canada (1993), Media Democracy Days (2001), and OpenMedia.ca (2007). Publications include *Remaking Media: The Struggle to Democratize Public Communication* (with W.K. Carroll, 2006) and *Journalism and Climate Crisis: Public Engagement, Media Alternatives* (with S. Forde, S. Gunster, and K. Foxwell-Norton, 2017). He writes for nationalobserver.com, rabble.ca, and other media.

KEVIN HOWLEY. Professor of Media Studies, DePauw University. His work has appeared in the *Journal of Radio Studies*, *Journalism: Theory, Practice and Criticism*, *Social Movement Studies*, and *Television and New Media*. He is the author of *Community Media: People, Places, and Communication Technologies* (2005), and editor of *Understanding Community Media* (2010) and *Media Interventions* (2013). His latest book is *Drones: Media Discourse and the Public Imagination* (2018).

NICHOLAS JOHNSON.* Author, *How to Talk Back to Your Television Set* (1970), and nine more books, including *Columns of Democracy* (2018) and *What Do You Mean and How Do You Know?* (2009). Commissioner, Federal Communications Commission (1966–1973); Professor, University of Iowa College of Law (1981–2014, media law and cyberlaw). More at http://www.nicholasjohnson.org/.

CHARLES L. KLOTZER. Founder, editor, and publisher emeritus of *St. Louis Journalism Review* and *FOCUS/Midwest*. The *St. Louis Journalism Review* has been transferred to Southern Illinois University, Carbondale, and is now the *Gateway Journalism Review*. Klotzer remains active at the *Review*.

NANCY KRANICH. Lecturer, School of Communication and Information, and special projects librarian, Rutgers University. Past president of the American Library Association (ALA), and convener of the ALA Center for Civic Life. Author of *Libraries and Democracy: The Cornerstones of Liberty* (2001) and "Libraries: Reuniting the Divided States of America" (2017).

DEEPA KUMAR. Professor of Media Studies, Rutgers University. Award-winning scholar and activist. Author of *Outside the Box: Corporate Media, Globalization, and the UPS Strike* (2007), *Islamophobia and the Politics of Empire* (2012), and about 75 journal articles, book chapters, and contributions in independent and establishment media. Past president of the Rutgers AAUP-AFT faculty union.

MARTIN LEE. Investigative journalist and author. Co-founder of Fairness & Accuracy In Reporting, and former editor of FAIR's magazine, *Extra!*. Director of Project CBD, a medical science information nonprofit. Author of *Smoke Signals: A Social History of Marijuana—Medical, Recreational, and Scientific* (2012), *The Beast Reawakens: Fascism's Resurgence from Hitler's Spymasters to Today's Neo-Nazi Groups and Right-Wing Extremists* (2000), and *Acid Dreams: The Complete Social History of LSD: The CIA, the Sixties, and Beyond* (with B. Shlain, 1985).

PETER LUDES. Professor of Mass Communication, Jacobs University, Bremen, 2002–2017. Visiting Professor at the University of Cologne, since 2018. Founder of the German Initiative on News Enlightenment (1997) at the University of Siegen. Recent publications on brutalization and banalization (2018) and collective myths and decivilizing processes (2020, with Stefan Kramer).

WILLIAM LUTZ. Professor Emeritus of English, Rutgers University. Former editor of the *Quarterly Review of Doublespeak*. Author of *Doublespeak: From Revenue Enhancement to Terminal Living: How Government, Business, Advertisers, and Others Use Language to Deceive You* (1989), *The Cambridge Thesaurus of American English* (1994), *The New Doublespeak: Why No One Knows What Anyone's Saying Anymore* (1996), and *Doublespeak Defined* (1999).

CONCHA MATEOS. Senior Lecturer in Visual Studies, Department of Communication Sciences, Universidad Rey Juan Carlos, Spain. Journalist for radio, television, and political organizations in Spain and Latin America. Academic researcher and activist. Coordinator for Project Censored research in Europe and Latin America.

DANIEL MÜLLER. Head of the Postgraduate Academy at the University of Siegen, in Germany. Researcher and educator in journalism, mass communication studies, and history at public universities for many years. Has published extensively on media history, media–minority relations in Germany, and on nationality policies and ethnic relations of the Soviet Union and the post-Soviet successor states, particularly in the Caucasus. Jury member of the German Initiative on News Enlightenment.

JACK L. NELSON.* Distinguished Professor Emeritus, Graduate School of Education, Rutgers University. Former member, Committee on Academic Freedom and Tenure, American Association of University Professors. Recipient, Academic Freedom Award, National Council for Social Studies. Author of 17 books, including *Critical Issues in Education: Dialogues and Dialectics*, 9th ed. (with S. Palonsky and M.R. McCarthy, 2021) and *Human Impact of Natural Disasters* (with V.O. Pang and W.R. Fernekes, 2010), and about 200 articles.

PETER PHILLIPS. Professor of Political Sociology, Sonoma State University. Director, Project Censored, 1996–2010. President, Media Freedom Foundation, 2010–2016. Editor or co-editor of 14 editions of *Censored*. Co-editor (with Dennis Loo) of *Impeach the President: The Case Against Bush and Cheney* (Seven Stories Press, 2006). Author of *Giants: The Global Power Elite* (Seven Stories Press, 2018).

MICHAEL RAVNITZKY. Attorney, writer, editor, engineer, and Freedom of Information Act expert who has developed tools to broaden access to public records in the public interest.

T.M. SCRUGGS. Professor Emeritus (and token ethnomusicologist), University of Iowa. Published in print, audio, and/or video format, on Central American, Cuban, and Venezuelan music and dance and US jazz. Involvement with community radio in Nicaragua, Venezuela, and the United States, including the KPFA (Berkeley, CA) Local Station Board and Pacifica National Board. Executive producer, The Real News Network, and board member, Truthout.

NANCY SNOW. Pax Mundi Professor of Public Diplomacy, Kyoto University of Foreign Studies, Japan. Professor Emeritus of Communications, California State University, Fullerton. Fellow, Temple University, Japan, Institute of Contemporary Asian Studies. Author or editor of 12 books, including *The SAGE Handbook of Propaganda* (2020) and a new edition of *The Routledge Handbook of Public Diplomacy* (with Nicholas J. Cull, 2020).

PAUL STREET. Researcher, award-winning journalist, historian, author, and speaker. Author of ten books to date: *This Happened Here: Neoliberals, Amerikaners, and the Trumping of America* (Routledge, October 2021); *Hollow Resistance: Obama, Trump and the Politics of Appeasement* (CounterPunch, 2020); *They Rule: The 1% vs. Democracy* (2014); *Crashing the Tea Party*, with Anthony R. DiMaggio (2011); *The Empire's New Clothes* (2010); *Barack Obama and the Future of American Politics* (2009); *Racial Oppression in the Global Metropolis* (2007); *Still Separate, Unequal* (2005); *Segregated Schools: Educational Apartheid in Post–Civil Rights America* (2005); and *Empire and Inequality* (2004). He writes regularly for *CounterPunch*.

SHEILA RABB WEIDENFELD.* Emmy Award–winning television producer. Former press secretary to Betty Ford and special assistant to the President; author, *First Lady's Lady*. President of DC Productions Ltd. Creator of snippetsofwisdom.com. Director of community relations of Phyto Management LLC and Maryland Cultivation and Processing LLC.

ROB WILLIAMS. Founding president of the Action Coalition for Media Education (ACME). Teaches media, communications, global studies, and journalism at Champlain and Saint Michael's Colleges and Northern Vermont University. Author of numerous articles on critical media literacy education. Publisher of the *Vermont Independent* online news journal. Author of *The Post (Truth) World* (2019) and *Media Mojo!* (2020), and co-editor of *Media Education for a Digital Generation* (with J. Frechette, 2016) and *Most Likely to Secede* (with R. Miller, 2013), about the Vermont independence movement.

*Indicates having been a Project Censored judge since our founding in 1976.

In Memoriam

With sadness, we note the passing of Ernesto Carmona Ulloa, Chilean author and journalist, longtime Project Censored judge, and translator of the Top 25 stories for Spanish readers. Ernesto was a dear colleague and friend to the Project and will be greatly missed.

We also note the passing of poet, artist, and cultural icon Lawrence Ferlinghetti, founder of City Lights Booksellers and Publishers in San Francisco, champion of free speech and expression, fierce opponent of censorship, and lifelong lover of books and the wisdom they impart.

How to Support Project Censored

Nominate a Story

To nominate a *Censored* story, forward the URL to mickey@projectcensored.org or andy@projectcensored.org. The deadline for nominating *Censored* stories for the next volume is March 31, 2022.

Criteria for Project Censored news story nominations:

1) A censored news story reports information that the public has a right and a need to know, but to which the public has had limited access.

2) The news story is recent, having been first reported no later than one year ago. Stories submitted for *State of the Free Press 2023* should be no older than April 2021.

3) The story is fact-based with clearly defined concepts and verifiable documentation. The story's claims should be supported by evidence—the more controversial the claims, the stronger the evidence necessary.

4) The news story has been published, either electronically or in print, in a publicly circulated newspaper, journal, magazine, newsletter, or similar publication from either a domestic or foreign source.

Make a Tax-Deductible Donation

We depend on tax-deductible donations to continue our work. Project Censored is supported by the Media Freedom Foundation, a 501(c)(3) nonprofit organization. To support our efforts on behalf of independent journalism and freedom of information, send checks to the address below or donate online at projectcensored.org. Your generous donations help us to oppose news censorship and promote media literacy.

Media Freedom Foundation
PO Box 1177
Fair Oaks, CA 95628
mickey@projectcensored.org
andy@projectcensored.org
Phone: (707) 241-4596

ABOUT THE EDITORS

ANDY LEE ROTH is the associate director of Project Censored and co-editor of 12 editions of this yearbook. He coordinates the Project's Campus Affiliates Program, a news media research network of several hundred students and faculty at two dozen colleges and universities across North America. His research and writing have been published in a variety of outlets, including *Index on Censorship*, *In These Times*, *YES! Magazine*, *Media, Culture & Society*, and the *International Journal of Press/Politics*. He earned a PhD in sociology at the University of California, Los Angeles, and a BA in sociology and anthropology at Haverford College. He lives in Winthrop, Washington with his sweetheart and their two marvelous cats.

MICKEY HUFF is the director of Project Censored and president of the nonprofit Media Freedom Foundation. To date, he has co-edited 13 editions of the Project's yearbook. He is also the co-author, with Nolan Higdon, of *United States of Distraction: Media Manipulation in Post-Truth America (and what we can do about it)* (City Lights Publishers, 2019). Huff received the Beverly Kees Educator Award as part of the 2019 James Madison Freedom of Information Awards from the Society of Professional Journalists, Northern California. He is a professor of social science, history, and journalism at Diablo Valley College, where he co-chairs the history program and is chair of the Journalism Department. Huff is executive producer and host of *The Project Censored Show*, the Project's weekly syndicated public affairs radio program. A musician and composer, he lives with his family in Fair Oaks, California.

For more information about the editors, to invite them to speak at your school or in your community, or to conduct interviews, please visit projectcensored.org.

Index

Popkin, Gabriel, 100, 101
Popular Front for the Liberation of Palestine, 238
Portland, OR, 8, 208, 225n48
Postmates, 235
poverty, xiii, xvii, 14, 17, 33–36, 48, 62, 64, 71, 100, 166, 218, 235, *see also* economics, inequality
Poynter Institute, xiv
prescription drugs, 10, 33–36, *see also* health
Prince Harry, *see* Mountbatten-Windsor, Harry
The Princess and the Frog (movie), 173
Princeton University, 171, 212, 215
prisons, 143, *see also* criminal justice system; police
for-profit prisons, 10, 70–74, 112, 113, 128–34
health in, 70–74
youth, 112, 113
privacy, *see* surveillance
Progressive Soapbox, 93, 94
Prohibition (US), 2
Project Censored, xv, 3, 10, 16, 22, 23, 25, 26, 28–31, 56, 66, 86, 90, 116n12–14, 127, 128, 134, 146, 153, 161, 193, 231, 240
Project South, 70, 72, 73
propaganda, xi, xiv, 12, 13, 16, 22, 58–61, 116n4, 170, 207, 216, 229–31, 235, 241–45
Proposition 22 (2020 California ballot initiative), 235, 236
Propwatch Project, 12, 16, 229, 230, 241, 243
ProQuest, 31
Protecting the Right to Organize Act (PRO Act) (US), 236
protests, *see* activism
Proud Boys (far-right organization), 201
Psaki, Jen, 8
Putin, Vladimir, 39, 40
Putin's People, 39, 40
QAnon, 13, 199, 205–208
Queens College, City University of New York, 62
QUEX Institute, 50, 51
racism, 9, 127, 173, 179, 181, 193, 222, 230, 236, *see also* Black peoples; Latinx peoples; police; voting; white supremacy
against women and children, 67–74, 96–98, 112, 113, 233, 190n15
and the US Capitol insurrection, 194, 199, 204–209, 220
colorism, 177, 178
policing, 107–110, 130, 157n62, 207
"Black Identity Extremists," 10, 128, 129, 144–48
police violence, 10, 16, 21, 25, 26, 45, 66–69, 120n77, 128, 138–44, 153, 156n40, 177, 209–214, 224n42, 248, *see also* Floyd, George
protests against, 2, 8, 10, 26, 67, 128, 129, 139, 142–48, 157n62, 193, 224n42, 256
Black Lives Matter, 7, 11, 44, 66, 68, 108, 109, 195, 208–212, 214, 247, 248
slavery, 67, 68, 177, 178, 232
voter suppression, 11, 12, 161, 175, 176, 187, 202, 215–19, 221
Rae, Addison, 172
Rahman, Susan, 134
Ratatouille (movie), 163
Readfearn, Graham, 52
Reagan, Ronald, 4, 200
Reconstruction (post–US Civil War), 221
Red Summer of 1919 (US), 2
Refinery29, 73
Reich, Robert, 221
Reinke, John, 159, 160, 186
religion, 23, 95, 102, 135, 147, 169, 255
American Gnosticism, 206, 207, *see also* QAnon
Christianity, 57, 104–106, 135, 137, 151, 152, 157n62, 169
Islam, 133, 240
Remkus, Ashley, 68

Reporters' Alert: Fresh Ideas for Journalists, 14
Reporters Without Borders (RSF), 7, 18n20
Republican Party (US), 12, 35, 82, 104, 131, 135, 138, 169, 175, 194, 196, 197, 200, 206, 208, 211, 214–21, 243
Retail, Wholesale and Department Store Union, 60
Reuters, 41, 74, 106, 206
Ribeiro, Francisca, 52
Rideshare Drivers United (RDU), 234–36
riots, 209–212, *see also* police, violence; Capitol (US), failed insurrection
Rising Up with Sonali (radio show), 229, 245
Ritter, Madisen, 81–83
Roberts, Yvonne, 91
Rodino-Colocino, Michelle, 12, 229, 230, 232–37
Rodriguez, Alexander "A-Rod," 183
Rodriguez, Victor, 110–12
Roll Call (newspaper), 132
Rolling Stone, 144
Rome, Italy, 151, 152
The Room Where It Happened, 24
Rosé (musician), 172
Rosneft, 40
Ross, Daniel, 51
Roth, Andy Lee, 1–19, 21–126, 229–60
RT (formerly Russia Today), 88
Rubin, Dave, 175
Rubio, Marco, 131
Ruiz, Iván, 62
Rupar, Aaron, 217
Russia, 8, 39–41, 48, 52, 90, 221
Ryan, Liz, 112, 113
Sahara desert, 40
Sainato, Michael, 43
Saint Mary's College, Notre Dame, 93, 112, 114
Saint Michael's College, 69, 102
Salisbury University, 96
Salt Lake City, UT, 69
Samuel, Sigal, 86, 123n105
San Diego, CA, 234
San Francisco State University (SFSU), 55, 74, 138, 238, 240
San José, CA, 143
Sanchez, Julia, 112, 113
Sanders, Bernie, 195
Santa Barbara County, CA, 180
Santa Rosa, CA, 43
Santayana, George, 174
satellites, x, 87–90
Saturday Night Live (television show), 163
Saudi Arabia, 166
Save America Rally, 241
Saxon, Shani, 96, 98, 112, 113, 141
Sayers, Dorothy L., 250
Scalise, Steve, 216
Schaff, Erin, 100, 101
Schector, Hailey, 144
Schumer, Chuck, 131, 200
Schwanebeck, Rachael, 10, 127–58
Seattle, WA, 58, 59
Sechin, Igor, 40
Secret Agent (television show), 251
sedition, 2, 198, 199, 215, 216, *see also* Capitol (US), failed insurrection
Sedition Act of 1918 (US), 2
seed sovereignty, 27, 74–78
Senate (US), 35, 131, 138, 147, 157n62, 197, 200, 218
Sessions, Jeff, 133
sexism, *see* women and girls
Shapiro, Ben, 135
Sharlet, Jeff, 205, 224n35
Shield, Charli, 74, 75
Shorenstein Center on Media, Politics and Public Policy, 69

With the publication of *State of the Free Press 2022*, Project Censored proudly launches the Censored Press, the publishing imprint of Project Censored and its nonprofit sponsor, the Media Freedom Foundation. Building on the Project's yearbook series, website, weekly radio show, and other educational programs, the Censored Press advances the Project's promotion of independent investigative journalism, media literacy, and critical thinking.

In addition to this volume, the Censored Press's first releases will include *The Media and Me: A Guide to Critical Media Literacy for Young People*, co-authored by Ben Boyington, Allison T. Butler, Nolan Higdon, Mickey Huff, and Andy Lee Roth, and illustrated by Peter Glanting (Fall 2022); *State of the Free Press 2023* (December 2022); and *Going Remote: An Educator's Journey through the Digital Exodus*, written and illustrated by Adam Bessie and Peter Glanting, a book of graphic journalism (late 2022/early 2023) based on a chapter published in *State of the Free Press 2021*.

The Censored Press's development is guided by a distinguished founding editorial board that includes Nora Barrows-Friedman, Mischa Geracoulis, Mickey Huff, Veronica Liu, Andy Lee Roth, T.M. Scruggs, and Dan Simon. The Censored Press benefits from a robust partnership with Seven Stories Press, the Project's longtime publisher and stalwart ally, which will print and distribute Censored Press titles.

The support of several founding donors has ensured that the Censored Press will be a sustainable publishing imprint, but your additional support will allow us to undertake even more publishing projects and provide new opportunities for reporting, teaching, and thinking critically! Learn more at censoredpress.org.